Cloud Native Security

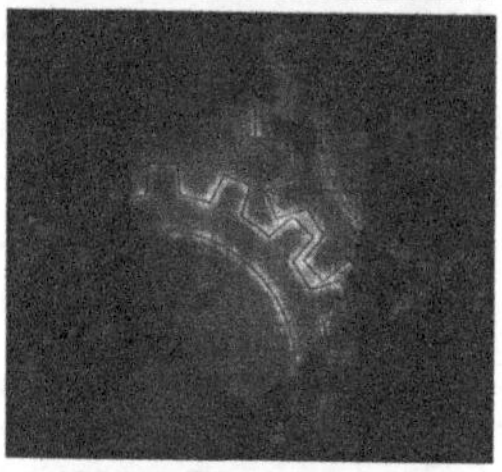

Cloud Native Security

Chris Binnie
Rory McCune

WILEY

Published by John Wiley & Sons, Inc., Hoboken, New Jersey.

Published simultaneously in Canada.

ISBN: 978-1-119-78223-0
ISBN: 978-1-119-82453-4 (ebk)
ISBN: 978-1-119-78224-7 (ebk)

For general information on our other products and services or for technical support, please contact our Customer Care Department within the United States at (800) 762-2974, outside the United States at (317) 572-3993 or fax (317) 572-4002.

Wiley also publishes its books in a variety of electronic formats. Some content that appears in print may not be available in electronic formats. For more information about Wiley products, visit our web site at `www.wiley.com`.

Library of Congress Control Number: 2021939557

Cover image: © non-exclusive/Getty Images
Cover design: Wiley

SKY10027980_070721

Cyber Security. . . Cybernetics. . . Kubernetes

The word Cybernetics *comes from the Greek word* kybernetes, *meaning rudder, pilot, a device used to steer a boat, or to support human governance.*

. . . Norbert Wiener defined cybernetics as "the study of control and communication in the animal and the machine."

Dan C. Marinescu, Complex Systems and Clouds, 2017

About the Authors

Chris Binnie is a technical consultant who has worked with critical Linux systems over a period of almost two-and-a-half decades. He has worked on banking and government server estates, on-premise and in the cloud. In addition to building an autonomous system network in 2005 and serving live HD video to 77 countries via a media streaming platform, which he architected and built on AWS in 2012, he has written two Linux books and written for *Linux* magazine and *ADMIN* magazine for a number of years. He has five years of experience in DevOps security consultancy roles and thrives on the challenge of explaining the complex in a clear and concise manner. Outside of work, Chris enjoys extolling the virtues of the unerring Ockham's razor.

Rory McCune has worked in the information and IT security arena for the past 20 years in a variety of roles. These days he spends most of his work time on cloud native security. He's an active member of the container security community having delivered presentations at a variety of IT and information security conferences. He has also presented at major containerization conferences, is an author of the CIS Benchmarks for Docker and Kubernetes and has authored and delivered container security training at conferences around the world. When he's not working, Rory can generally be found out walking and enjoying the scenery of the Scottish Highlands.

About the Technical Editor

Christina Kyriakidou is a full-time consulting IT architect and occasional blogger who has worked with numerous clients across the UK and Europe on supported and upstream Open Source software for more than 10 years. She has been working with container technologies since 2016 (when "gears" and "cartridges" were relevant) and is passionate about this world because it is a balance of new technologies and wide applicability. These days she spends most of her work time on educating customers about container platforms and automation, both on-premise and in the cloud.

Contents at a Glance

Contents

Introduction

There is little doubt that we have witnessed a dramatic and notable change in the way that software applications are developed and deployed in recent years.

Take a moment to consider what has happened within the last decade alone. Start with the mind-blowing levels of adoption of containers, courtesy of Docker's clever packaging of Linux container technologies. Think of the pivotal maturation of cloud platforms with their ever-evolving service offerings. Remember the now-pervasive use of container orchestrators to herd multiple catlike containers. And do not forget that software applications have been teased apart and broken down into portable, microservice-sized chunks.

Combined, these significant innovations have empowered developers by offering them a whole new toolbox from which their software can be developed, and a reliable platform that their applications can be deployed upon.

In hand with the other recent milestone innovations in computing, such as the growth of Unix-like operating systems and the birth of the web and the internet as a whole, Cloud Native technologies have already achieved enough to merit a place in the history books. However, as with all newly formed tech, different types of security challenges surface and must be addressed in a timely fashion.

Cloud Native security is a complex, multifaceted topic to understand and even harder to get right. Why is that? The answer lies with the multiple, diverse components that need to be secured. The cloud platform, the underlying host operating system, the container runtime, the container orchestrator, and then the applications themselves each require specialist security attention.

Bear in mind too, that the securing and then monitoring of the critical nuts and bolts of a tech stack needs to happen 24 hours a day, all year round. For those who are working in security and unaccustomed to Cloud Native technologies, their limited breadth of exposure can make the challenge that they are suddenly faced with a real eye-opener.

Among the more advanced attackers, there are many highly adaptive, intelligent, and ultimately extremely patient individuals with a vast amount of development and systems experience who have the ability to pull off exceptional compromises, including those of the highest-profile online services. These individuals, who may also be well-funded, are extremely difficult to keep out of a cloud estate. Only by continually plugging every security hole, with multiple layers of defense, is it possible to hope to do so. They are the attackers, however, that can usually be kept at arm's length. At the highest level, so-called nation-state attackers are advanced enough that many security teams would struggle to even identify if a compromise had been successful.

Insomnia-inducing concerns aside, the good news is that it is possible to increase the effort involved for an attacker to successfully exploit a vulnerability significantly. This can be achieved using a combination of open source tools and shifting security to the left in the software lifecycle in order to empower developers with greater visibility of threats and therefore giving them more responsibility for the code that makes it into production.

Shifting security to the left, as championed by DevSecOps methodologies, is a worthwhile pursuit, especially when coupled with the interjection of security logic gates into CI/CD pipelines that determine whether to pass or fail software builds. Combined with multiple build tests, wherever they might be needed within the software lifecycle, this approach is highly effective and has been growing in popularity exponentially.

Meeting the Challenge

The authors of *Cloud Native Security* have both worked in the technology and security space for more than 20 years and approach such challenges from different perspectives. For that reason, this book is divided into four distinct sections that together will arm the reader with enough security tooling knowledge, coupled with niche know-how, to improve the security posture of any Cloud Native infrastructure.

The key areas explored in detail within this book are the high-level building blocks already mentioned in the introduction. Part I focuses on container runtime and orchestrator security, Part II on DevSecOps tooling, Part III on the securing and monitoring of cloud platforms, and finally Part IV looks at advanced Kubernetes security.

There is ostensibly less Linux hardening information in this book than the other facets because Linux is more mature than the other components in a Cloud Native stack, fast approaching its 30th birthday. However, it would be unfair not to mention that almost every component involved with Cloud Native technologies starts with Linux in one shape or form. It is an often-overlooked

cornerstone of security in this space. For that reason, a chapter is dedicated to ensuring that the very best advice, based on industry-consensus, is employed when it comes to using automation to harden Linux.

Today's popular cloud platforms are unquestionably each different, but the security skills required to harden them can be transposed from one to another with a little patience. Amazon Web Services (AWS) is still the dominant cloud provider, so this book focuses on AWS; readers working on other cloud platforms, however, will find enough context to work with them in a similar manner. From a Linux perspective, the hands-on examples use Debian derivatives, but equally other Linux distributions will match closely to the examples shown.

Coverage of container security issues often incorrectly focuses solely only on static container image analysis; however, within this book readers will find that the information relating to container runtime threats are separated away cleanly from orchestrator threats for much greater clarity.

This book explores concepts and technologies that are more accessible to less experienced readers within the first three sections. And, on a journey through to the last section where more advanced attacks on Kubernetes are delved into, the latter chapters are constructed to help encourage the reader to absorb and then research further into the complex concepts.

It is the hope that security professionals will gain a diverse mix of the required niche knowledge to help secure the Cloud Native estates that they are working on. Equally, as today's developers are consistently required to learn more about security, they too can keep abreast of the challenges that their roles will increasingly involve.

With this in mind, it has been an enjoyable experience collecting thoughts to put them down on paper. The reader's journey now begins with a look at the innards of a Linux container. Not all DevOps engineers can confidently explain what a container is from a Linux perspective. That is something that this book hopes to remedy, in the interests of security.

What Does This Book Cover?

Here's a chapter-by-chapter summary of what you will learn in *Cloud Native Security*:

Chapter 1: What Is A Container? The first chapter in Part I discusses the components that comprise a Linux container. Using hands-on examples, the chapter offers the perspective of these components from a Linux system's point of view and discusses common types of containers in use today.

Chapter 2: Rootless Runtimes This chapter looks at the Holy Grail of running containers, doing so without using the `root` user. An in-depth examination of Docker's experimental rootless mode, followed by an in-depth look at Podman being run without using the superuser, helps demonstrate the key differences between the runtimes.

Chapter 3: Container Runtime Protection This chapter looks at a powerful open source tool that can provide impressive guardrails around containers. The custom policies can be used to monitor and enforce against unwanted anomalies in a container's behavior.

Chapter 4: Forensic Logging This chapter examines a built-in Linux Auditing System that can provide exceptional levels of detail. Using the auditing system, it is possible to walk, step-by-step, through logged events after an attack to fully understand how a compromise was successful. In addition, misconfigurations and performance issues can be identified with greater ease.

Chapter 5: Kubernetes Vulnerabilities This chapter looks at a clever tool that uses a number of detailed checks to suggest suitable security and compliance fixes to Kubernetes clusters. Such advice can be useful for auditing both at installation time and in an ongoing fashion.

Chapter 6: Container Image CVEs By using the best of three Common Vulnerability and Exploit scanning tools, or a combination of them, it is possible to capture a highly detailed picture of the vulnerabilities that require patching within static container images.

Chapter 7: Baseline Scanning (or, Zap Your Apps) This chapter is the first of Part II, "DevSecOps Tooling," and explores the benefits of performing baseline tests within a CI/CD pipeline to highlight issues with applications.

Chapter 8: Codifying Security This chapter demonstrates a tool that can utilize popular attack applications using custom policies to test for vulnerabilities within newly built services and applications in CI/CD tests.

Chapter 9: Kubernetes Compliance This chapter details a tool that is compatible with CI/CD tests that will inspect a Kubernetes cluster using hundreds of different testing criteria and then report on suitable fixes to help with its security posture.

Chapter 10: Securing Your Git Repositories This chapter looks at two popular tools to help prevent secrets, tokens, certificates, and passwords from being accidentally stored within code repositories using the `git` revision control system. Both suit being called from within CI/CD pipelines.

Chapter 11: Automated Host Security This chapter explores an often-overlooked aspect of Cloud Native security, the Linux hosts themselves. By automating the hardening of hosts either once or by frequently enforcing security controls, using a configuration management tool like Ansible, it is possible to help mitigate against attackers gaining a foothold and additionally create predictable, reliable, and more secure hosts.

Chapter 12: Server Scanning With Nikto This chapter offers a valuable insight into a tool that will run thousands of tests against applications running on hosts in order to help improve their security posture. It can also be integrated into CI/CD pipeline tests with relative ease.

Chapter 13: Monitoring Cloud Operations The first chapter of Part III, "Cloud Security," suggests solutions to the day-to-day monitoring of cloud infrastructure and how to improve Cloud Security Posture Management (CSPM). Using Open Source tools, it is quite possible to populate impressive dashboards with highly useful, custom metrics and save on operational costs at the same time.

Chapter 14: Cloud Guardianship This chapter examines a powerful tool that can be used to automate custom policies to prevent insecure configuration settings within a cloud environment. By gaining a clear understanding of how the tool works, you are then free to deploy some of the many examples included with the software across the AWS, Azure, and Google Cloud platforms.

Chapter 15: Cloud Auditing This chapter shows the installation and use of popular auditing tools that can run through hundreds of both Linux and cloud platform compliance tests, some of which are based on the highly popular CIS Benchmarks.

Chapter 16: AWS Cloud Storage This chapter looks at how attackers steal vast amounts of sensitive date from cloud storage on a regular basis. It also highlights how easy it is for nefarious visitors to determine whether storage is publicly accessible and then potentially download assets from that storage. In addition, the chapter identifies a paid-for service to help attackers do just that using automation.

Chapter 17: Kubernetes External Attacks This chapter is the first of Part IV, "Advanced Kubernetes and Runtime Security." It delves deeply into API Server attacks, a common way of exploiting Kubernetes, as well as looking at other integral components of a Kubernetes cluster.

Chapter 18: Kubernetes Authorization with RBAC This chapter discusses the role-based access control functionality used for authorization within a Kubernetes cluster. By defining granular access controls, you can significantly restrict the levels of access permitted.

Chapter 19: Network Hardening This chapter explores how networking can be targeted by attackers in a Kubernetes cluster and the modern approach to limiting applications or users moving between network namespaces.

Chapter 20: Workload Hardening This chapter builds upon the knowledge learned in the earlier chapters of the book and takes a more advanced approach to the hardening of workloads in Kubernetes.

A Few Conventions

This book follows the time-honored tradition of setting coding-language keywords, modifiers, and identifiers (including URLs), when they appear in running text, in the same `fixed-space font` used for displayed code listings and snippets.

We have also had to make a couple of changes from what you will see on your screen to fit the format of a printed book. First, although Linux command screens typically show white type on a dark background, that scheme does not reproduce well in printed captures. For legibility, we have reversed those screens to black-on-white.

Also note that the width of a printed page does not hold as many characters as a Linux command or output line. In cases where we have had to introduce line breaks that you would not see on the screen, we have made them at meaningful points; and in the rare instances where in entering code you would need to omit a line break we have shown, we tell you so explicitly.

Companion Download Files

As you work through the examples in this book, you will see that most of them are command-line interactions, where you enter a single command and see its output. For the automated tasks demonstrated in Chapter 19, YAML files are available for download from `http://www.wiley.com/go/cloudnativesecurity`.

How to Contact the Publisher

If you believe you have found a mistake in this book, please bring it to our attention. At John Wiley & Sons, we understand how important it is to provide our customers with accurate content, but even with our best efforts an error may occur.

To submit your possible errata, please email it to our Customer Service Team at `wileysupport@wiley.com` with the subject line "Possible Book Errata Submission."

Part

I

Container and Orchestrator Security

The Cloud Native Computing Foundation, often abbreviated as the CNCF (`www.cncf.io`), reported in its 2020 survey that "the use of containers in production has increased to 92%, up from 84% last year, and up 300% from our first survey in 2016" and also that "Kubernetes use in production has increased to 83%, up from 78% last year." The report (`www.cncf.io/wp-content/uploads/2020/12/CNCF_Survey_Report_2020.pdf`) takes note of a number of useful facts that demonstrate that the way modern applications are developed and hosted is continuing to evolve using Cloud Native technologies and methodologies. A significant component, as the survey demonstrates, involves containerization, and for that reason the first six chapters of this book explore the security of containers and container orchestrators. The final part of the book examines this topic using more advanced examples and scenarios.

In This Part

CHAPTER

1

What Is A Container?

Linux containers as we know them today have been realized through a series of incremental innovations, courtesy of a disparate group of protagonists. Destined for a place in the history books, containers have brought significant change to the way that modern software is now developed; this change will be intriguing to look back upon in the coming years ahead.

In simple terms, a *container* is a distinct and relatively isolated unit of code that has a specific purpose. As will be repeated later, the premise of a container is to focus on one key process (such as a web server) and its associated processes. If your web server needs to be upgraded or altered, then no other software components are affected (such as a related database container), making the construction of a technology stack more modular by design.

In this chapter, we will look at how a container is constructed and some of its fundamental components. Without this background information it is difficult to understand how to secure a containerized server estate successfully. We will start by focusing on the way software runs containers; we call that software the *container runtime*. We will focus on the two most prominent runtimes, Docker and Podman. An examination of the latter should also offer a valuable insight into the relatively recent advances in container runtimes.

As we work through the book, we will look at this area again from a more advanced perspective with an eye firmly on security mitigation. Purposely, rather than studying historical advances of Linux containers, this chapter focuses on identifying the components of a container that security personnel should be concerned about.

Common Misconceptions

In 2014–15, the clever packaging of system and kernel components by Docker Inc. led to an explosion of interest in Linux containers. As Docker's popularity soared, a common misconception was that containers could be treated in the same way as virtual machines (VMs). As technology evolved, this became partially true, but let us consider what that misconception involved to help illustrate some of the security challenges pertinent to containers.

Along the same lines as most VMs, less-informed users trusted that Customer A had no access to Customer B's resources if each customer ran its own containers. This implicit trust is understandable. Hardware virtualization is used often on Linux systems, implemented with tools like the popular Kernel-based Virtual Machine, or KVM (`www.linux-kvm.org`), for example. Virtual machines using such technologies can run on the same physical machine and do indeed share significant levels of segregation, improving their security posture significantly. Helpful information is provided in a white paper by a long-standing commercial brand, VMware, that offers a detailed look at how this works.

```
www.vmware.com/content/dam/digitalmarketing/vmware/en/pdf/
whitepaper/techpaper/vmw-white-paper-secrty-vsphr-hyprvsr-uslet-101
.pdf
```

This type of virtualization is not to be confused with *paravirtualization*, utilized by software such as Xen (`xenproject.org`), where guest operating systems (OSs) can share hardware on a modified host OS.

NOTE **Xen is able to support hardware virtualization and paravirtualization. You can find more information on the subject here:**

`wiki.xen.org/wiki/Xen_Project_Software_Overview#PV_.28x86.29`

In Figure 1.1 we can see the difference between containers and virtual machines. The processes shown are those relevant to a running application. Using our web server example again, one process might be running a web server listening on an HTTP port and another for HTTPS. As mentioned, to maintain the desired modularity, containers should service a specific single task (such as a web server). Normally, they will run a main application's process alone, along with any required associated processes.

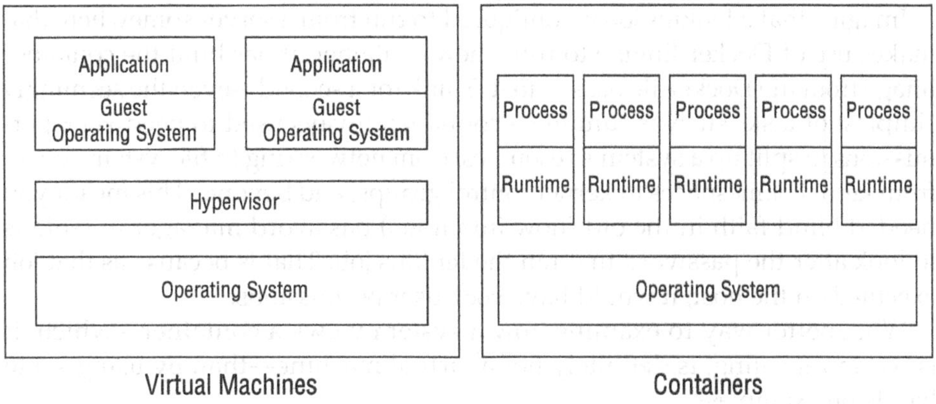

Figure 1.1: How virtual machines and containers reside on a host

It should be clear that a Linux container is an entirely different animal than a VM. A saying that appears to have gained popularity at Red Hat during the explosion of container popularity noted earlier is that fundamentally "containers are Linux." One interpretation of such a statement is that if you can appreciate how a Linux system is constructed at a nuts-and-bolts level and understand how to slice up a system into small segments, each of which uses native Linux components, then you will have a reasonable chance of understanding what containers are. For a more specific understanding of where that phrase comes from, visit this Red Hat blog page that explains the motivation behind the phrase: `www.redhat.com/en/blog/containers-are-linux`.

From the perspective of an underlying host machine, the operating system is not only slicing memory up to share among containers, segmenting the networking stack, dividing up the filesystem, and restricting full access to the CPU; it is also hiding some of the processes that are running in the process table. How are all those aspects of a Linux system controlled centrally? Correct, via the kernel. During the massive proliferation of Docker containers, it became obvious that users did not fully appreciate how many of the components hung together.

For example, the Docker runtime has been improved over time with new security features (which we look at in more detail in Chapter 2, "Rootless Runtimes"); but in older versions, it needed to run as the `root` user without exception. Why? It was because in order to slice up the system into suitable container-shaped chunks, superuser permissions were needed to convince the kernel to allow an application like Docker to do so.

One example scenario (which is common still to this day) that might convey why running as the `root` user is such a problem involves the popular continuous integration/continuous development (CI/CD) automation tool, Jenkins.

TIP **Security in the CI/CD software development pipeline is the subject of the chapters in Part II of this book, "DevSecOps Tooling."**

Imagine that a Jenkins job is configured to run from a server somewhere that makes use of Docker Engine to run a new container; it has built the container image from the Dockerfile passed to it. Think for a second—even the seemingly simplest of tasks such as running a container always used to need `root` permissions to split up a system's resources, from networking to filesystem access, from kernel namespaces to kernel control groups, and beyond. This meant you needed blind faith in the old (now infamous) password manager in Jenkins to look after the password that ran the Jenkins job. That is because as that job executed on the host, it would have `root` user permissions.

What better way to examine how a system views a container—which, it is worth repeating, is definitely not a virtual machine—than by using some hands-on examples?

Container Components

There are typically a number of common components on a Linux system that enable the secure use of containers, although new features, or improvements to existing kernel and system features, are augmented periodically. These are Linux security features that allow containers to be bundled into a distinct unit and separated from other system resources. Such system and kernel features mean that most containers spawned, without adding any nonstandard options to disable such security features, have a limited impact on other containers and the underlying host. However, often unwittingly containers will run as the `root` user or developers will open security features to ease their development process. Table 1.1 presents key components.

Table 1.1: Common Container Components

COMPONENT	DESCRIPTION
Kernel namespaces	A logical partitioning of kernel resources to reduce the visibility that processes receive on a system.
Control croups	Functionality to limit usage of system resources such as I/O, CPU, RAM, and networking. Commonly called *cgroups*.
SElinux/AppArmor	Mandatory Access Control (MAC) for enforcing security-based access control policies across numerous system facets such as filesystems, processes, and networking. Typically, SElinux is found on Red Hat Enterprise Linux (RHEL) derivatives and AppArmor on Debian derivatives. However, SElinux is popular on both, and AppArmor appears to be in experimental phase for RHEL derivatives such as CentOS.
Seccomp	Secure Computing (seccomp) allows the kernel to restrict numerous system calls; for the Docker perspective, see `docs.docker.com/engine/security/seccomp`.

COMPONENT	DESCRIPTION
Chroot	An isolation technique that uses a pseudo root directory so that processes running within the chroot lose visibility of other defined facets of a system.
Kernel capabilities	Checking and restricting all system calls; more in the next section.

Kernel Capabilities

To inspect the innards of a Linux system and how they relate to containers in practice, we need to look a little more at kernel capabilities. The kernel is important because before other security hardening techniques were introduced in later versions, Docker allowed (and still does) the ability to disable certain features, and open up specific, otherwise locked-down, kernel permissions.

You can find out about Linux kernel capabilities by using the command `$ man capabilities` (or by visiting `man7.org/linux/man-pages/man7/capabilities.7.html`).

The manual explains that capabilities offer a Linux system the ability to run permission checks against each system call (commonly called *syscalls*) that is sent to the kernel. Syscalls are used whenever a system resource requests anything from the kernel. That could involve access to a file, memory, or another process among many other things, for example. The manual explains that during the usual run of events on traditional Unix-like systems, there are two categories of processes: any privileged process (belonging to the `root` user) and unprivileged processes (which don't belong to the `root` user). According to the Kernel Development site (`lwn.net/1999/1202/kernel.php3`), kernel capabilities were introduced in 1999 via the v2.1 kernel. Using kernel capabilities, it is possible to finely tune how much system access a process can get without being the `root` user.

By contrast, *cgroups* or *control groups* were introduced into the kernel in 2006 after being designed by Google engineers to enforce quotas for system resources including RAM and CPU; such limitations are also of great benefit to the security of a system when it is sliced into smaller pieces to run containers.

The problem that kernel capabilities addressed was that privileged processes bypass all kernel permission checks while all nonroot processes are run through security checks that involve monitoring the user ID (UID), group ID (GID), and any other groups the user is a member of (known as *supplementary groups*). The checks that are performed on processes will be against what is called the *effective UID* of the process. In other words, imagine that you have just logged in as a nonroot user `chris` and then elevate to become the `root` user with an `su-` command. Your "real UID" (your login user) remains the same; but after you elevate to become the superuser, your "effective UID" is now 0, the UID for the `root` user. This is an important concept to understand for security, because security controls need to track both UIDs throughout their lifecycle on a system. Clearly you don't want a security application telling you that the root user is attacking your system, but instead you need to know the "real UID," or the login user chris in this example, that elevated to become the root user instead. If you are ever doing work within a container for testing and changing the USER instruction in the Dockerfile that created the container image, then the id command is a helpful tool, offering output such as this so you can find out exactly which user you currently are:

```
uid=0(root) gid=0(root) groups=0(root)
```

Even with other security controls used within a Linux system running containers, such as namespaces that segregate access between pods in Kubernetes and OpenShift or containers within a runtime, it is highly advisable never to run a container as the root user. A typical Dockerfile that prevents the root user running within the container might be created as shown in Listing1.1.

Listing 1.1: A Simple Example Dockerfile of How to Spawn a Container as Nonroot

```
FROM debian:stable
USER root
RUN apt-get update && apt-get install -y iftop && apt-get clean
USER nobody
CMD bash
```

In Listing 1.1, the second line explicitly states that the root user is initially used to create the packages in the container image, and then the nobody user actually executes the final command. The USER root line isn't needed if you build the container image as the root user but is added here to demonstrate the change between responsibilities for each USER clearly.

Once an image is built from that Dockerfile, when that image is spawned as a container, it will run as the nobody user, with the predictable UID and GID of 65534 on Debian derivatives or UID/GID 99 on Red Hat Enterprise Linux derivatives. These UIDs or usernames are useful to remember so that you can check that the permissions within your containers are set up to suit your needs. You might need them to mount a storage volume with the correct permissions, for example.

Now that we have covered some of the theory, we'll move on to a more hands-on approach to demonstrate the components of how a container is constructed. In our case we will not use the dreaded --privileged option, which to all intents and purposes gives a container root permissions. Docker offers the following useful security documentation about privileges and kernel capabilities, which is worth a read to help with greater clarity in this area:

```
docs.docker.com/engine/reference/run/
#runtime-privilege-and-linux-capabilities
```

The docs describe Privileged mode as essentially enabling "...access to all devices on the host as well as [having the ability to] set some configuration in AppArmor or SElinux to allow the container nearly all the same access to the host as processes running outside containers on the host." In other words, you should rarely, if ever, use this switch on your container command line. It is simply the least secure and laziest approach, widely abused when developers cannot get features to work. Taking such an approach might mean that a volume can only be mounted from a container with tightened permissions onto a host's directory, which takes more effort to achieve a more secure outcome. Rest assured, with some effort, whichever way you approach the problem there will be a possible solution using specific kernel capabilities, potentially coupled with other mechanisms, which means that you don't have to open the floodgates and use Privileged mode.

For our example, we will choose two of the most powerful kernel capabilities to demonstrate what a container looks like, from the inside out. They are `CAP_SYS_ADMIN` and `CAP_NET_ADMIN` (commonly abbreviated without `CAP_` in Docker and kernel parlance).

The first of these enables a container to run a number of sysadmin commands to control a system in ways a `root` user would. The second capability is similarly powerful but can manipulate the host's and container network stack. In the Linux manual page (`man7.org/linux/man-pages/man7/capabilities.7.html`) you can see the capabilities afforded to these `--cap-add` settings within Docker.

From that web page we can see that Network Admin (`CAP_NET_ADMIN`) includes the following:

- Interface configuration
- Administration of IP firewall
- Modifying routing tables
- Binding to any address for proxying
- Switching on promiscuous mode
- Enabling multicasting

We will start our look at a container's internal components by running this command:

```
$ docker run -d --rm --name apache -p443:443 httpd:latest
```

We can now check that TCP port 443 is available from our Apache container (Apache is also known as `httpd`) and that the default port, TCP port 80, has been exposed as so:

```
$ docker ps
IMAGE  COMMAND              CREATED          STATUS PORTS                    NAMES
httpd  "httpd-foreground" 36 seconds ago Up 33s 80/tcp, 443->443/tcp apache
```

Having seen the slightly redacted output from that command, we will now use a second container (running Debian Linux) to look inside our first container with the following command, which elevates permissions available to the container using the two kernel capabilities that we just looked at:

```
$ docker run --rm -it --name debian --pid=container:apache \
--net=container:apache --cap-add sys_admin debian:latest
```

We will come back to the contents of that command, which started a Debian container in a moment. Now that we're running a Bash shell inside our Debian container, let's see what processes the container is running, by installing the `procps` package:

```
root@0237e1ebcc85: /# apt update; apt install procps -y
root@0237e1ebcc85: /# ps -ef
UID          PID  PPID  C STIME TTY          TIME CMD
root           1     0  0 15:17 ?        00:00:00 httpd -DFOREGROUND
daemon         9     1  0 15:17 ?        00:00:00 httpd -DFOREGROUND
daemon        10     1  0 15:17 ?        00:00:00 httpd -DFOREGROUND
daemon        11     1  0 15:17 ?        00:00:00 httpd -DFOREGROUND
root          93     0  0 15:45 pts/0    00:00:00 bash
root         670    93  0 15:51 pts/0    00:00:00 ps -ef
```

We can see from the `ps` command's output that `bash` and `ps -ef` processes are present, but additionally several Apache web server processes are also shown as `httpd`. Why can we see them when they should be hidden? They are visible thanks to the following switch on the `run` command for the Debian container:

```
--pid=container:apache
```

In other words, we have full access to the `apache` container's process table from inside the Debian container.

Now try the following commands to see if we have access to the filesystem of the `apache` container:

```
root@0237e1ebcc85: cd /proc/1/root
root@0237e1ebcc85: ls
bin  boot  dev etc  home  lib lib64  media  mnt  opt  proc  root  run  sbin
srv  sys  tmp  usr  var
```

There is nothing too unusual from that directory listing. However, you might be surprised to read that what we can see is actually the top level of the Apache container filesystem and not the Debian container's. Proof of this can be found by using this path in the following `ls` command:

```
root@0237e1ebcc85: ls usr/local/apache2/htdocs
usr/local/apache2/htdocs/index.html
```

As suspected, there's an HTML file sitting within the `apache2` directory:

```
root@0237e1ebcc85:/proc/1/root# cat usr/local/apache2/htdocs/index.html
<html><body><h1>It works!</h1></body></html>
```

We have proven that we have visibility of the Apache container's process table and its filesystem. Next, we will see what access this switch offers us:`--net=container:apache`.

Still inside the Debian container we will run this command:

```
root@0237e1ebcc85:/proc/1/root# ip a
1: lo: <LOOPBACK,UP,LOWER_UP> mtu 65536 qdisc noqueue state UNKNOWN group
default
    link/loopback 00:00:00:00:00:00 brd 00:00:00:00:00:00
    inet 127.0.0.1/8 scope host lo
       valid_lft forever preferred_lft forever
10: eth0@if11: <BROADCAST,MULTICAST,UP,LOWER_UP> mtu 1500 qdisc noqueue
state UP
    link/ether 02:42:ac:11:00:02 brd ff:ff:ff:ff:ff:ff link-netnsid 0
    inet 172.17.0.2/16 brd 172.17.255.255 scope global eth0
       valid_lft forever preferred_lft forever
```

The slightly abbreviated output from the `ip a` command offers us two network interfaces, `lo` for the loopback interface and `eth0`, which has the IP address 172.17.0.2/16.

Let's exit the Debian container by pressing Ctrl+D and return to our normal system prompt to run a quick test. We named the container `apache`, so using the following `inspect` command we can view the end of the output to get the IP address for the Apache container:

```
$ docker inspect apache | tail -20
```

Listing 1.2 shows slightly abbreviated output from that command, and lo and behold in the `IP Address` section we can see the same IP address we saw from within the Debian container a moment ago, as shown in Listing 1.2: `"IPAddress": "172.17.0.2"`.

Listing 1.2: The External View of the Apache Container's Network Stack

```
"Networks": {
                "bridge": {
                    "IPAMConfig": null,
                    "Links": null,
                    "Aliases": null,
                    "NetworkID": [...snip...]
                    "Gateway": "172.17.0.1",
                    "IPAddress": "172.17.0.2",
                    "IPPrefixLen": 16,
                    "IPv6Gateway": "",
```

```
                        "GlobalIPv6Address": "",
                        "GlobalIPv6PrefixLen": 0,
                        "MacAddress": "02:42:ac:11:00:02",
                        "DriverOpts": null
                    }
                }
            }
        }
]
```

Head back into the Debian container now with the same command as earlier, shown here:

```
$ docker run --rm -it --name debian --pid=container:apache \
--net=container:apache --cap-add sys_admin debian:latest
```

To prove that the networking is fully passed across to the Debian container from the Apache container, we will install the `curl` command inside the container:

```
root@0237e1ebcc85:/# apt update; apt install curl -y
```

After a little patience (if you've stopped the Debian container, you'll need to run `apt update` before the `curl` command for it to work; otherwise, you can ignore it) we can now check what the intertwined network stack means from an internal container perspective with this command:

```
root@0237e1ebcc85:/# curl -v http://localhost:80
<html><body><h1>It works!</h1></body></html>
```

And, not straight from the filesystem this time but served over the network using TCP port 80, we see the HTML file saying, "It works!"

As we have been able to demonstrate, a Linux system does not need much encouragement to offer visibility between containers and across all the major components of a container. These examples should offer an insight into how containers reside on a host and how easy it is to potentially open security holes between containerized workloads.

Again, because containers are definitely not the same as virtual machines, security differs greatly and needs to be paid close attention to. If a container is run with excessive privileges or punches holes through the security protection offered by kernel capabilities, then not only are other containers at serious risk but the host machine itself is too. A sample of the key concerns of a "container escape" where it is possible to "break out" of a host's relatively standard security controls includes the following:

- Disrupting services on any or all containers on the host, causing outages
- Attacking the underlying host to cause a denial of service by causing a stress event with a view to exhaust available resources, whether that be RAM, CPU, disk space capacity, or I/O, for example
- Deleting data on any locally mounting volumes directly on the host machine or wiping critical host directories that cause system failure
- Embedding processes on a host that may act as a form of advanced persistent threat (APT), which could lie dormant for a period of time before being taken advantage of at a later date

Other Containers

A little-known fact is that serverless technologies also embrace containerization, or more accurately lightweight virtualization when it comes to AWS Lambda. Making use of KVM as mentioned earlier, AWS uses Firecracker to provide what it calls MicroVMs. When launched, AWS explicitly stated that security was its top priority and ensured that multiple levels of isolation were introduced to provide defense in depth. From a performance perspective, remarkably the MicroVMs can apparently start up in about an eighth of a second. An active Open Source project, Firecracker is an intriguing technology:

`github.com/firecracker-microvm/firecracker`

As mentioned earlier, the security model is a familiar one, according to the AWS site: "The Firecracker process is jailed using cgroups and seccomp BPF, and has access to a small, tightly controlled list of system calls."

Apparently, at least according to this page on the AWS forums (`forums.aws.amazon.com/thread.jspa?threadID=263968`), there are restrictions applied to the containerized service such as limitations on varying kernel capabilities. These are dropped for security purposes and might include various syscalls like PTRACE, which allow the monitoring of and potentially the control of other processes. Other more obvious services, such as SMTP, are disallowed to prevent spam from leaving a function. And removing the ability to use the `CAP_NET_RAW` capability makes it impossible to spoof IP addresses or use raw sockets for capturing traffic.

Another approach to running containers in a more secure fashion is to lean on hardware virtualization to a greater degree. One of the earlier pioneers of containerization was CoreOS (known for a number of other products, such as `etcd`, which is prevalent in most modern Kubernetes distributions). They created a container runtime called `rkt` (which was pronounced "rock-it"), that is sadly now deprecated. The approach from `rkt` was to make use of KVM as a hypervisor. The premise (explained at `coreos.com/rkt/docs/latest/running-kvm-stage1.html`) was to use KVM, which provides efficient hardware-level virtualization, to spawn containers rather than `systemd-nspawn` (`wiki.debian.org/nspawn`), which can create a slim namespaced container. The sophisticated `rkt` offered what might be called *hard tenancy* between containers. This strict isolation enabled true protection for Customer B if Customer A was compromised; and although containers are, again, not virtual machines, `rkt` bridged a gap where previously few other security innovations had succeeded.

A modern approach being actively developed, similar to that of `rkt`, is called Kata Containers (`katacontainers.io`) via the Open Stack Foundation (OSF). The marketing strapline on the website confidently declares that you can achieve the "speed of containers" and still have the "security of VMs." Along a similar vein to `rkt`, MicroVMs are offered via an Open Source runtime. By using hardware virtualization the isolation of containerized workloads can be comfortably assured. This post from Red Hat about SElinux alerations for Kara Containers is informative: `www.redhat.com/sysadmin/selinux-kata-containers`. Its customers apparently include internet giants such as Baidu, which uses Kata Containers in production, and you are encouraged to investigate their offering further.

Finally, following a slight tangent, another interesting addition to this space is courtesy of AWS, which, in 2020, announced the general availability of an Open Source Linux distribution called Bottlerocket (`aws.amazon.com/bottlerocket`). This operating system is designed specifically to run containers with improved security. The premise for the operational side of Bottlerocket is that creating a distribution that contains only the minimal files required for running containers reduces the attack surface significantly. Coupled with SElinux, to increase isolation between containers and the underlying host, the usual suspects are present too: cgroups, namespaces, and seccomp. There is also device mapper functionality from `dm-verity` that provides integrity checking of block devices to prevent the chances of advanced persistent threats taking hold. While time will tell if Bottlerocket proves to be popular, it is an interesting development that should be watched.

Summary

In this chapter, we looked at some of the key concepts around container security and how the Linux kernel developers have added a number of features over the years to help protect containerized workloads, along with contributions from commercial entities such as Google.

We then looked at some hands-on examples of how a container is constructed and how containers are ultimately viewed from a system's perspective. Our approach made it easy to appreciate how any kind of privilege escalation can lead to unwanted results for other containers and critically important system resources on a host machine.

Additionally, we saw that the USER instruction should never be set to `root` within a container and how a simple Dockerfile can be constructed securely if permissions are set correctly for resources, using some forethought. Finally, we noted that other technologies such as serverless also use containerization for their needs.

CHAPTER 2

Rootless Runtimes

In Chapter 1, "What Is A Container?," we looked at the components that make up a container and how a system is sliced up into segments to provide isolation for the standard components that Linux usually offers.

We also discussed the likely issues that could be caused by offering a container excessive privileges. It became clear that, having examined a container's innards, opening up as few Linux kernel capabilities as possible and stoically avoiding the use of Privileged mode was the way to run containers in the most secure fashion.

In this chapter, we continue looking at developments in the container space that have meant it is no longer necessary to always use the `root` user to run the underlying container runtime(s). Consider that for a moment. In Chapter 1 we discussed how a compromised container can provide a significant threat to the underlying operating system (OS) and other containers running on the host. Additionally, we looked at how the `root` user on the host transposed directly to the `root` user within a container. If the container was subject to a compromise, then any resources that the container could access were also accessible on the host; and most alarmingly, they would have superuser permissions. For a number of years, to improve the Linux container security model, developers made great efforts to run containers without providing `root` user permissions. Relatively recent runtime innovations have meant that the Holy Grail is now a reality.

In the first half of this chapter, we will look at an experimental feature available from Docker (`www.docker.com`), known as *rootless mode*, which apparently is soon to be a stable feature. Following that we will explore another prominent container runtime, called Podman (`podman.io`), that offers similar functionality with some welcome extra features.

Docker Rootless Mode

Docker, beginning with v19.03 (`docs.docker.com/engine/release-notes/#19030`), offers a clever feature it calls *rootless mode*, in which Docker Engine doesn't require superuser privileges to spawn containers. Rootless mode appears to be an extension of a stable feature called *user namespaces*, which helped harden a container. The premise of that functionality was to effectively fool a container into thinking that it was using a host's user ID (UID) and group ID (GID) normally, when from a host's perspective the UID/GID used in the container was being run without any privileges and so was of much less consequence to the host's security.

With rootless mode there are some prerequisites to get started; these have to do with mapping unprivileged users with kernel namespaces. On Debian derivatives, the package we need is called `uidmap`, but we will start (as the `root` user) by removing Docker Engine and its associated packages with this command (be careful only to do this on systems that are used for development, for obvious reasons):

```
$ apt purge docker
```

Then, continuing as the superuser, we will install the package noted earlier with this command:

```
$ apt install uidmap
```

Next, we need to check the following two files to make sure that a less-privileged user (named `chris` in this instance) has 65,536 UIDs and GIDs available for re-mapping:

```
$ cat /etc/subuid
chris:100000:65536
$ cat /etc/subgid
chris:100000:65536
```

The output is what is expected, so we can continue. One caveat with this experimental functionality is that Docker Inc. encourages you to use an Ubuntu kernel. We will test this setup on a Linux Mint machine with Ubuntu 18.04 LTS under the hood.

If you want to try this on Debian Linux, Arch Linux, openSUSE, Fedora (v31+), or CentOS, then you will need to prepare your machine a little more beforehand. For example, although Debian is the underlying OS for Ubuntu, there are clearly notable differences between the two OSs; to try this feature on Debian, you would need to adjust the kernel settings a little beforehand. The required kernel tweak would be as follows, relating to user namespaces:

```
kernel.unprivileged_userns_clone=1
# add me to /etc/sysctl.conf to persist after a reboot
```

You would also be wise to use the `overlay2` storage driver with this command:

```
$ modprobe overlay permit_mounts_in_userns=1
# add me to /etc/modprobe.d to survive a reboot
```

There are a few limitations that we will need to look at before continuing. The earlier user namespace feature had some trade-offs that meant the functionality was not suited for every application. For example, the `--net=host` feature was not compatible. However, that is not a problem, because the feature is a security hole; it is not recommended, because the host's network stack is opened up to a container for abuse. Similarly, we saw that the same applied when we tried to share the process table with the `--pid` switch in Chapter 1. It was also impossible to use `--read-only` containers to prevent data being saved to the container's internal filesystem, which disabled a welcome security control. And, the avoid-at-all-costs Privileged mode was not possible in this setup either.

For rootless mode, however, the limitations are subtly different. In Table 2.1 we can see some of the limitations.

Table 2.1: Rootless Mode Limitations and Restrictions

RESTRICTED FUNCTIONALITY	DESCRIPTION/WORKAROUND
Control groups	Known as *cgroups*, these were used to throttle containers to quotas for host services such as CPU, I/O, and RAM but are not available in rootless mode.
AppArmor	On Ubuntu derivatives or those OSs that use AppArmor, it is not possible to use the mandatory access controls in AppArmor.
Checkpoint	An experimental feature for snapshotting containers; checkpoints will not work in rootless mode: `docs.docker.com/engine/reference/commandline/checkpoint`.
Overlay v1	It appears that the original `overlay` storage driver is not compatible. Use `overlay2` instead: `docs.docker.com/storage/storagedriver/overlayfs-driver`.

Continues

Table 2.1 (continued)

RESTRICTED FUNCTIONALITY	DESCRIPTION/WORKAROUND
Privileged ports	Sometimes known as root ports, privileged ports are any network ports below 1024 and for security reasons can only be exposed to the network by the `root` user. It is, however, possible to use the `setcap` command apparently to do this, but you should research the potentially unintended consequences: `$ setcap cap_net_bind_service=ep $HOME/bin/rootlesskit.`
Ping command	On some Linux distributions it may not be possible to use the `ping` command without adding `net.ipv4.ping_group_range = 0 2147483647` to the file `/etc/sysctl.conf.`
Networking	You need to enter the correct namespace for the host to have visibility of the IP address of the container using `nsenter` (`man7.org/linux/man-pages/man1/nsenter.1.html`), and the same applies to the host's networking as per user namespaces. The `--net=host` option won't work without extra effort or conceding security trade-offs.

The contents of Table 2.1 are not intended to put you off using rootless mode but instead give an insight into the lengths that the developers at Docker have had to go to in order to make this functionality a reality. There are unquestionably trade-offs, but that is almost always the case when security controls are introduced. You might have only one lock on the front door of your house, for example, but to be fully insurable your door probably needs two locks, which means paying for a second lock, fitting it, and carrying a second key with you when you have left the house.

Installing Rootless Mode

To get started we need to download an installation script as supplied by Docker. It can be found at `get.docker.com/rootless` and, as with all online content, the script should be read through to check for any security implications that you do not want to be exposed to before applying it. And, having read the comments at the top of the script, you need to run a `diff` command on the contents of the script `github.com/docker/docker-install/blob/master/rootless-install.sh` before using the script at the other URL (choose the Raw option for the displayed format on GitHub for easy copying):

```
$ diff -y get-docker.sh install.sh
```

This Docker functionality is being actively developed, so if you have trouble with one version of the installation script, try the other, which might be a more stable version.

It should go without saying at this juncture that we do not need to be the `root` user for the running containers. As a result, at this stage we will become the `chris` user with this command:

```
$ sudo -i chris
```

Clearly, you should alter the username to suit your own needs, potentially using your nonprivileged login user.

We will run the slightly more stable `get.docker.com` version of the script this way, saving it to `install.sh` as a filename:

```
$ curl https://get.docker.com/rootless > install.sh
```

Now, make it executable and run the script:

```
$ chmod +x install.sh ; ./install.sh
```

After the short process is completed, you are greeted with Docker Engine client and server version information; for example, the client is installed as follows to match the server version:

```
Client: Docker Engine - Community
 Version:           19.03.12
 API version:       1.40
 Go version:        go1.13.10
```

In Listing 2.1 we can see the tail end of the installation script's output.

Listing 2.1: Rootless Mode Docker Has Installed and Is Offering the User Information

```
# Docker binaries are installed in /home/chris/bin
# WARN: dockerd is not in your current PATH or pointing to /home/chris/
bin/dockerd
# Make sure the following environment variables are set (or add them to
~/.bashrc):
export PATH=/home/chris/bin:$PATH
export DOCKER_HOST=unix:///home/chris/rootless/docker.sock

#
# To control docker service run:
# systemctl --user (start|stop|restart) docker
#
```

Take a look at the post-install advice in Listing 2.1. The binaries have been installed within your user's home directory under the `bin/` directory. You can confirm that they are there with an `ls` command.

The next thing to do is create three environment variables, as follows:

```
$ export XDG_RUNTIME_DIR=/home/$USER/rootless
$ export PATH=/home/$USER/bin:$PATH
$ export DOCKER_HOST=unix:///home/$USER/rootless/docker.sock
```

In the previous examples, for ease, `$USER` is used in place of `chris`.

You can also specify a different directory name here if you prefer. Before running the next command, we will need a directory to store our running container content and configuration, so create one now:

```
$ mkdir rootless
```

Now we can run this command to get rootless mode going, noting that we are using the preferred `overlay2` storage driver:

```
$ bin/dockerd-rootless.sh --experimental --storage-driver overlay2
```

Listing 2.2 shows the end of the output, describing how `/home/chris/rootless/docker.sock` has connected to Docker Engine in rootless mode.

Listing 2.2: Docker in Rootless Mode Has Run Successfully

```
WARN[2020-08-24T15:51:34.554236269+01:00]
Not using native diff for overlay2, this may cause degraded performance
for building images: failed to set opaque flag on middle layer: operation
not permitted  storage-driver=overlay2
INFO[2020-08-24T15:51:34.555462723+01:00] Docker daemon
commit=48a66213fe graphdriver(s)=overlay2 version=19.03.12
INFO[2020-08-24T15:51:34.556309674+01:00]
Daemon has completed initialization
INFO[2020-08-24T15:51:34.602091497+01:00] API listen on
/home/chris/rootless/docker.sock
```

If you run the following command, you will see the processes running for Docker, as the less privileged user:

```
$ ps -ef | grep docker
```

Listing 2.3 shows the results.

Listing 2.3: Rootless Mode Docker Processes Running in the Background

```
chris     9286  9213  0 15:51 pts/0    00:00:00
rootlesskit --net=vpnkit --mtu=1500 --slirp4netns-sandbox=auto
--slirp4netns-seccomp=auto --disable-host-loopback --port-driver=builtin
--copy-up=/etc --copy-up=/run bin/dockerd-rootless.sh --experimental
--storage-driver overlay2
```

```
chris     9295  9286  0 15:51 pts/0    00:00:00 /proc/self/exe --net=vpnkit
--mtu=1500 --slirp4netns-sandbox=auto --slirp4netns-seccomp=auto
--disable-host-loopback --port-driver=builtin --copy-up=/etc
--copy-up=/run bin/dockerd-rootless.sh --experimental
--storage-driver overlay2
chris      9325  9295  0 15:51 pts/0    00:00:04 dockerd --experimental
--storage-driver overlay2
chris      9343  9325  0 15:51 ?        00:00:03 containerd --config /
home/chris/rootless/docker/containerd/containerd.toml --log-level info
```

To start a rootless mode container, we need to point Docker Engine precisely at where the Docker socket file is located. Within a second terminal, we will run the following commands to spawn a rootless Apache container:

```
$ systemctl --user start docker
$ export XDG_RUNTIME_DIR=/home/chris/rootless; \
export DOCKER_HOST=unix:///home/chris/rootless/docker.sock; \
export PATH=/home/chris/bin:$PATH

$ docker run -d -p 8000:80 httpd
Unable to find image 'httpd:latest' locally
latest: Pulling from library/httpd
bf5952930446: Already exists
3d3fecf6569b: Pull complete
b5fc3125d912: Pull complete
679d69c01e90: Pull complete
76291586768e: Pull complete
Digest:
sha256:3cbdff4bc16681541885ccf1524a532afa28d2a6578ab7c2d5154a7abc182379
Status: Downloaded newer image for httpd:latest
a8a031f6a3a3827eb255e1d92619519828f0b1cecfadde25f802a064c6258138
```

Excellent. That is what success looks like when the Docker runtime downloads an image and spawns a container in rootless mode. Note that if you had not chosen TCP port 8000 but instead a port lower than 1024 (normally TCP port 80 for web servers), then you would have received an error because, as a nonroot user, we can't open a privileged or root port.

Also, take note that this feature is very new, and the process to getting rootless Docker to work may vary between builds. You have been warned!

If you run into trouble and need to start again, then carefully as the `root` user you can try the following command (after trying to execute it as your lower privileged user first) to kill off related processes:

```
$ pkill rootlesskit; pkill dockerd; pkill experimental; pkill containerd
```

This should stop all the processes so you can start fresh.

Let's do one final test to show that we have a container running in rootless mode that would be accessing the web server. A reminder that unfortunately network namespaces work differently when using rootless mode. Instead, you can try a few other familiar commands such as the following:

```
$ docker ps
CONTAINER ID IMAGE COMMAND              STATUS        PORTS
a8a031f6a3a3 httpd "httpd-foreground" Up 15 minutes 0.0.0.0:8000->80/tcp
```

In the slightly abbreviated output, you can see that Apache's `httpd` container is running as hoped. To prove that the networking is different with this implementation, we can use this command to check our container's IP address (replacing `a8a031f6a3a3` with the name or hash ID of your container):

```
$ docker inspect a8a031f6a3a3 | grep IPAddress
"IPAddress": "172.17.0.2",
            "MacAddress": "02:42:ac:11:00:02",
                    "IPAddress": "172.17.0.2",
```

We can see that the container is using 172.17.0.2 as its IP address, but now try to connect to the exposed port, TCP port 8000:

```
$ nc -v 172.17.0.2 8000
```

Nothing happens. The connection does not work using the `netcat` tool, so we can see that there's definitely a change in the way standard networking is running. According to the documentation cited earlier, this is expected behavior and occurs because "the daemon is namespaced inside RootlessKit's network namespace." We are not using privileged ports (lower than port 1024), so it is possible to access the container's exposed port; but as you might have guessed, we must do so via the host's network stack. For some potentially helpful context, if you're familiar with Kubernetes, this functionality is called NodePort, where a container directly uses a host port on the host's IP Address so that the container is accessible from outside of the cluster (more can be found at `kubernetes.io/docs/concepts/services-networking/service`). The following `netcat` command will work and will not just quietly fail this time:

```
$ nc -v localhost 8000
Connection to localhost 8000 port [tcp/*] succeeded!
```

And, to prove that is the correct container that responded to our `netcat` request, we can use the `curl` command to check that port on our `localhost` too:

```
$ curl localhost:8000
<html><body><h1>It works!</h1></body></html>
```

We have completed the installation of rootless mode using Docker and additionally successfully proven the networking service of a container running as the user chris. The next steps to continue exploring this improvement to container security would be running a number of containers of varying types to check limitations that this mode introduces in a more complex environment.

Running Rootless Podman

For a more mature version of Docker Engine being run without the root user, let's look at another container runtime that can achieve that, too.

Some industry commentators were surprised when Red Hat applied extra development efforts to a runtime called Podman, as it appeared to come out of the blue (developers.redhat.com/blog/2018/08/29/intro-to-podman). Red Hat has now gone a step further and reportedly removed official support for the Docker package for Red Hat Enterprise Linux v8.0. It has been said that keeping up with feature and security updates for the Community Edition of Docker was a driver in the decision to go it alone. Indeed, Red Hat has created even a podman-docker RPM package that links Docker to Podman for people who are comfortable using Docker commands (access.redhat.com/documentation/en-us/red_hat_enterprise_linux/8/html-single/building_running_and_managing_containers/index). Maintaining autonomy and avoiding reliance on a third party were also apparently factors; Red Hat customers made it clear that their preference was for the container runtime to be either integral to the operating system or integral with OpenShift.

Another valuable Podman feature is its ability to run daemonless. Consider that for a moment. Rather than running an application all year round on critical systems (which in itself represents a superuser-run attack vector), it is possible to use the container runtime only when it is needed. It is a clever and welcome addition to Podman's offering. For backward compatibility, the venerable Podman happily runs container images compliant with the Open Container Initiative (OCI; see www.opencontainers.org), and it is compatible with Docker images, too.

And, with Red Hat Enterprise Linux v8.0 there has been a clearer focus on helping users move away from Docker in Kubernetes to use CRI-O (cri-o.io), which is now one of the preferred container runtimes in Kubernetes thanks to its lightweight and more secure nature. An interesting Red Hat blog entry can be found at developers.redhat.com/blog/2019/01/29/podman-kubernetes-yaml.

It is safe to say that Podman handles the running of containers differently than Docker. Instead of using containerd (the popular runtime) and containerd-shim (the runtime used for daemonless containers that acts a type of parent that shepherds a container's child processes), it uses a `conmon` process for every running container. According to Red Hat (as described at `developers.redhat.com/blog/2019/01/15/podman-managing-containers-pods/`), `conmon` is a small program written in the C language that monitors the parent process of each container. If the container stops or fails, then it dutifully passes on the exit code. Additionally, `conmon` is responsible for allowing the `tty` to be attached to a container, and `conmon` also provides the daemonless functionality that Podman achieves. It manages this by continuing to run, even when Podman has stopped, which cleverly keeps a detached container alive in the background. There is more information on how that works here: `developers.redhat.com/blog/2019/01/15/podman-managing-containers-pods`.

Setting Up Podman

We are going to use the Ubuntu 20.04 Long Term Support (LTS) release to run Podman as rootless. This is because according to the docs (`github.com/containers/podman/blob/master/docs/tutorials/rootless_tutorial.md`), if you read this important note about the `fuse-overlayfs` package, you need at least version 0.7.6: "This especially needs to be checked on Ubuntu distributions as `fuse-overlayfs` is not generally installed by default and the 0.7.6 version is not available natively on Ubuntu releases prior to 20.04."

To install Podman, notably this time as the `root` user, we will first add a source to the `apt` package manager this way as one long command which should go on one line:

```
$ echo "deb
https://download.opensuse.org/repositories/devel:/kubic:/libcontainers:/
stable/xUbuntu
_20.04/ /" | sudo tee /etc/apt/sources.list.d/devel:kubic:libcontainers:
stable.list
```

If you're not using Ubuntu 20.04, then alter the 20.04 string in the previous command. If you want to try other Linux distributions, then you can use this page: `podman.io/getting-started/installation`.

Next, we need to add the repository's key to our keyring as a trusted source (changing 20.04 if required again) which is one line command:

```
$ curl -L
https://download.opensuse.org/repositories/devel:/kubic:/libcontainers:/stable/
xUbuntu_18.04/Release.key | sudo apt-key add -
```

A successful response is `OK`.

Now, refresh your packages and upgrade any that require upgrading:

```
$ sudo apt-get update; sudo apt-get upgrade -y
```

We should now be able to install Podman as follows:

```
$ apt-get -y install podman
```

Note the output from that command, shown here, so you can get an idea of the underlying components used:

```
Recommended packages:
crun slirp4netns varlink
The following NEW packages will be installed
catatonit conmon containernetworking-plugins containers-common
containers-golang containers-image crun libyajl2 podman
podman-plugins runc slirp4netns uidmap varlink
```

Check that Podman has installed correctly:

```
$ podman -v
podman version 2.0.4
```

We need to check our UID and GID mapping settings files to run rootless containers next. Run these commands and delete any entries (only on a development system!) to check that they are empty:

```
$ cat /etc/subuid
$ cat /etc/subgid
```

This is the point where you might want to create a specific user for running rootless containers. Simply use the `adduser` command with a username of your choice, such as `poduser`, and follow the prompts:

```
$ sudo adduser poduser
```

We will stick with user `chris`, however, for continuity.

Now we want to populate the `subuid` and `subgid` files in the `/etc` directory. Use this command to set the ranges of UIDs and GIDS that you want to use, changing the name of the user at the end to suit your requirements:

```
$ sudo usermod --add-subuids 200000-201000 --add-subgids 200000-201000 chris
```

Without any more tweaking or fiddling, we are ready to run Podman in rootless mode. It has been a particularly painless process so far.

First, however, remember that Podman is not running as a daemon. Take a look with this command (to be really sure, run this as the `root` user to see any hidden processes in the process table, and not only as the `chris` user):

```
$ ps -ef | grep podman
```

The only output you should see is the `grep` command that you've just run. But, if we run this Podman command, we should see a service ready and waiting:

```
$ podman ps
CONTAINER ID  IMAGE   COMMAND  CREATED  STATUS  PORTS   NAMES
```

It looks remarkably familiar, just as Docker Engine would output. Using the `chris` user we can start up a container using another familiar command for Apache:

```
$ podman run -it -p 8000:80 httpd:latest
```

We have not added the `-d` switch to that command, and Listing 2.4 shows the `STDOUT` logging (output straight to the terminal).

Listing 2.4: Podman Running Rootless with Little Effort

```
AH00558: httpd: Could not reliably determine the server's fully
qualified domain name, using 10.0.2.100. Set the 'ServerName' directive
globally to suppress this message
AH00558: httpd: Could not reliably determine the server's fully
qualified domain name, using 10.0.2.100. Set the 'ServerName' directive
globally to suppress this message
[Tue Aug 29 14:09:20.303062 2020] [mpm_event:notice]
[pid 1:tid 140532155102336] AH00489: Apache/2.4.46 (Unix) configured
-- resuming normal operations
[Tue Aug 29 14:09:20.304849 2020] [core:notice]
[pid 1:tid 140532155102336] AH00094: Command line:
'httpd -D FOREGROUND'
```

Just as we did before with Docker in rootless mode, let's see how our networking is set up. We will open up another terminal (as the `chris` user) and try this command:

```
$ podman ps
CONTAINER ID  IMAGE                   COMMAND            CREATED
e09883662c2b docker.io/library/httpd:latest httpd-foreground
```

The abbreviated output proves we have `httpd` running as hoped. It is worth noting that other standard users will not have visibility of Podman container processes, but the user `chris` certainly does. We can see the container is definitely running, and not as the `root` user:

```
$ ps -ef | grep podman
```

The abbreviated output from that command shows, among other entries:

```
chris       6069    6035  podman run -it -p 8000:80 httpd:latest
```

Do we need to access the container via the host's network, as we did with Docker? We can test with this command:

```
$ curl localhost 8000
<html><body><h1>It works!</h1></body></html>
```

The answer is yes, we've exposed a nonprivileged port (TCP port 8000) and can access the container via the `localhost`. If you get stuck, check firewalling rules or other container runtimes that are still installed.

One difference between Docker and Podman in rootless mode is that Podman does not allocate an IP address by default. Using the previous `podman ps` command, we can see our container's hash ID is `e09883662c2b`. The next command should offer us internal IP addresses, but not in Podman containers:

```
$ podman inspect e098 | grep IP
"IPAddress": "",
              "IPPrefixLen": 0,
              "IPv6Gateway": "",
              "GlobalIPv6Address": "",
              "GlobalIPv6PrefixLen": 0,
              "LinkLocalIPv6Address": "",
              "LinkLocalIPv6PrefixLen": 0,
```

The top line in the output demonstrates that an IP address doesn't appear to be allocated, even though from a container's perspective an IP address is actually allocated via `slirp4netns` (the component that provides userspace networking functionality that was installed earlier). The container can apparently only communicate over the network with the host and beyond (and not other containers). There is more information at `github.com/rootless-containers/slirp4netns`. Thanks to the fact that Podman provides no default networking bridge, this is a limitation when using `slirp4netns`, which is part and parcel or using rootless mode.

If you need to run the `ping` command from a rootless container for any reason, you might need to tweak the kernel. You can temporarily adjust the tunable kernel setting with this syntax:

```
$ sysctl -w "net.ipv4.ping_group_range=0 2000000"
```

To make sure this setting survives reboots, you should add the following command to copy it to a file:

```
$ echo "net.ipv4.ping_group_range=0 2000000" >> /etc/sysctl.conf
```

The documentation encourages you to delve into the `/usr/share/containers` directory. As a low-privileged user, you should be able to read the files but not necessarily edit them, as these are for the sysadmin to edit. The files are as follows:

```
containers.conf  seccomp.json
```

If you look inside the directory `/etc/containers`, then you can apparently override the settings in the previous directory. The file listing looks like this:

```
containers.conf  policy.json      registries.conf  registries.d/
storage.conf
```

Note that Podman reads these configuration files in this order, with the last overriding the previous file's settings potentially:

```
/usr/share/containers/containers.conf
/etc/containers/containers.conf
$HOME/.config/containers/containers.conf
```

The `containers.conf` file contains a number of user-tunable settings. You can configure *cgroups* (control groups) and resource quotas such as RAM and CPU, and you can also define which kernel capabilities are included. In Listing 2.5 we can see many default capabilities have been commented out, which means they are not in use but are instead replaced by Podman's corresponding default settings.

Listing 2.5: Some Additional Kernel Capabilities That Can Be Uncommented for Containers to Use

```
# List of default capabilities for containers.
# If it is empty or commented out,
# the default capabilities defined in the container engine will
# be added.
#
# default_capabilities = [
#     "AUDIT_WRITE",
#     "CHOWN",
#     "DAC_OVERRIDE",
#     "FOWNER",
#     "FSETID",
#     "KILL",
#     "MKNOD",
#     "NET_BIND_SERVICE",
#     "NET_RAW",
#     "SETGID",
#     "SETPCAP",
#     "SETUID",
#     "SYS_CHROOT",
# ]
```

The `storage.conf` file is a comprehensive way of tweaking your rootless container storage options. You can remap UIDs and GIDs if required so they appear differently inside and outside your containers to suit your volume mounting needs.

There are also settings for the `devicemapper` logging levels, which can help debug storage driver issues if required.

Inside the `registries.conf` file it is also possible to set up your image registry settings. In that file you can see the following:

```
[registries.search]
registries = ['docker.io', 'quay.io']
```

And, in the `registries.d/` directory you can configure the settings required to access those container image registries with authentication, for example.

Summary

In this chapter, we have proven that running containers without relying on the exposure of the `root` user is thankfully now no longer a distant reality when running containerized workloads.

Our first container runtime, Docker Engine, needs some more fine-tuning to get rootless mode working but did successfully launch a fully functional container, without needing the `root` user. The second runtime, Podman, not only does not need to run around the clock as a daemon but additionally took little effort, using Ubuntu 20.04, to install. Its configuration also looks like a logical process in addition. Remember that not only is Podman capable of running with less privileges, but it is also a highly versatile, lightweight, and daemonless container runtime that can be used in a number of scenarios as the `root` user too.

Watch this space carefully. Although the nascent rootless innovations still need a little more work, rootless Podman is growing increasingly mature. Thanks to Red Hat's reach within enterprise environments, it is used extensively in OpenShift v4.0 platforms and is indeed battle-hardened as a production container runtime.

CHAPTER 3

Container Runtime Protection

In previous chapters, we looked at the need to get the permissions correctly configured to protect other containers running on a host and indeed the host itself. In Chapter 6, "Container Image CVEs," we will also look at protecting against common vulnerabilities and exploits (CVEs) to plug security holes in container images. The third major aspect of container security is at least as important from an operational perspective. That is the need to capture and potentially automatically remediate any issues when anomalous behavior is discovered from your running containers.

Only a handful of trustworthy and battle-worn container runtime security applications exist. Of those there is one Open Source tool that stands out from the crowd. Created by a company called Sysdig (`sysdig.com`) in 2016 and a member of the Cloud Native Computing Forum (CNCF), Falco (`falco.org`) excels at both container and host security rules enforcement and alerting. Of the more popular commercial tools there are Prisma Cloud Compute Edition (formerly Twistlock prior to acquisition) and Aqua from AquaSec.

Falco (`sysdig.com/opensource/falco`) offers exceptional Open Source functionality that can be used to create rulesets to force containers to behave in precisely the way you want. It also integrates with Kubernetes API Audit Events, which means that all sorts of orchestrator actions can be secured in addition. You can find more information here:

```
falco.org/docs/event-sources/kubernetes-audit.
```

In this chapter, we will look at installing Falco and then explore its features and how it can help secure our container runtime and underlying hosts, in the same way that some commercial products do, but without any associated fees. We will also explore using some of its rulesets and how to make changes to them yourself.

Running Falco

Following true Cloud Native methodology, we will use a container image to spawn Falco. That said, there are Linux `rpm`, `deb`, and binary files that you can install or execute directly, too, which appears to be the preferred route for their installation.

You can run Falco either on a host or by a userland container that additionally needs to access a pre-installed driver on the underlying host. Falco works by tapping into the kernel with elevated permissions to pick up the kernel's system calls (syscalls), and the driver is needed to offer that required functionality. We also need to provide Falco with the requisite permissions to enable such functionality. As described in Chapter 1, "What Is A Container?," for a container runtime we define these permissions using kernel capabilities. To get an idea of what is available, you could do worse than looking over some of the names of the kernel capabilities in the manual (using the command `man capabilities`). Various versions of the manual are online too, such as this:

```
man7.org/linux/man-pages/man7/capabilities.7.html
```

To protect the underlying host, we will run Falco with as few privileges as possible. Be warned, however, that you will need a kernel version of v5.8 or higher to make use of the extended Berkeley Packet Filter (eBPF) driver without running a one-off `--privileged` container to install that driver to the underlying host(s) that Falco will run on. The Berkeley Packet Filter has been extended to allow increased access to the networking stack to applications via the kernel.

If you are lucky enough to have a kernel of v5.8 or later, the way around the one-off driver installation is to add the `CAP_SYS_BPF` option to your running container at startup time, which the more modern kernels will support. Add it using this command-line switch:

```
--cap--add SYS_BPF
```

For this demonstration, we will not assume that you have that kernel version, so we will install the driver on a host where we will use the one-off container method. The commands are as follows:

```
$ docker pull falcosecurity/falco-driver-loader:latest
$ docker run --rm -it --privileged -v /root/.falco:/root/.falco \
-v /proc:/host/proc:ro -v /boot:/host/boot:ro \
```

```
-v /lib/modules:/host/lib/modules:ro \
-v /usr:/host/usr:ro -v /etc:/host/etc:ro \
falcosecurity/falco-driver-loader:latest
```

As you can see, we are using the insecure `--privileged` switch to gain the elevated permissions required to install the Falco driver. Listing 3.1 shows part of the output from the command, in which Dynamic Kernel Module Support (DKMS) is called into action on Debian derivatives and a kernel module is used.

Listing 3.1: DKMS Assisting with the Privileged Kernel Module Installation

```
Building module:
cleaning build area...
make -j4 KERNELRELEASE=4.15.0-20-generic
-C /lib/modules/4.15.0-20-generic/build
M=/var/lib/dkms/falco/85c88952b018fdbce246422[...snip]/build...
cleaning build area...
DKMS: build completed.
falco.ko:
Running module version sanity check.
 - Original module
   - No original module exists within this kernel
 - Installation
   - Installing to /lib/modules/4.15.0-20-generic/kernel/extra/
```

Although the kernel version (4.15.0.20-generic) seems like a long way off from version 5.8, around version v4.19 the versions jumped to v5.4. To check that the process has automatically loaded up the kernel module as hoped, we can run this `lsmod` command:

```
$ lsmod | grep falco
falco                  634880  0
```

As we can see, `falco` is present in the list of loaded modules, so we can continue to proceed. Obviously, if you installed packages directly onto the host as the `root` user, this step would not be needed, but it is important to illustrate that container protection security tools also have trade-offs, and suffice to say functionality like rootless mode will not accommodate such functionality without some heartache. Relinquishing an undefined security control, such as having a common attack vector across all hosts, to onboard a security tool to protect running containers is a necessary evil; in this case, the kernel module is essential to Falco's functionality. Be aware that you are allowing the tool to tap into the very lowest level of a host's innards (and its running containers), so you need to be completely sure that the security product to which you are offering privileged access is fully trustworthy. On a large, containerized estate, with orchestrators and potentially tens of thousands of running containers on differing varieties of hosts, the fact that you are adding another attack vector to each and every host in the estate needs to be carefully considered. You are effectively opening up a predictable security hole (that is, it is predictable if an attacker knows that a privileged container runs on each host) that can be exploited throughout the estate if a vulnerability is found.

Next, to run our Falco container, we will run the following long command all on one line ideally to enable the kernel capability `CAP_SYS_PTRACE`. According to the `SYS_PTRACE` man page (`man7.org/linux/man-pages/man2/ptrace.2.html`), we can control and manipulate other processes with this privilege as well as move data into the memory space of processes.

```
$ docker run --rm -it --security-opt apparmor:unconfined \
--cap-add SYS_PTRACE \
--pid=host $(ls /dev/falco* | xargs -I {} echo --device {}) -v
/var/run/docker.sock:/var/run/docker.sock \
falcosecurity/falco-no-driver:latest
```

Note that we're demonstrating Falco on a Linux Mint machine (which is based on Ubuntu 18.04), and this command uses AppArmor effectively to stop rogue processes accessing several locked-away parts of a system. To use it, we also need to add the following switch to provide the required permissions to our container:

```
--security-opt apparmor:unconfined
```

As demonstrated in Chapter 1, you might also recognize that the container is offered the ability to access the host's process table namespace with the `--pid` switch on the Docker command.

Think about this for a moment. From a security vendor's perspective, AppArmor has clearly made an effort to reduce the attack surface its product brings to each host. However, from an organization's point of view, there's definitely a significant trade-off. We are effectively switching off all the protection afforded by AppArmor for this container and offering the tool the ability to poison or break other processes. That applies not just to our container runtime but our host(s) as a whole. Do not be mistaken; Falco is certainly not alone when it comes to this elevated permissions requirement for runtime protection.

After we have run the previous command, its brief output includes information as follows:

```
2020-08-09T12:27:54+0000: Falco initialized with configuration file
/etc/falco/falco.yaml
2020-08-09T12:27:54+0000: Loading rules from file
/etc/falco/falco_rules.yaml:
2020-08-09T12:27:54+0000: Loading rules from file
/etc/falco/falco_rules.local.yaml:
2020-08-09T12:27:54+0000: Loading rules from file
/etc/falco/k8s_audit_rules.yaml:
```

Thanks to the fact that we entered the command as shown earlier, without adding `-d` to daemonize the container and `detach` the terminal from it, the `STDOUT` output (direct to the terminal) immediately starts listing some useful insights into what's happening on the host machine. Let's see what we can expect from Falco by looking at some of the output now. The first example is related to filesystem access:

```
2020-08-09T13:35:47.930163243+0000: Warning Sensitive file opened for
reading by non-trusted program (user=<NA> program=pkexec
command=pkexec
/usr/lib/x86_64-linux-gnu/cinnamon-settings-daemon/csd-backlight-helper
--set-brightness 828 -b firmware -b platform
-b raw file=/etc/pam.d/common-account parent=csd-power
gparent=cinnamon-sessio ggparent=lightdm gggparent=lightdm
container_id=host image=<NA>)
```

We can see that "Sensitive file opened for reading by non-trusted program" has flagged an issue. Let's try to spawn a container from an image:

```
2020-08-09T13:45:46.935191270+0000: Notice A shell was spawned in a
container with an attached terminal (user=root <NA> (id=8f31495aeedf)
shell=bash parent=<NA> cmdline=bash terminal=34816
container_id=8f31495aeedf image=<NA>)
```

As we can see, Bash was used to access a running container. The flagged issue is listed as "A shell was spawned in a container with an attached terminal."

Another flagged issue, this time more specific to the host, is as shown here:

```
2020-08-09T13:48:37.040867784+0000: Error File below / or /root opened
for writing (user=root command=bash parent=sudo
file=/root/.bash_history-18236.tmp program=bash container_id=host
image=<NA>)
2020-08-09T13:48:37.041053025+0000: Warning Shell history had been
deleted or renamed (user=root type=rename command=bash
fd.name=<NA> name=<NA> path=<NA>
oldpath=/root/.bash_history-18236.tmp host (id=host))
```

We can see that in the `/root` directory a process has written to a temporary file while the `.bash_history` file, used to record typed Bash commands, was probably opened/closed and appended to.

Another example alert might be this container warning:

```
2020-08-09T15:41:28.324617000+0000: Notice Container with sensitive
mount started (user=root command=container:3369c68859c6
dangly_goldwasser (id=3369c68859c6)
image=falcosecurity/falco-no-driver:latest
mounts=/var/run/docker.sock:/var/run/docker.sock::true:rprivate)
```

We can see that a volume has been mounted by none other than Falco itself so that it can mount the Docker socket to tap into Docker Engine.

Configuring Rules

Next, we will look at how Falco's rulesets are constructed. Here is a more desktop-oriented rule, which should prevent applications (other than Skype or WebEx) from accessing the local camera:

```
- rule: access_camera
  desc: a process other than skype/webex tries to access the camera
  condition: evt.type = open and fd.name = /dev/video0 and not proc.name
  in (skype, webex)
  output: Unexpected process opening camera video device
 (command=%proc.cmdline)
  priority: WARNING
```

As we can see, the rule consists of a name and description followed by three criteria. They are the `condition` Falco should look out for, the `output` it should report, and the `priority` level of the output.

Here is a container-specific rule to examine a bit closer:

```
- rule: change_thread_namespace
  desc: an attempt to change a program/thread\'s namespace
  (commonly done as a part of creating a container) by calling setns.
  condition: syscall.type = setns and not proc.name in
  (docker, sysdig, dragent)
  output: "Namespace change (setns) by unexpected program
  (user=%user.name command=%proc.cmdline container=%container.id)"
  priority: WARNING
```

This rule pays close attention to a container moving between namespaces. The `setns` syscall that is marked as important is used to change namespace. The rule, however, ignores the event if `docker`, `sysdig`, or `dragent` initiate it.

Another example is a case study that Sysdig wrote about to help explain how a CVE could be mitigated using Falco, at the end of 2019. It was CVE-2019-14287 (`cve.mitre.org/cgi-bin/cvename.cgi?name=CVE-2019-14287`) that allowed a simple command to be run to make the `sudo` command run commands as the `root` user. To exploit the CVE, it was apparently as simple as using the `sudo` command as follows:

```
$ sudo -u#-1
```

In Listing 3.2 we can see the rule that the Sysdig team concocted to detect and then block the exploit within the CVE.

Listing 3.2: Detecting and Blocking the "sudo" CVE

```
- rule: Sudo Potential bypass of Runas user restrictions
   (CVE-2019-14287)
  desc: [...snip...] This can be used by a user with sufficient sudo
  privileges to run commands as root even if the Runas specification
  explicitly disallows root access as long as the ALL keyword is listed
  first in the Runas specification
  condition: >
     spawned_process and
     proc.name="sudo" and
     (proc.cmdline contains "-u#-1" or proc.cmdline contains
  "-u#4294967295")
  output: "Detect sudo exploit (CVE-2019-14287)
  (user=%user.name command=%proc.cmdline container=%container.info)"
  priority: CRITICAL
  tags: [filesystem, mitre_privilege_escalation]
```

Source: sysdig.com/blog/detecting-cve-2019-14287

Changing Rules

If you run the Docker command to check the help output, you are offered a number of useful choices to remember, as shown here:

```
$ docker run -it falcosecurity/falco-no-driver:latest falco --help
```

And you can list all the rules currently loaded up into Falco with this syntax:

```
$ docker run -it falcosecurity/falco-no-driver:latest falco -L
```

The output includes the rule name along with a description such as this example:

```
Rule                                 Description
----                                 -----------
Create Symlink Over Sensitive Files Detect symlink over sensitive files
```

Although there are certainly more graceful ways of editing rules and configuration for Falco (which we will look at in a moment), if you use the container approach to run Falco, it is possible to extract the rules file that you want to change and save it to the local machine. Then you can simply mount the local machine volume when Falco fires up, and your changing configuration and rules will be loaded up.

You can initially copy the files out of the container with this command, where a `docker ps` command has given you the hash ID of your container previously:

```
$ docker cp 1f7591607c7d:/etc/falco/falco_rules.yaml .
```

Simply repeat the previous command for these files:

`falco_rules.local.yaml, falco.yaml, k8s_audit_rules.yaml`

As you might imagine, you should place your own custom rules within the `falco_rules.local.yaml` file, which, barring comments, is mostly empty and not overwritten with version upgrades.

To load up changes, mount your volume as so with the additional `-v $(pwd):/etc/falco/` option that mounts the `/etc/falco` directory from inside the container to your current working directory on your local machine:

```
$ docker run --rm -it --security-opt apparmor:unconfined \
--cap-add SYS_PTRACE \
--pid=host $(ls /dev/falco* | xargs -I {} echo --device {}) -v
$(pwd):/etc/falco/ \
-v /var/run/docker.sock:/var/run/docker.sock \
falcosecurity/falco-no-driver:latest
```

The bundled rules are impressive and well worth a look. Listing 3.3 shows a Kubernetes example.

Listing 3.3: Unwanted Service Exposure via a NodePort Is Captured in Kubernetes

```
- rule: Unexpected K8s NodePort Connection
  desc: Detect attempts to use K8s NodePorts from a container
  condition: (inbound_outbound) and fd.sport >= 30000
   and fd.sport <= 32767 and container and not nodeport_containers
  output: Unexpected K8s NodePort Connection (command=%proc.cmdline
   connection=%fd.name container_id=%container.id
    image=%container.image.repository)
  priority: NOTICE
  tags: [network, k8s, container, mitre_port_knocking]
```

It's not 100% clear, but the commercial, enterprise method used to update rules appears to be connecting to a back end. Rather than extracting the configuration and rules files from a running container, Falco also offers the ability to install rules in a different way. On Docker Hub (`hub.docker.com/r/sysdig/falco_rules_installer`), there is a container image created by Sysdig that will allow you to update rules via a running container. Its purpose is to first validate existing rules and then inspect any custom rules and deploy them to a suitable back end. The command would look like this, for example:

```
$ docker run --rm --name falco-rules-installer -it \
-e DEPLOY_HOSTNAME=https://my-sysdig-backend.com \
-e DEPLOY_USER_NAME=test@sysdig.com \
-e DEPLOY_USER_PASSWORD=<my password> \
-e VALIDATE_RULES=yes -e DEPLOY_RULES=yes \
-e CREATE_NEW_POLICIES=no \
-e SDC_SSL_VERIFY=True sysdig/falco_rules_installer:latest
```

For our purposes, though, copying rules out of a running container makes sense. For the host-installed version, you can also pass the `-c` switch to point the daemon at a different configuration file. It is also quite possible to point, multiple times, at directories where your rules reside with the `-r` switch, too.

Macros

Falco also employs the concept of using macros. The example that their documentation offers for a simple macro is as follows:

```
- macro: in_container
  condition: container.id != host and proc.name = sh
```

This example could be reused across multiple rules without having to explicitly rewrite it each time and offer significant time-savings.

Lists

It is also possible to use lists so that collections of items can be grouped together more easily to make them more repeatable. The following is one example:

```
- list: common_binaries
  items: [netcat, iftop, ngrep]
```

Here, we can avoid explicitly writing all the binaries for Linux shells and instead just refer to a list of `shell_binaries`.

Getting Your Priorities Right

The following are categories for rule priorities:

```
EMERGENCY, ALERT, CRITICAL, ERROR, WARNING,
NOTICE, INFORMATIONAL, DEBUG
```

These categories will allow you to sort alerts into a more meaningful set of results and allow the ability to react accordingly. As we saw in the other rules, within your rules, you would add a line such as this within the following example pseudocode stanza:

```
- rule: A custom rule
  desc: Rule description
  condition: container.privileged=true
  priority: WARNING
```

Tagging Rulesets

You can also group rules and alerts with tags to help with identifying issues more clearly. The tagging also offers the ability to explicitly run only certain rules with the relevant tags, for example. The previous example is shown expanded next to include tags. The `-T` switch disables rules with a certain tag, and the lowercase `-t` switch means that you will only run those rules with the tags listed after that switch.

```
- rule: A custom rule
  desc: Rule description
  condition: container.privileged=true
  priority: WARNING
  tags: [database, cis]
```

Outputting Alerts

In addition to the standard Unix-like `syslog` log forwarding, there are other ways to receive alerts from Falco. To use `syslog`, you can simply tweak your configuration this way:

```
syslog_output:
  enabled: true
```

But to use ChatOps alerts, via Slack, for example, Sysdig has created a repository in GitHub (`github.com/falcosecurity/falcosidekick`) to assist with just that.

The documentation describes the service that the code will provide as "a simple daemon for enhancing available outputs for Falco." The list of compatible recipients is lengthy and includes most of the usual suspects, such as Slack, Datadog, AWS Lambda, Opsgenie, Rocketchat, and SMTP for email.

A nice touch is that you can even spawn it as another container; to do that, you would use syntax such as this:

```
$ docker run -d -p 2801:2801 -e SLACK_WEBHOOKURL=XXXXX \
falcosecurity/falcosidekick
```

Additionally, the documentation provides lots of pointers on how to tweak each of the webhook outputs to your needs and enjoy real-time messaging as you want in order to set off emergency pagers at 4 a.m. or just report innocuous events to a chat channel.

Summary

There is no doubt that Falco offers extensive security functionality for both container runtime and hosts. It also plays nicely with Kubernetes, and as of version v0.13.0 API Audit Events can be captured as an event source so that Falco can be rolled out across a cluster to offer genuine insight into what containers and hosts are getting up to in the quiet hours. Supported Kubernetes actions from Falco include the creation and deletion of resources (pods, deployments, daemon sets, and so on), changes to ConfigMaps and secrets, volume mounts, host networking, granting cluster-admin access, and using ConfigMaps for overly sensitive information.

Even the Open Source version of Falco is an impressive, battle-hardened piece of software. And, its commercial products have a notable enterprise client list using the paid-for Enterprise Falco and Sysdig Secure products. If you are to trust your cloud estate with security tools running with elevated permissions, then clearly it makes sense to use the most reputable tool that you can find on the market to avoid bouts of insomnia.

CHAPTER

4

Forensic Logging

In previous chapters, we looked at ensuring that containers ran with minimal permissions and saw how to catch and enforce anomalous behavior from containers. However, as any seasoned professional will tell you, security is far more than just enforcement.

Thanks to the clever design of the Linux kernel, there is a relatively straightforward way of monitoring precisely how your container runtime and orchestrator interact with their underlying hosts. It is possible to log not only every action that a system makes but in fact every system call (syscall), which occurs when a process requests something from the kernel, on a running system.

Why would you do this? There are at least two particularly good reasons. First, an audit trail offers you the ability to trace how an attacker compromised, or partially compromised, a container or a host. The forensic analysis that you can perform on such logs allows you to walk step-by-step through any event and, with enough understanding of what each step entails, retrace the footsteps of an attacker. Second, having such a high level of detailed operational data available to you can make performance tuning and application debugging possible. You can see exactly what an application is doing and then fine-tune it in response.

In this chapter, we will look at what is described as the "userspace component to the Linux Auditing System," according to the man page. The venerable `auditd` is a way of interacting with the Linux Auditing System to write system events to disk. This command allows you to define the number of days to store log files, where any log file older than the number of days is automatically deleted. It is also possible to prevent changes to the logging configuration (which an attacker would want to do in order to hide their actions) without the root user first causing a reboot. Bear in mind that if you implement `auditd` rules as recommended, then you should be monitoring, as part of your security concerns, irregular reboots after you have set it up for this reason.

Things to Consider

We will look at how to manage a sane number of log files locally, on the host that `auditd` is set up on, to avoid flooding your disks with potentially very noisy log files. On a busy Kubernetes host, for example, with containers being stopped and started, your logs can fill up rapidly. When using `auditd`, make sure that you monitor your initial logging activity closely. You may find that if logs are too noisy, instead of keeping 30 days of logs locally, you decide to store them for far fewer days. If you are working in a large organization that can afford to store voluminous logging data, you can also use `syslog` to forward such logs upstream to a system such as Splunk (`www.splunk.com`), or you could create your own Syslog receivers and then purge your older log files.

One less-than-obvious capacity issue is that you need to pay close attention to the ordering of your `auditd` monitoring rules. This is because every single kernel/system interaction will be logged to disk if you choose to use wide-ranging rules. If you are familiar with the kernel's Netfilter (commonly used for firewalling) and its Userland companion IPtables, rules are processed in order, from the top down. The same applies here; in other words, if your first `auditd` rule satisfies more than 50% of syscalls, then the subsequent rules will not be processed for the majority of the time. As a result of this, your `auditd` ruleset is processed much more efficiently, and syscalls are acted upon faster, speeding up your system.

This issue is not quite as significant on modern cloud servers, whose CPU specifications provide considerably better performance than older hardware could achieve. However, in production systems this issue should always be factored in. It is a contentious issue because virtual machines hosted on-site can act quite differently than those provisioned in the cloud, where more tenants generally share the compute and I/O resources.

Think for a moment about what takes place when an event is logged to disk. The fact that the auditing system is built into the kernel means the capture of an event is not the issue, but when dealing with many potential log entries per second, the resulting I/O is relatively expensive. If you're in any doubt, Red Hat provides a useful page that talks about disk I/O affecting non-SSD drives, titled "Is there any system performance penalty to enable auditing?"

(access.redhat.com/solutions/666333). This unrelated page (linux-audit.com/tuning-auditd-high-performance-linux-auditing) encourages you to consider ignoring events to speed up the processing of your auditd ruleset.

Let's take a look at how to set up auditd, and we can return to this consideration later.

Salient Files

We will begin with a look at the files that make up the auditd package. It is safe to say that auditd is more commonly found by default on Red Hat Enterprise Linux than some other Linux distributions. That said, the following command shows a Debian server hosting the package without issue. Thanks to the fact that the Ubuntu implementation of auditd will be the same as Debian's, we will use a Debian (Buster) server for this chapter. The only difference is that Debian bundles two simple example files. The nice thing about auditd is that when it comes to Linux distributions that are members of the same family, as Ubuntu and Debian are, the configuration will be the same. Indeed, it is common that configuration can be transposed between other Linux distributions (for Red Hat Enterprise Linux derivatives for example) with ease, too (potentially with the exclusion of file paths and per-distribution package names). This is because auditd is merely translating what are relatively standard kernel event activities back to a human-readable format.

```
$ dpkg -l | grep audit
ii  auditd                          1:2.8.4-3               amd64
User space tools for security auditing
ii  libaudit-common                 1:2.8.4-3               all
Dynamic library for security auditing—common files
ii  libaudit1:amd64                 1:2.8.4-3               amd64
Dynamic library for security auditing
ii  libauparse0:amd64               1:2.8.4-3               amd64
Dynamic library for parsing security auditing
```

Take note at this stage that the majority of your auditd configuration will reside within the /etc/audit directory:

```
$ ls /etc/audit
auditd.conf  auditd.conf.dpkg-dist  audit.rules  audit.rules.prev  audit-
stop.rules  rules.d/
```

We will begin by looking at the syslogauditd.confsyslog file first, as you can see that syslogauditd.conf.dpkg-distsyslog exists as a reminder of the original configuration should we need it. That reminder to keep copies of the default files is timely, because as you will see there are some heavily nuanced rulesets to fine-tune, and until you are used to the syntax, typos can be commonplace.

Also worth pointing out is that the nomenclature of filenames is not quite what you might expect; for example, one of the files in the output just shown is named `audit.rules` and not, for example, `auditd.rules` to keep you on your toes.

Inside the main configuration file, `auditd.conf`, we will start by focusing on a few lines that we will alter. You could achieve this by using Ansible (see the idempotency information for `auditd` in Chapter 11, "Automated Host Security") quite easily using search-and-replace functionality when hardening an Amazon Machine Image (AMI) in AWS or some other type of Linux server. Alternatively, you can build it in your kickstart/build file or image. In Listing 4.1, we can see the contents of the configuration file that we will combine with a lengthy (in most cases) rules file.

Listing 4.1: Contents of the Main Configuration File, `auditd.conf`

```
#
# This file controls the configuration of the audit daemon
#

log_file = /var/log/audit/audit.log
log_format = RAW
log_group = root
priority_boost = 4
flush = INCREMENTAL
freq = 20
num_logs = 5
disp_qos = lossy
dispatcher = /sbin/audispd
name_format = NONE
##name = mydomain
max_log_file = 50
max_log_file_action = ROTATE
space_left = 75
space_left_action = SYSLOG
action_mail_acct = root
admin_space_left = 50
admin_space_left_action = SUSPEND
disk_full_action = SUSPEND
disk_error_action = SUSPEND
##tcp_listen_port =
tcp_listen_queue = 5
tcp_max_per_addr = 1
##tcp_client_ports = 1024-65535
tcp_client_max_idle = 0
enable_krb5 = no
krb5_principal = auditd
##krb5_key_file = /etc/audit/audit.key
```

The first line to pay attention to within Listing 4.1 is `num_logs = 5`. As you would expect, this sets the number of log files you can save locally to a host before rotating them. For ease of file access and portability we will set that to num_logs = 20. Next, we will consider what the maximum log file size in megabytes should grow to until it is rotated. If you work out the sums, then if we leave max_log_file = 50 and multiply that number by 20, then we should never use more than 1GB of disk space. For more information, you can check the man page for this configuration file (linux.die.net/man/8/auditd.conf).

The next setting, admin_space_left, is interesting, although it is a configuration option that is not unique to this logging daemon in Linux. It configures the amount of spare disk capacity left for emergencies so that your system will perform some action before your system falls over due to a lack of disk space. It offers a last chance to save a system from downtime before services fail due to a stress event, such as a denial-of-service attack or a misbehaving application, that starts using up all your disk space. Note that the space_left setting must be higher than this one, which triggers a warning of some sorts that is forwarded to an email address, or syslog for example, via the space_left_action when issues arise. The next three actions do not need much explanation:

```
admin_space_left_action = SUSPEND
disk_full_action = SUSPEND
disk_error_action = SUSPEND
```

The default admin_space_left_action tells auditd what to do when disk space is critically close. Table 4.1 shows the options for this action.

Table 4.1: Actions for auditd When Disks Are Filling Up Rapidly

ACTION	DESCRIPTION
ignore	Disks will continue to fill up and auditd won't act at all.
syslog	A warning alert will be written to the syslog daemon.
email	If you set up action_mail_acct, with an email address, then syslog and the recipient will both receive a warning.
suspend	This forces auditd to stop writing events to disk, limiting your security logging. The auditd daemon should come to life when disk space is available again and doesn't actively sleep.
single	Use single to drop the system to single-user mode. This means your system drops off the network, and other than mounting local disk mounts, you're telling your system to essentially halt for troubleshooting. This option is more drastic than other settings but is a good failsafe to protect a system potentially.

Breaking the Rules

Next, let's move on to how our all-important rulesets are constructed. As we are interested in microservices and containers, we will create a rule to monitor Docker Engine in order to pick up some of its actions in our audit logs. To do this we will add a single line to the `audit.rules` file (in addition to the defaults, which will be explained shortly):

```
-w /usr/bin/docker -p rwxa -k docker-daemon
```

Let's break the contents of that line down into segments for a moment.

First, the `-w` switch stands for a rule that "watches" for changes in the filesystem. In other words, when the file that `auditd` is watching does something it will be captured; in this case, the file being monitored is Docker's binary.

Next, the `-p` switch identifies the permissions that we want to capture, such as read access. You should finely tune which permissions you want to capture. Writing to a file is more invasive than reading from it usually, for example. In Table 4.2 we can see the simple options that the "permissions" section of the command means.

Table 4.2: The Different Permissions You Can Apply

PERMISSION	OPTION
`-r`	Logs read accesses of a file
`-w`	Logs write accesses of a file
`-x`	Captures executions of a file
`-a`	Logs attribute changes to a file

As Table 4.2 demonstrates, our previous example captures read, write, execute, and attribute changes to the Docker binary.

Finally, `-k` stands for the keyname, which is essentially a label so that you can sort through the audit logs more easily. You might have one rule for Docker executions and one for its attributes changing, respectively named `docker-run` and `docker-attrib-alert`.

To sum up, the *watches* or *filesystem* rules look like this:

```
-w path-to-file -p permissions -k keyname
```

Our second type of rule is called a *syscall* rule. It starts with an `-a` instead of a `-w`. The syntax is as follows:

```
-a action,list -S syscall -F field=value -k keyname
```

Here we are checking for specific system calls made to the kernel. One example might be related to the request to change the system's hostname, which we can capture this way (entered on a single, long line; we have split it here to fit the page):

```
-a always,exit -F arch=b64 -S sethostname -S setdomainname \
-k system-files
```

Starting from the left, the `-a` switch can be either `always` log or `never` log followed by a comma (and there is never a space before the next entry, which in this case is `exit`). The `exit` represents the current value of the `list` option, which can be any of the following: `task`, `entry`, `exit`, `user`, or `exclude`. The `task` option is not used often, because it is seen only when `fork` or `clone` syscalls are fired.

Table 4.3 illustrates the `list` options that you can use.

Table 4.3: List Options Available for `fork` and `clone` Syscalls

LIST OPTION	DESCRIPTION
`task`	Uncommon; only captured during `fork` or `clone` syscalls.
`entry`	Applies whenever a syscall entry is triggered. It may be deprecated in favor of the greater visibility available via `exit`.
`exit`	Used for exits, and because `entry` can't be used to check certain aspects, the `exit` option is commonly used for filters more often. All fields are available to exits. This example checks for volume mounts: `-a always,exit -F arch=b64 -S mount -F auid>=1000 -F auid!=4294967295 -k mounts`
`user`	Userspace event filtering. You can use `uid`, `auid`, `gid`, and `pid`.
`exclude`	Switches off some events combined with `msgtype` to stop the kernel from capturing them. For example, here we're not logging current working directory alerts, which are always known as `cwd`: `-a always,exclude -F msgtype=CWD`

The `-S` switch can be the syscall name or its number, but humans usually prefer a recognizable name. For efficiency, you can add more than one syscall per rule, and it is recommended that you chain rules together. The `-F` helps fine-tune the command. For example, if you wanted to avoid monitoring the account UID (user ID) with 500, then your `-F` switch could be `-F uid!=500`.

From a container perspective, using the `msgtype` option to avoid container actions can be useful to explore.

The final rule type that we will look at is an execution command of sorts that "controls" the `auditd` configuration settings. These include deleting currently loaded rules prior to re-applying an updated set of rules or controlling the kernel backlog queue. In almost all but one particularly important control rule, these tend to be set up at the top of the `audit.rules` file. We will look at that control rule a little later on in this chapter, which deals with immutability, which is commonly added at the end of the rules file.

Now that we have gained a better understanding of the types of rules involved with `auditd`, let's return to the directory structure once more before looking at how to query the logs in a sane, manageable way.

Key Commands

As a quick reminder, a directory listing for the main configuration directory `/etc/auditd` looks like this:

```
$ ls /etc/audit
auditd.conf  auditd.conf.dpkg-dist  audit.rules  audit.rules.prev
audit-stop.rules  rules.d/
```

The file `auditd.conf` is where we will tune how the `auditd` daemon will behave; the second file, `auditd.conf.dpkg-dist`, is the original so you can refer back to it.

Pay particular attention here. The `audit.rules` file within the `rules.d/` directory is where our critical config will take place, and a file of the same name in the directory just shown will be the currently running rules, as parsed by `auditd` to set them live within the kernel. The `audit.rules.prev` file is a reminder of your last-known-good ruleset and written automatically when you apply new rules. Note at this point that, for obvious reasons, these files are all owned by the `root` user and can only be written to by `root`. The file `audit-stop.rules` contains the following comment and contents:

```
# These rules are loaded when the audit daemon stops
# if configured to do so.
# Disable auditing
-e 0
# Delete all rules
-D
```

This configuration is essentially clearing the decks and removing any logging and previously loaded-up rules. Bear those commands in mind because they will be present in our main rules file in one form or another shortly.

Inside the `rules.d/` directory there are two files present:

```
audit.rules  audit.rules.dpkg-dist
```

Again, the OS has written a reminder of the original `dpkg-dist` rules should we need them to recover a ruleset.

The Rules

Remember that we are looking at the rules before they are parsed by `auditd` when we are inside the `rules.d/` directory. We should customize this file with our own rules, because changes will not be picked up in the `audit.rules` file in the directory just shown. The `rules.d/` directory is useful because when you sort your rules into sections (one for file access, another for logins, and so on), all files ending with the extension `.rules` in that directory are parsed. Splitting up complex sets of rules into multiple files makes tweaking or enabling/disabling them more manageable. If we look at the top of the contents of that file, we can see the following:

```
# This file contains the auditctl rules that are loaded
# whenever the audit daemon is started via the initscripts.
# The rules are simply the parameters that would be passed
# to auditctl. Path: /etc/audit/rules.d/audit.rules
```

Contrast that to the comments at the top of the file in the directory shown earlier (`/etc/audit`) by the same name, as shown here:

```
$ cat ./audit.rules
## This file is automatically generated from /etc/audit/rules.d
```

It is important to get the differences clear in your mind, particularly if you are automating `auditd` through a configuration management tool such as Ansible, for example. Should you get caught up in confusion around these paths, all hell can break loose if you do not edit the correct file but then query the expected running config. One useful way to remember the difference is that you can add lots of custom comments to the `audit.rules` file in the `rules.d/` directory, but the parsed rules in the `/etc/audit/audit.rules` file will have all the comments stripped out when they rules are parsed.

We will go back up a directory level now and look at the `/etc/audit/audit.rules` file in more detail.

The top of the `audit.rules` file in the `/etc/audit` directory, after the comments, starts this way:

```
-D
-b 320
```

The `-D` flag clears all running rules in their entirety, so for an imperceptibly small amount of time when you refresh rules, there will not be any rules present. The second line shows `-b 320` (Ubuntu uses `-b 8192` by default) is the tunable parameter to tell the system how much buffer to permit `auditd` to use. This is the buffer within the kernel, and as you would expect, the bigger the buffer, the more memory that you will commit from the system's pool. In our example, `320` is a very small memory commitment from the system and would suit systems with less RAM available.

This leads us nicely to the `auditctl` command, which was mentioned a moment ago. You can keep an eye on statistics from a running `auditd` using the `-s` command shown here:

```
$ auditctl -s
enabled 2
failure 1
```

```
pid 325
rate_limit 0
backlog_limit 320
lost 0
backlog 0
backlog_wait_time 15000
loginuid_immutable 0 unlocked
```

To determine how much buffer your system needs to capture all of your system's activity (or at least the activity that your rules apply to), you need to pay attention to the `backlog` value displayed by this command. The `backlog_limit` should be greater than the backlog value to ensure smooth operation. The `lost` metric shows how many events the system could not capture. Clearly this value should be nominal.

As a rule of thumb, in general you should make the buffer larger for busier systems. We can also see from that command's output that an event `failure` was recorded. You can cause the system to panic, log to `syslog`, or silently ignore the failure should `auditd` fail to record an event. When buffers get filled up, the failure option settings are checked by the kernel. To set the way `auditd` handles failures, use `audit_set_failure`. Table 4.4 shows the options for that setting.

Table 4.4: Options for `audit_set_failure`

OPTION	VALUE	DESCRIPTION
0	AUDIT_FAIL_PRINTK	This is the default and will drop failure events to the "syslog."
1	AUDIT_FAIL_SILENT	Using this option means no action is taken upon failure.
2	AUDIT_FAIL_PANIC	The machine uses the panic function to freeze the machine.

We will continue looking at the `auditctl` command now and return to a list of example rules after that.

Parsing Rules

Before we get into the detail of example rules, we will look at how to interact with `auditd` and ask the rules to be parsed and then loaded into the system.

To demonstrate that our example command is successful, we will delete all existing rules manually (remember the `-D` line in the configuration file mentioned earlier?) and use the `auditctl` command to do that. Let's verify that it works now, as shown here:

```
$ auditctl -D
No rules
```

The first thing to note is that there are no rules set up. Second, because we are able to alter rules without a reboot, we can tell that the "immutable rules" option (which you should ensure is present when you are fully happy with your rules in order to increase security) is not enabled. For more information regarding this excellent security feature (which does add operational overhead, as downtime is required to make changes), see the "Immutable Rules" sidebar.

IMMUTABLE RULES

To prevent unwanted, nefarious changes to the auditing rules, something an attacker would definitely be keen to do, the sophisticated `auditd` can be set up to require a reboot before allowing even the `root` user the ability to do so.

The workflow for making a change to rules on a running `auditd` system that has immutable rules enabled already is as follows.

Edit the `/etc/audit/audit.rules` file and set the `-e` option at the end of the `rules.d/auditd.rules` file from `2` to `1` (or if you prefer, then you can comment out that line stating as so: `#  -e  2`). Next, run these commands, noting the comments for each of them, for an explanation:

```
$ augenrules --check # make sure that we edited the correct rules file
  /sbin/augenrules: Rules have changed and should be updated

$ augenrules --load # load the adjusted rules file

$ reboot
```

To re-enable immutable rules, you simply edit the `/etc/audit/audit.rules` file again and change rules as required. Once you are finished, add the `-e  2` option back to the bottom of the `/etc/audit/audit.rules` file (or remove the `#` comment) and then run the `augenrules  --load` command shown earlier to enable immutability.

Let's look at a simple example of a rules file now.

Inside the `rules.d/` directory we will add a short rules file to demonstrate `auditd` in action. We will call the file `audit.rules` as you would if you were combining all your rules into a single file. At the start of the file we delete previous rules (so that none exist) and then load a `login` monitoring rule. In Listing 4.2 we can see what our file would look like.

Listing 4.2: A Simple Rules File to Catch User Logins

```
# First rule—delete all
-D
# Increase the buffers to survive stress events such as DDoS attacks.
# Make this larger (e.g. 8192) for busy systems
-b 320
# Login and Logout events are captured
-w /var/log/lastlog -p wa -k catch-logins
```

```
# Don't enable immutability
#(if you set this to "2" you need a reboot to make changes)
-e 1
```

Notice that we have used a `watch` rule that will check the login system file for changes and then dutifully log them.

To apply the file's rules, by parsing them into machine-friendly rules with comments stripped out, we use this command first to sanity-check that the system is happy with their syntax:

```
$ augenrules --check
```

This command will spot any rules that have changed in your `rules.d/` directory and parse those rules to populate your `/etc/audit/audit.rules` file. If you get confused, the difference in the contents of the two rules files is that comments are present in the `rules.d/` version. The `--check` option is really useful if you transpose rulesets between Linux distributions that use subtly different file paths for some files.

The next command parses and applies the rules from our `rules.d/` directory:

```
$ augenrules --load
```

Let's check to test whether applying our rules worked. The contents of our generated rules file as follows, without comments as hoped around the custom rules:

```
$ cat /etc/audit/audit.rules
## This file is automatically generated from /etc/audit/rules.d
-D
-b 320
-w /var/log/lastlog -p wa -k catch-logins
-e 1
```

And, back to the useful `auditctl` command, we will list, with the `-l` switch, the running configuration with this command:

```
$ auditctl -l
-w /var/log/lastlog -p wa -k catch-logins
```

Excellent. We can see that a single `watch` rule has been applied. Let's test it with a login. Note that we have added the key `catch-logins` so that we can find entries more easily within the log file `/var/log/audit/audit.log`. If we run this command before a login event has taken place, we will see the updating of our rule as shown here under `CONFIG_CHANGE`:

```
$ cat /var/log/audit/audit.log | grep 'catch-logins'
type=CONFIG_CHANGE msg=audit(1595611642.941:886):  auid=1000 ses=17
subj==unconfined op=add_rule key="catch-logins" list=4 res=1
```

We can then view this new entry after a login event has taken place:

```
$ cat /var/log/audit/audit.log | grep 'catch-logins'
type=SYSCALL msg=audit(1595611885.636:969): arch=c000003e syscall=257
success=yes exit=10 a0=ffffff9c a1=7ffd65998d60 a2=42 a3=180 items=2
ppid=532 pid=6596 auid=1000 uid=0 gid=0 euid=0 suid=0 fsuid=0 egid=0
sgid=0 fsgid=0 tty=(none) ses=97 comm="sshd" exe="/usr/sbin/sshd"
subj==unconfined key="catch-logins"
```

That logging entry contains a lot of information, even for one single login event. You can see why on a busy system it is critical to rotate logs proficiently in order to use `auditd` correctly considering that is just one entry. If you are familiar with Linux, then much of the log entry shown here will be reasonably familiar. For example, it notes that the Secure Shell (SSH) executable `sshd` is used, among other things.

But take note of the `auid` field, which is particularly useful. It stands for "audit user ID" or more accurately, as described in Chapter 1, "What Is a Container?," the "real UID" as opposed to the "effective UID." Remember that when someone logs into a system, they are given this ID, which then gets applied to any processes that user then runs. And if such a user elevates their privileges to the `root` user, for example, even then this ID is still traceable. Clearly this is really important for post-compromise searching.

Earlier in the chapter we saw a `watch` rule for Docker. Let's generate some logs from containers to get a sense of how audit data is collected. Note that the "key" or label is `docker-daemon` so that we can search for it more easily:

```
-w /usr/bin/docker -p rwxa -k docker-daemon
```

The following command will fire up `nginx`. Its image is not present on the local machine, so it will need to be pulled down from Docker Hub:

```
$ docker run -d -p80:80 nginx
Unable to find image 'nginx:latest' locally
latest: Pulling from library/nginx
[..snip. . .]
Digest: sha256:0e188877aa60537d1a1c6484b8c3929cfe09988145327ee47e8e91dd
Status: Downloaded newer image for nginx:latest
330d5ac4745555fe655c7d3169d32fee0cd717ac57f184f794f975662ecea0f5
```

In our `auditd` log we are offered this information having searched for `docker` and not just the key `docker-daemon` to get as much information from other rules too in addition:

```
$ cat /var/log/audit/audit.log | grep docker
```

Broader results than you might expect in the normal running of Docker from such a command are as follows; it shows when the Docker service came online and when it was stopped, via `systemd` entries, for example:

```
type=SERVICE_START msg=audit(1595360007.681:75): pid=1 uid=0
auid=4294967295 ses=4294967295 msg='unit=docker comm="systemd"
exe="/lib/systemd/systemd" hostname=? addr=? terminal=? res=success'
type=SERVICE_STOP msg=audit(1595360007.681:76): pid=1 uid=0
auid=4294967295 ses=4294967295 msg='unit=docker comm="systemd"
exe="/lib/systemd/systemd" hostname=? addr=? terminal=? res=success'
```

We can tell that the "unit file" for `systemd` (an application's startup profile or object you might say) is indeed called `docker` as shown earlier from this command and output:

```
$ systemctl list-unit-files | grep docker
docker.service                              enabled
docker.socket                               enabled
```

Pay close attention to the timestamp in brackets. Using the timestamps, it is easy to keep track of groups of events that occur within the same second. For example, to convert the time just shown into a human-readable format, enter this command:

```
$ date -d@1595677083
Sat 25 Jul 12:38:03 BST 2020
```

However, as you can imagine, we need a much more efficient way, with greater clarity, of checking the events in audit logs due to their volume. The sophisticated `auditd` offers a few ways to do just that.

Monitoring

The first way to check potentially mountainous volumes of logs that `auditd` provides is via the command `ausearch`. Let's use the `-i`, or "interpret," switch:

```
$ ausearch -i | grep -i "docker"
```

Do not be confused by the `-i` switch on the `grep` command, it is included only in the event that case-sensitivity means that some logs are not displayed for some reason. The `-i` instructs `grep` to search for uppercase and lowercase matches. In Listing 4.3, we can see a tiny sample of the formatted version of the logs, using the `ausearch` command, heavily abbreviated as you might guess.

Listing 4.3: Sample Output of Docker Running Behind the Scenes, Courtesy of the `ausearch` Command

```
type=PROCTITLE msg=audit(25/07/20 12:50:14.724:597):
proctitle=/sbin/iptables -w2 -t nat -A DOCKER -p tcp -d 0/0—dport 80
-j DNAT—to-destination 172.17.0.2:80   -i docker0
type=PROCTITLE msg=audit(25/07/20 12:50:14.744:598):
proctitle=/sbin/iptables -w2 -t filter -A DOCKER   -i docker0
-o docker0 -p tcp -d 172.17.0.2—dport 80 -j ACCEPT
type=EXECVE msg=audit(25/07/20 12:50:09.816:595):
argc=5 a0=docker a1=run a2=-d a3=-p80:80 a4=nginx
type=PROCTITLE msg=audit(25/07/20 12:52:14.843:621):
proctitle=docker rmi -f nginx
```

If you look closely at Listing 4.3, you can see how Docker works behind the scenes, namely, using `iptables` to set up its networking stack for what then becomes our `nginx` container. Separate from the first two commands (which were located in different parts of the log file), as well as nicely converted timestamps, we can see the options that the Docker binary used to create the container:

```
a0=docker a1=run a2=-d a3=-p80:80 a4=nginx
```

Then, on the final line, we can see that we have cleaned up the image from the system by using the Docker `rmi` command to remove the image, deleting it locally.

Other useful commands that come with `auditd` include the `aulastlog` command, which quickly checks to see when users have logged in. Here is an example:

```
$ aulastlog
Username         Port          From            Latest
root                                           **Never logged in**
daemon                                         **Never logged in**
bin                                            **Never logged in**
sys                                            **Never logged in**
sync                                           **Never logged in**
```

If you're familiar with the `last` command, then it is a similar idea. Use the `-u` switch to search for a specific user:

```
$ aulastlog -u chris
```

Another command along the same vein is `aulast`, which offers system uptime information, for example:

```
$ aulast
reboot   system boot  4.15.0-20-generi Wed Jul 22 20:08—crash
```

Probably one of the most powerful and commonly used of the built-in `auditd` commands is `aureport`, which summarizes events very clearly. In Listing 4.4 we can see what this command offers on its own, without switches.

Listing 4.4: The `aureport` Command, Run Without Using Any Options

```
$ aureport
Summary Report
======================
Range of time in logs: 21/07/20 20:21:45.071–25/07/20 15:06:13.443
Selected time for report: 21/07/20 20:21:45–25/07/20 15:06:13.443
Number of changes in configuration: 950
Number of changes to accounts, groups, or roles: 0
Number of logins: 0
Number of failed logins: 0
Number of authentications: 8
Number of failed authentications: 3
Number of users: 4
Number of terminals: 8
Number of host names: 1
Number of executables: 15
Number of commands: 16
Number of files: 17
Number of AVC's: 0
Number of MAC events: 0
Number of failed syscalls: 0
Number of anomaly events: 20
Number of responses to anomaly events: 0
Number of crypto events: 0
Number of integrity events: 0
Number of virt events: 0
Number of keys: 13
Number of process IDs: 751
Number of events: 4643
```

As Listing 4.4 demonstrates, it is possible to get an overview easily with `aureport`. However, the other options it provides are also worth exploring. Add the `-au` (authorized events) switch to that command, for example. In the redacted output displayed in Listing 4.5 there is a useful level of detail provided. The redaction shown is to prevent the leaking of usernames and IP addresses to protect the innocent.

Listing 4.5: The `auth` Switch for `aureport`

```
Authentication Report
============================================
# date time acct host term exe success event
============================================
1. 07/06/20 22:51:25 <USER> <IP ADDRESS> ftp /usr/sbin/ftpd yes 607217
2. 08/06/20 01:37:08 <USER> <IP ADDRESS ftp /usr/sbin/ftpd yes 609264
3. 08/06/20 03:01:40 <USER> <IP ADDRESS ftp /usr/sbin/ftpd yes 610287
4. 08/06/20 03:02:12 <USER> <IP ADDRESS ftp /usr/sbin/ftpd yes 610302
5. 08/06/20 03:02:43 <USER> <IP ADDRESS ftp /usr/sbin/ftpd yes 610305
6. 08/06/20 03:03:14 <USER> <IP ADDRESS ftp /usr/sbin/ftpd yes 610320
```

When you generate reports, be warned that you will need a little patience and expect the log searching to take a little while. Piping the output into the `less` command is useful or exporting results to a file, as shown here when using the `-x` switch for filtering logs with executed file events:

```
$ aureport -x | less
Executable Report
====================================
# date time exe term host auid event
====================================
1. 21/07/20 20:21:45 /lib/systemd/systemd ? ? -1 30
2. 21/07/20 20:21:45 /lib/systemd/systemd ? ? -1 31
```

In Listing 4.6 we can see the output from the file-related events, via the `-f` switch.

Listing 4.6: A Summary of Recent File Events as Captured by `auditd`

```
$ aureport -f
File Report
===============================================
# date time file syscall success exe auid event
===============================================
1. 25/07/20 12:38:03 /root/.bash_history 92 yes /bin/bash 1000 351
2. 25/07/20 12:39:37 /root/.bash_history 92 yes /bin/bash 1000 360
3. 25/07/20 12:47:11 /root/.bash_history 92 yes /bin/bash 1000 576
4. 25/07/20 12:47:10 /usr/bin/docker 59 yes /usr/bin/docker 1000 575
```

Another useful option for checking which processes have been run on a system is `-p`. A slightly abbreviated example is as follows, this time for a different machine that was used for a Kubernetes lab environment:

```
$ auditctl -p
Process ID Report
======================================
# date time pid exe syscall auid event
======================================
10. 06/07/20 17:11:34 27621 /usr/bin/dpkg 82 1000 2672
128. 06/07/20 17:15:32 482 /var/lib/minikube/v1.18.3/kubectl 24 10 35
312. 06/07/20 17:17:44 29853 /usr/bin/minikube 263 1000 2899
```

Note that in the output the micro-Kubernetes distribution, Minishift, has been seen executing its bundled `kubectl` binary and also its main `minikube` binary.

The 27621, 4284, and 28853 entries in this case are the process IDs (the `pid`), and we can then use them to search the log for other activities undertaken by that process with this command:

```
$ ausearch -p 27621
```

In Listing 4.7 we can see just one entry in the output of what the `ausearch` command offers us, demonstrating the extensive detail that `auditd` can provide.

Listing 4.7: The Abbreviated `ausearch` Output per pid

```
time->Sun Jul 26 17:11:36 2020
type=PROCTITLE msg=audit(1595779896.548:27584):
procttle=2F7573722F62696E2F64706B67002D2D7374617475732D6664
003733002D2D6E6F2D747269676767657273002D2D756E7061636B002D2D6
175746F2D6465636F6E666967757265002D2D7265637572736976665002F
746D702F6170742D64706B672D696E7374616C6C2D343169796B7A
type=PATH msg=audit(1595779896.548:27584): item=1
name="/var/lib/dpkg/updates/0086" inode=1465005 dev=fd:01
mode=0100644 ouid=0 ogid=0 rdev=00:00 nametype=DELETE cap_
fp=0000000000000000 cap_fi=0000000000000000 cap_fe=0 cap_fver=0
type=PATH msg=audit(1595779896.548:27584): item=0
name="/var/lib/dpkg/updates/" inode=1442359 dev=fd:01
mode=040755 ouid=0 ogid=0 rdev=00:00 nametype=PARENT
cap_fp=0000000000000000 cap_fi=0000000000000000 cap_fe=0 cap_fver=0
type=CWD msg=audit(1595779896.548:27584): cwd="/"
type=SYSCALL msg=audit(1595779896.548:27584): arch=c000003e
syscall=87 success=yes exit=0 a0=5589a36d19f0 a1=5589a1938034
a2=5589a36d1a06 a3=4 items=2 ppid=27593 pid=27621 auid=1000 uid=0
gid=0 euid=0 suid=0 fsuid=0 egid=0 sgid=0 fsgid=0 tty=pts1 ses=2
comm="dpkg" exe="/usr/bin/dpkg" key="delete"
```

Finally, let's try summarizing activities within a certain time period, using the `-ts` (time start) and `-te` (time end) switches and this command:

```
$ aureport -ts yesterday -te now—summary
Summary Report
======================
Range of time in logs: 24/07/20 11:40:52.741—25/07/20 15:42:34.837
Selected time for report: 24/07/20 00:00:00—25/07/20 15:42:39
Number of changes in configuration: 683
Number of changes to accounts, groups, or roles: 0
Number of logins: 0
Number of failed logins: 0
Number of authentications: 7
```

Ordering and Performance

As previously mentioned, you need to make sure you are not overloading the `audit.rules` file with too many rules, just adding those that are useful to you. This is because *every* syscall is captured and matched against *any* rules that are present before continuing being processed.

Equally, it is important to order your rules carefully. Rules are processed from the top down as mentioned earlier. On a busy containerized system you might put the Docker rule that we looked at earlier directly under the "backlog" buffer setting, as your first rule at the top, if it is the busiest application or service associated with a rule, for example.

If you search online, there are many examples of rules. Although not all will apply to your Linux distribution, `auditd` is not shy about telling you when a file that you are trying to watch does not exist or if you are trying to apply a 64-bit rule to a 32-bit system, for example. Therefore, test any rules that you want to use and then keep thinking about the ordering of your rules file as you apply newer rules.

Getting your ordering correct can indeed make a difference to a busy system's performance, even though modern hardware is usually relatively capable of dealing with large numbers of rules in many scenarios.

To get started with `auditd`, you would be wise, however, to start with just a handful of rules and consider the benchmarking suggestions near the start of this chapter. There is evidence that chaining rules together can improve performance significantly, but each and every scenario will be different, and as a result it is difficult to offer full examples here. However, there are a number of excellent collections of rulesets in GitHub, one being here: `github.com/linux-audit/audit-userspace/tree/master/rules`. Its parent page is here and offers more options: `github.com/Neo23x0/auditd`.

Summary

In this chapter, we explored the highly sophisticated auditing system included within the Linux kernel and the userland tools that we can use to query the logs that it generates.

In addition to the ability of being able to query certain types of events, in varying ways, you can select specific time periods too.

Coupled with the immutable rules capability, meaning attackers must force a reboot to alter your running configuration, by deploying `auditd` on a busy system (never mind one running an orchestrator and multiple containers), the `auditd` system provides an excellent view of precisely what your systems are doing all year round. There are numerous documents online to assist with tuning rulesets to suit your needs should you need to reference them further.

Having spent some time watching the worker nodes on your containerized estate's `auditd` logs, you should be able to pinpoint any unwelcome traffic interaction between your containers. This is referred to as *east-west traffic*, where lateral container traffic takes place. It might be due to a misconfiguration or be causing an unwelcome (often invisible) performance issue within your container orchestrator. In the event that per-host communication or host-to-host communication is not as intended, having generated reports and whittled down specific events using `auditd`, it should quickly become obvious that a sophisticated monitoring system such as `auditd` can be successfully utilized for many more uses beyond just forensic analysis.

CHAPTER

5

Kubernetes Vulnerabilities

As the number of containers that you are running continues to increase over time, it becomes imperative that a container orchestrator of some description is used to manage them. The dynamic nature of orchestrators, such as Red Hat's OpenShift or Docker Swarm, means that their configuration is inherently complex, and they can be difficult to secure correctly. The most popular container orchestrator, Kubernetes, is what this book focuses on and for good reason due to its provenance.

Kubernetes (`kubernetes.io`) heralds from Google and began life as Borg (`research.google/pubs/pub43438`). Over the course of the next decade or so Kubernetes became Open Sourced, and its popularity, having run years of containerized workloads for Google's own services in one form or another, gained maturity to the extent that thousands of household names started hosting their online applications with it over subsequent years.

Gaining a deeper insight into how secure your Kubernetes cluster's configuration is can save all sorts of headaches that might otherwise have arisen. There's a clever piece of open source software called `kube-hunter` (`github.com/aquasecurity/kube-hunter`), from Aqua Security (`www.aquasec.com`), which can offer genuinely valuable hardening hints and tips for your cluster. In this chapter, we will first create a Kubernetes cluster for test purposes and then explore what `kube-hunter` can tell us about it.

Mini Kubernetes

Let's get started by creating a mini Kubernetes cluster using an outstanding micro Kubernetes distribution, k3s (`k3s.io`). Apparently, k3s is half the size of memory footprint than K8s, the popular abbreviation for Kubernetes and hence the unusual name.

If you are not aware of k3s, it is definitely a welcome addition to the Kubernetes family. A running cluster can use just 40MB of RAM, and it is an ideal addition to Internet of Things (IoT) infrastructure thanks to its tiny footprint.

The installation is a simple as this:

```
$ curl -sfL https://get.k3s.io | sh -
```

For security reasons, you do not have to execute the script that the `curl` command pulls down immediately, so remove the pipe and the `-sh` switch to check that you are happy with its contents first before installing to a system as per its instructions. The binary itself, required to install a cluster, is a staggeringly small 100MB in size. You have to give credit to the team at Rancher (`rancher.com`) that created k3s.

If you are curious about how the cluster operates, you are thinking along the right lines. Instead of using Kubernetes' most popular key:value configuration database, `etcd` (`etcd.io`), k3s uses `sqlite3` by default. That said, `etcd` and MySQL and Postgres can also be used if required. k3s offers a full-blown, production-ready cluster that can be installed in seconds, and exploring it is highly recommended. It is an excellent way to test applications in Kubernetes without having to leave a lab running round the clock, in the event that it might be needed in the future for testing.

When you run that installation command mentioned earlier, you are presented with a long list of container-related output mixed in with shell script output. Listing 5.1 shows the output from the installation process.

Listing 5.1: Getting Started with Installing k3s

```
[INFO]  Finding release for channel stable
[INFO]  Using v1.18.6+k3s1 as release
[INFO]  Downloading hash https://github.com/rancher/k3s/releases/
download/v1.18.6+k3s1/sha256sum-amd64.txt
[INFO]  Downloading binary https://github.com/rancher/k3s/releases/
download/v1.18.6+k3s1/k3s
[INFO]  Verifying binary download
[INFO]  Installing k3s to /usr/local/bin/k3s
[INFO]  Creating /usr/local/bin/kubectl symlink to k3s
[INFO]  Creating /usr/local/bin/crictl symlink to k3s
[INFO]  Skipping /usr/local/bin/ctr symlink to k3s, command exists in
PATH at /usr/bin/ctr
[INFO]  Creating killall script /usr/local/bin/k3s-killall.sh
```

```
[INFO]  Creating uninstall script /usr/local/bin/k3s-uninstall.sh
[INFO]  env: Creating environment file
/etc/systemd/system/k3s.service.env
[INFO]  systemd: Creating service file
/etc/systemd/system/k3s.service
[INFO]  systemd: Enabling k3s unit
Created symlink /etc/systemd/system/multi-user.target.wants/k3s.service
/etc/systemd/system/k3s.service.
[INFO]  systemd: Starting k3s
```

The download from GitHub takes a little while on a slow connection, but otherwise, using Ubuntu 18.04 as the host to install k3s upon, the cluster installs seamlessly and quickly. If you get any `CrashLoopBackOff` errors with your containers, check your `iptables` rule clashes. You might need to disable `firewalld`, for example, and wait a minute or two for the containers to restart:

```
$ systemctl stop firewalld
```

Try running a `kubectl` command as the `root` user to see if you are connecting to the cluster correctly:

```
$ kubectl version
```

If that does not work, then run this command:

```
$ export KUBECONFIG=/etc/rancher/k3s/k3s.yaml
```

If that still does not work, then the issue might be with existing `iptables` rules. You can flush all rules (if you are certain that you want to) as so with this command:

```
$ iptables -t nat -F; iptables -t mangle -F; iptables -F; iptables -X
```

Let's check that we have some containers running with this command, now that we have confirmed `kubectl` is working:

```
$ kubectl get pods --all-namespaces
```

In Listing 5.2 we can see a slightly abbreviated view of what pods are present in a standard installation, including the ingress controller to allow traffic into the cluster, `traefik`.

Listing 5.2: All the Pods from All the Namespaces in a Standard k3s Installation

```
NAMESPACE    NAME                              READY   STATUS      AGE
kube-system provisioner-gkrbh                  1/1     Running     19s
kube-system metrics-server-7566d56c8-nfz57     1/1     Running     19s
kube-system helm-install-traefik-kwfdc         0/1     Completed   2m
kube-system coredns-8655855d6-8gdx8            1/1     Running     19s
kube-system svclb-traefik-9vjqr                2/2     Running     36s
kube-system traefik-758cd5fc85-xwz45           1/1     Running     37s
```

As we can see in Listing 5.2, we are all set and have a single-node cluster running and available. Other common Kubernetes components are present, including `coredns` (`coredns.io`), which provides local DNS lookups to be resolved to local cluster resource names. The whole process took less than two minutes. If you see any container restarts that then complete correctly after some retrying, then it is probably down to your CPU taking its time to finish off other tasks. Adding worker nodes is not complex when it comes to k3s, but we will just test against a master node for now. Incidentally, to uninstall k3s, use this command when you no longer need your lab:

```
$ /usr/local/bin/k3s-uninstall.sh
```

Let's quickly prove that we have a Kubernetes master node running as hoped with this command:

```
$ kubectl get nodes
NAME    STATUS   ROLES    AGE     VERSION
kilo    Ready    master   5m18s   v1.18.6+k3s1
```

Great, that looks promising and that is near enough the latest version. Note that, in the k3s lexicon, the master node is referred to as a k3s server and the worker/minion/slave nodes are referred to as k3s agents. Let's turn to our Kubernetes security tool now, the sophisticated `kube-hunter`.

Options for Using *kube-hunter*

We will now look at the ways you can use `kube-hunter`. There are different options for the deployment method, which allows you to choose how to implement scans with `kube-hunter`. You also have to make a choice about the scope of your scans and whether, as you will shortly see, you will scan only local Kubernetes clusters or remote clusters. Finally, you will be asked to confirm if you would like to enable the risky automated attack mode or just run passive scans. Let's look at these three options now.

Deployment Methods

You have three options for deploying `kube-hunter` to hunt for security issues within Kubernetes. In Table 5.1 we can see how these three options might be put to use best.

Table 5.1: Deployment Methods for `kube-hunter`

DEPLOYMENT METHOD	DESCRIPTION
Host	This requires a version of Python v3 and `pip`, the Python package manager, present on the host.
Container	You can also use "host networking" with Docker to insecurely access all the host machine's network stack so that network interface scanning can occur.
Pod	Kubernetes uses the concept of pods as opposed to containers (a *pod* is simply one or more containers). Gain an inside-cluster perspective to see the damage that a nefarious pod might be able to cause within your cluster.

Scanning Approaches

As mentioned, there are three different scanning approaches to how you might use `kube-hunter`: remote, interface, and network scans. For a comprehensive audit, for example, you might choose to use all three of the scanning approaches combined, with a variety of deployment methods, as shown in Table 5.2.

Table 5.2: Scanning Options That You Can Try in `kube-hunter`

SCANNING APPROACH	DESCRIPTION
Remote	An installation on a host connected to your network can scan remote machines for any cluster hosted outside of your local network, using an attacker's perspective. Or, armed with the local IP address of a node, you can use this internally too.
Interface	This permits the scanning of all of the host's local network interfaces when hunting for interesting Kubernetes components.
Network	Use this option to run a scan on a specific network CIDR only, e.g., 10.10.10.0/24.

Hunting Modes

Finally, and most importantly, there are two main hunting modes that you can use with `kube-hunter`, as shown in Table 5.3.

Table 5.3: Hunting Modes in `kube-hunter`

MODE	DESCRIPTION
Active	Once vulnerabilities have been highlighted, `kube-hunter` will then attempt to exploit those vulnerabilities. Active mode is turned off by default and must be enabled with the `--active` switch. Take exceptional care using this hunting option and only ever run it against your own clusters.
Passive	No changes will be made to your cluster if issues are discovered.

As you can see, you should avoid running active mode in production environments, and you should not attempt to run `kube-hunter` over other people's clusters without explicit permission.

Container Deployment

We can install `kube-hunter` via a container (you will need Docker running as well as k3s) and scan the local machine using the `interface` option, as shown in Table 5.2. In Listing 5.3 we can see an abbreviated view of what happens when you run the displayed command. As Listing 5.3 demonstrates, once the container image has been pulled, you are presented with an interactive menu. Before proceeding, however, there is a caveat about using this approach.

Listing 5.3: Abbreviated Output of Using the Single Container Approach with `kube-hunter` Offering a Welcome Interactive Menu

```
$ docker run -it --rm --network host aquasec/kube-hunter

Unable to find image 'aquasec/kube-hunter:latest' locally
latest: Pulling from aquasec/kube-hunter
[..snip. . .]
530cb0749284: Pull complete
Digest:
sha256:fee4656ab3b4db[...snip...] 126a96887505cns
Status: Downloaded newer image for aquasec/kube-hunter:latest
Choose one of the options below:
1. Remote scanning      (scans one or more specific IPs or DNS names)
2. Interface scanning   (scans subnets on all local network interfaces)
3. IP range scanning    (scans a given IP range)
Your choice:2
```

The `kube-hunter` documentation explains that within the container there is a proprietary plugin that sends the scanning results to Aqua Security. You can pick up results from this address, having entered your email address: `kube-hunter.aquasec.com`.

Note that when uploading data to generate nicely formatted reports, you need to accept Aquasec's terms, found here: `kube-hunter.aquasec.com/eula.html`.

If you are not keen on the sharing of vulnerability information and accepting proprietary terms and conditions, you can build a container locally using the provided Dockerfile, within the GitHub repository, so it won't include the closed source plugin. The Dockerfile is here: `github.com/aquasecurity/kube-hunter/blob/master/Dockerfile`.

With `kube-hunter` installed, let's try scanning all of the host's interfaces using the interactive menu, by choosing Option 2. In Figure 5.1 we can see heavily abbreviated results from the interface scan.

```
+----------------------+-------------------+--------------------+
| Unrecognized K8s API | 10.42.0.0:6443    | A Kubernetes API   |
|                      |                   | service            |
+----------------------+-------------------+--------------------+
| Metrics Server       | 10.42.0.2:443     | The Metrics server |
|                      |                   | is in charge of    |
|                      |                   | providing resource |
|                      |                   | usage metrics for  |
|                      |                   | pods and nodes to  |
|                      |                   | the API server     |
+----------------------+-------------------+--------------------+
| Metrics Server       | 10.42.0.2:443     | The Metrics server |
|                      |                   | is in charge of    |
|                      |                   | providing resource |
|                      |                   | usage metrics for  |
|                      |                   | pods and nodes to  |
|                      |                   | the API server     |
+----------------------+-------------------+--------------------+
| Kubelet API          | 192.168.1.48:10250 | The Kubelet is the |
|                      |                   | main component in  |
|                      |                   | every Node, all pod |
|                      |                   | operations goes    |
|                      |                   | through the kubelet |
+----------------------+-------------------+--------------------+
| Kubelet API          | 172.18.0.1:10250  | The Kubelet is the |
|                      |                   | main component in  |
|                      |                   | every Node, all pod |
|                      |                   | operations goes    |
|                      |                   | through the kubelet |
+----------------------+-------------------+--------------------+
| Kubelet API          | 172.17.0.1:10250  | The Kubelet is the |
|                      |                   | main component in  |
|                      |                   | every Node, all pod |
|                      |                   | operations goes    |
|                      |                   | through the kubelet |
+----------------------+-------------------+--------------------+
```

Figure 5.1: The excellent `kube-hunter` has found Kubernetes components but isn't sure what Kubernetes distribution that k3s is.

Inside Cluster Tests

Let's try the pod deployment approach now to gain a better internal overview of our cluster. In Listing 5.4 we can see the `job.yaml` file's contents (`raw.githubusercontent.com/aquasecurity/kube-hunter/master/job.yaml`) that will enable us to consume the YAML file as a batch job and then deploy a pod within the k3s cluster.

Listing 5.4: The Contents of `job.yaml` from `kube-hunter`'s GitHub Repository

```
apiVersion: batch/v1
kind: Job
metadata:
  name: kube-hunter
spec:
  template:
    spec:
      containers:
```

```
      -name: kube-hunter
          image: aquasec/kube-hunter
          command: ["python", "kube-hunter.py"]
          args: ["-pod"]
        restartPolicy: Never
  backoffLimit: 4
```

After copying that content into a local file named `job.yaml`, we can use the next command to ingest the configuration:

```
$ kubectl create -f job.yaml
job.batch/kube-hunter created
```

The command's output looks promising. We can check which resources our "job" is consuming and where, using this command:

```
$ kubectl describe job kube-hunter
```

The end of that command's output offers us this required information:

```
Normal  SuccessfulCreate  37s   job-controller
Created pod: kube-hunter-r4z4k
```

Armed with the pod name designated to run that Kubernetes job, we can then see the rigorous `kube-hunter`'s output with a reference to the pod's name from earlier within this command:

```
$ kubectl logs kube-hunter-r4z4k
```

As the results are so comprehensive, we will look at them in sections. In Listing 5.5 we can see the top of the logs output.

Listing 5.5: The Top Section of the Results

```
2020-07-27 11:42:06,152 INFO kube_hunter.modules.report.collector
Started hunting
2020-07-27 11:42:06,152 INFO kube_hunter.modules.report.collector
Discovering Open Kubernetes Services
2020-07-27 11:42:06,168 INFO kube_hunter.modules.report.collector
Found vulnerability "Read access to pod's service account token"
in Local to Pod (kube-hunter-r4z4k)
2020-07-27 11:42:06,169 INFO kube_hunter.modules.report.collector
Found vulnerability "CAP_NET_RAW Enabled" in Local to
Pod(kube-hunter-r4z4k)
2020-07-27 11:42:06,169 INFO kube_hunter.modules.report.collector
Found vulnerability "Access to pod's secrets" in Local to
Pod (kube-hunter-r4z4k)
2020-07-27 11:42:09,587 INFO kube_hunter.modules.report.collector
Found open service "Kubelet API" at 10.42.0.1:10250
2020-07-27 11:42:09,635 INFO kube_hunter.modules.report.collector
Found open service "Metrics Server" at 10.42.0.2:443
2020-07-27 11:42:09,733 INFO kube_hunter.modules.report.collector
```

```
Found open service "Metrics Server" at 10.42.0.1:6443
2020-07-27 11:42:17,118 INFO kube_hunter.modules.report.collector
Found open service "API Server" at 10.43.0.1:443
2020-07-27 11:42:17,199 INFO kube_hunter.modules.report.collector
Found vulnerability "K8s Version Disclosure" in 10.43.0.1:443
2020-07-27 11:42:17,202 INFO kube_hunter.modules.report.collector
Found vulnerability "Access to API using service account token"
in 10.43.0.1:443
```

Interestingly, the output from `kube-hunter` demonstrates that what appeared to be an unknown Kubernetes distribution is actually behaving in the way that `kube-hunter` is familiar with. The main comments on discovered vulnerabilities are actually relating to the Kubernetes job that we just used to execute `kube-hunter`.

We can see, for example, "Read access to pod's service account token" was noted. Additionally, `CAP_NET_RAW Enabled` (which gives unbridled access to forge all kinds of packets, bind to any IP address, and allow "transparent" proxying) is also allowed to be used by the pod that we created. A little further later in Listing 5.5 we can also see "K8s Version Disclosure" has been captured as an issue too.

In Figure 5.2, we can see some of the vulnerabilities that we just mentioned explained at the end of the output from the pod.

ID	LOCATION	CATEGORY	VULNERABILITY	DESCRIPTION	EVIDENCE
KHV005	10.43.0.1:443	Information Disclosure	Access to API using service account token	The API Server port is accessible. Depending on your RBAC settings this could expose access to or control of your cluster.	b'{"kind":"APIVersions","versions":["v1" ...
KHV002	10.43.0.1:443	Information Disclosure	K8s Version Disclosure	The kubernetes version could be obtained from the /version endpoint	v1.18.6+k3s1
None	Local to Pod (kube-hunter-r4z4k)	Access Risk	CAP_NET_RAW Enabled	CAP_NET_RAW is enabled by default for pods. If an attacker manages to compromise a pod, they could potentially take advantage of this capability to perform network attacks on other pods running on the same node	
None	Local to Pod (kube-hunter-r4z4k)	Access Risk	Access to pod's secrets	Accessing the pod's secrets within a compromised pod might disclose valuable data to a potential attacker	['/var/run/secrets/kubernetes.io/service ...
KHV050	Local to Pod (kube-hunter-r4z4k)	Access Risk	Read access to pod's service account token	Accessing the pod service account token gives an attacker the option to use the server API	eyJhbGciOiJSUzI1NiIsImtpZCI6IlRJMk1rSS1r ...

Figure 5.2: We need the vulnerability IDs so that we can look up more details within the `kube-hunter` Knowledge Base.

The left column here shows that there are Knowledge Base IDs offered for most of the issues spotted. You should be able to explore the vulnerability Knowledge Base (KB) at this address but it seems sometimes the KB site is unavailable: `aquasecurity.github.io/kube-hunter`.

In Figure 5.3, we can see what happens when we enter KHV002 into the Knowledge Base. We are greeted with much more useful detail and given advice about any potential risks.

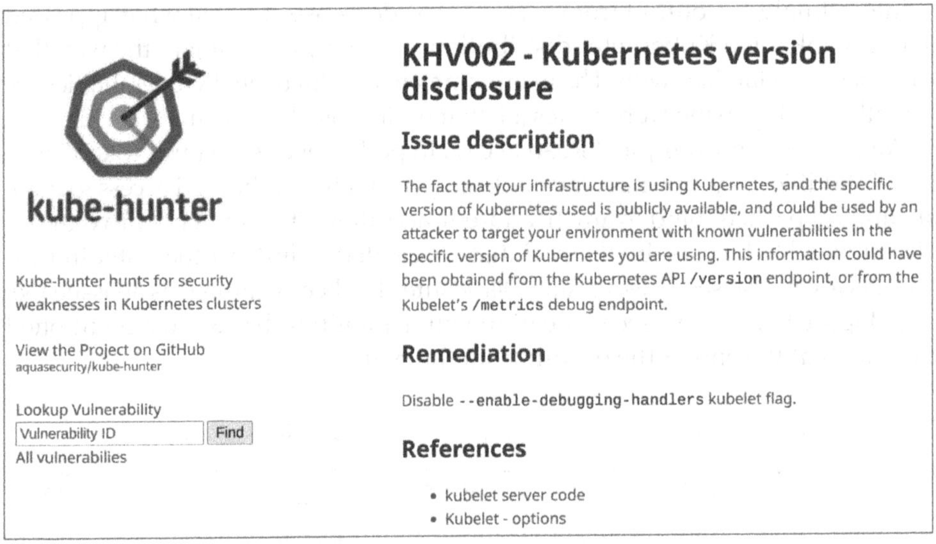

Figure 5.3: Looking up KHV002 in the Knowledge Base offers more detail.
Source: aquasecurity.github.io/kube-hunter/kb/KHV002.html

Fear not if the KB site is unavailable, however; Aqua dutifully lists all of the KB code and the relevant advice within its GitHub repository (`github.com/aquasecurity/kube-hunter/tree/main/docs/_kb`). In the case of our example, the URL is `github.com/aquasecurity/kube-hunter/blob/main/docs/_kb/KHV047.md`.

The remediation advice offered by the Knowledge Base is helpful. Exposing something as simple as a software version has long been known to give attackers useful tips about the bugs of a running system. You are advised to disable the `--enable-debugging-handlers` option in Kubernetes to make your cluster more suitable for production.

Minikube vs. *kube-hunter*

In Chapter 9, "Kubernetes Compliance," we will install the Minikube Kubernetes distribution to test another Aqua Security product, `kube-bench`, which tests for compliance. Check that chapter for installing Minikube if you want to test `kube-hunter` against it.

To begin testing against another Kubernetes distribution, to avoid any compatibility issues of running two clusters on one lab machine, we can almost instantaneously tear down k3s by using this command:

```
$ /usr/local/bin/k3s-uninstall.sh
```

If you follow the Minikube install process offered in Chapter 9, you should be able to start up Minikube with this command:

```
$ minikube start --driver=none
```

WARNING **A reminder that you should stop this instance of Minikube after using the lab, as it is effectively running in Privileged mode and therefore potentially insecure in this installation mode.**

If that command is successful, you should be able to see this at the tail of the output:

```
Verifying Kubernetes components..
Enabled addons: default-storageclass, storage-provisioner
Done! kubectl is now configured to use "minikube"
```

Returning now to the `job.yaml` file that we just looked at, let's attempt to install it into our Minishift cluster where a pod will be used to run the job through to completion.

Assuming that you still have the YAML file on hand, we can run the following command (if not, its contents are shown earlier and available in the GitHub repository for `kube-hunter`):

```
$ kubectl create -f job.yaml
job.batch/kube-hunter created
```

That looks as if it was successful. Let's describe the job again with this command:

```
$ kubectl describe job kube-hunter
```

We can see that the job ran, and among the output we are told the pod's name is as follows:

```
Created pod: kube-hunter-thf9n
```

Check its logs again using this command:

```
$ kubectl logs kube-hunter-thf9n
```

As expected, the results are different from k3s's but not as dramatically as we might initially thought. In Figure 5.4 we can see that we are running a different version of Kubernetes from the one we used with k3s, but essentially most of the internal findings in this case were related to the permissions offered to the `kube-hunter` pod that we just ran and not actually to the cluster itself.

```
+--------+--------------------+--------------------+--------------------+--------------------+--------------------+
| ID     | LOCATION           | CATEGORY           | VULNERABILITY      | DESCRIPTION        | EVIDENCE           |
+--------+--------------------+--------------------+--------------------+--------------------+--------------------+
| KHV005 | 10.96.0.1:443      | Information        | Access to API using| The API Server port| b'{"kind":"APIVersio|
|        |                    | Disclosure         | service account    | is accessible.     | ns","versions":["v1"|
|        |                    |                    | token              |     Depending on   | ...                |
|        |                    |                    |                    | your RBAC settings |                    |
|        |                    |                    |                    | this could expose  |                    |
|        |                    |                    |                    | access to or control|                   |
|        |                    |                    |                    | of your cluster.   |                    |
+--------+--------------------+--------------------+--------------------+--------------------+--------------------+
| KHV002 | 10.96.0.1:443      | Information        | K8s Version        | The kubernetes     | v1.18.3            |
|        |                    | Disclosure         | Disclosure         | version could be   |                    |
|        |                    |                    |                    | obtained from the  |                    |
|        |                    |                    |                    | /version endpoint  |                    |
+--------+--------------------+--------------------+--------------------+--------------------+--------------------+
```

Figure 5.4: An internal view of Minishift is a slight improvement over k3s's.

Let's return to the network interface scanning again and then test Minishift this time. We rerun this Docker command using the container approach noted earlier and choose Option 2 for "interface":

```
$ docker run -it --rm --network host aquasec/kube-hunter
```

This time, for example, we can see that `etcd` is present for the storage, whereas we know that k3s uses `sqlite3` by default. The information reported for `etcd`, along with the IP address and port number in the findings that an attacker needs, is as follows:

> "Etcd is a DB that stores cluster's data, it contains configuration and current state information, and might contain secrets".

Also noted is that there is no mention of `kube-hunter` not recognizing the Kubernetes distribution, although the distribution is not named directly.

Having said that, however, the "host" install discussed earlier using the `pip` package manager returns the same result:

```
$ pip install kube-hunter
Collecting kube-hunter
  Could not find a version that satisfies the requirement kube-hunter
  from versions: )
No matching distribution found for kube-hunter
```

Getting a List of Tests

Running `kube-hunter` via a container again, we can generate a list of tests that the tool performs, using the following command:

```
$ docker run -it --rm --network host aquasec/kube-hunter --list
```

The `--list` switch generates a list of "passive" or "normal" hunters, and it contains an impressive number of items that `kube-hunter` will run through. Some examples are as follows:

```
* Kubelet Discovery
  Checks for the existence of a Kubelet service, and its open ports
```

```
* Port Scanning
  Scans Kubernetes known ports to determine open endpoints for discovery
* Kubelet Secure Ports Hunter
  Hunts specific endpoints on an open secured Kubelet
```

If you are interested in just listing "active" hunting criteria, then this is the command for the container option:

```
$ docker run -it --rm --network host aquasec/kube-hunter—list—active
```

Again, the "passive" testing criteria is displayed, but this time a slightly shorter list of "active" test criteria is also shown. Here are some examples:

```
* Arp Spoof Hunter
  Checks for the possibility of running an ARP spoof attack from within
  a pod (results are based on the running node)
* Etcd Remote Access
  Checks for remote write access to etcd, will attempt to add a new key
  to the etcd DB
* Prove /var/log Mount Hunter
  Tries to read /etc/shadow on the host by running commands inside a pod
  with host mount to /var/log
```

The "active" list of testing criteria is impressive and definitely worth reading through before executing "active" scanning tests.

Summary

In this chapter, we looked at creating a local, lightweight Kubernetes distribution called k3s and ran the thorough `kube-hunter` over that distribution to check for vulnerabilities.

Following that we tested against the Minikube Kubernetes distribution and noted that `kube-hunter` was able to recognize the distribution, whereas it did not when it came to k3s. On both of our laboratory installations of Kubernetes, the excellent `kube-hunter` provided valuable insights into what an attacker might look for such as software versions and networking details about the running components of Kubernetes.

When you are a bit more familiar with `kube-bench`, within a fully blown Kubernetes test cluster (not a production cluster), it is recommended that you try some of the "active" scans to gain more knowledge about the inherent issues that Kubernetes might have. There is no question that `kube-hunter` is a valuable tool to have available to you when hardening your Kubernetes clusters.

CHAPTER

6

Container Image CVEs

Systems of all types are subject to *common vulnerabilities and exploits* (CVEs)—known software bugs that provide attackers a foothold to take advantage of. Container images are no exception and need to be monitored for CVEs, but they additionally require a patching strategy in which either developers themselves or a centralized team take ownership to ensure that containers do not run in a production environment without meeting the tolerated in-house criteria. Each CVE is assigned risk categories using standardized ratings. It is common that an in-house standard might allow containers to spawn from images only when Critical vulnerabilities are not present. Or, indeed, to disallow both High and Critical vulnerabilities, for example.

Identifying issues is just a small part of the process involved when container images contain CVEs. A mature and well-formulated strategy needs to be agreed upon and enforced. It is not enough to disseminate the plan among developer teams, which might take the easy way out and ignore issues; the strategy requires enforcement to make a difference on a large, containerized estate. And besides checking for CVEs with proprietary and Open Source products, the strategy must also check for the compliance of a container image, for example, whether it was created to run as the insecure `root` user, as discussed in previous chapters. CVEs will undoubtedly also be lurking in abundance within container image registries.

In this chapter, we will examine what a CVE entails, in definition and content, and look at three popular tools that can scan container images to identify where vulnerabilities exist. Additionally, you will learn how to scan images against CIS Benchmarks, and when we look at the third tool, we will look at how to install and set up an exceptional Open Source image registry that automatically scans images for CVEs as standard.

Understanding CVEs

Understanding how CVEs are scored is of critical importance so that you can gauge whether to follow the standardized approach or create your own scoring system in-house. One should always examine CVE scanning results as well as the actual use of a container image to make a thorough assessment.

Each estate is unique, and it is important to bear in mind that software vendors only suggest the criticality of the patch according to their own criteria and without having access to how a company might use their software. One example scenario might be that your organization runs microservices within a specific technology stack. On the back end, which only staff have access to within an air-gapped network segment, popular web servers run as containers. When CVEs are announced for these web servers and a critical CVE is discovered, a panic occurs because of the servers' public-facing nature. In this case, however, a maintenance window could be postponed until convenient, thanks to the fact that the CVE is not directly affecting production services that are client-facing, and the issue only affects back-end staff. The in-house scoring of such security issues would be specifically oriented to your own unique attack vectors.

The vulnerability scoring standard is called the Common Vulnerability Scoring System (CVSS) and is widely adopted for good reason. The specification is clear, well-thought-out, and updated by the CVSS Special Interest Group. You can find more information at `www.first.org/cvss/specification-document` about the current version, v3.1. The document explains that the scope is not just for software but hardware and firmware in addition. The standard defines three key groups of metrics. The first of these, the Base score, is related to a vulnerability's key characteristics and its severity. The Temporal metrics are focused on how a vulnerabilities severity may alter over a period of time, such as whether exploit code is available in the wild and successful compromises have been witnessed. Finally, the Environmental metric can adjust the other metrics if a specific computing environment is affected. The last thing to note is that CVSS scoring ranges from 0.0 to 10.0. One area of CVEs to pay attention to is the common language used throughout. For example, if a CVE can allow a remote compromise over the network, then the attack vector will be listed as "network," and the Base Score will likely be increased as a result. Other common terminology might include denial-of-service (DoS) attacks in the common parlance and if a vulnerability might not actively cause a compromise directly but instead cause a service to fail permanently or intermittently. Figure 6.1 summarizes the CVE vulnerability levels.

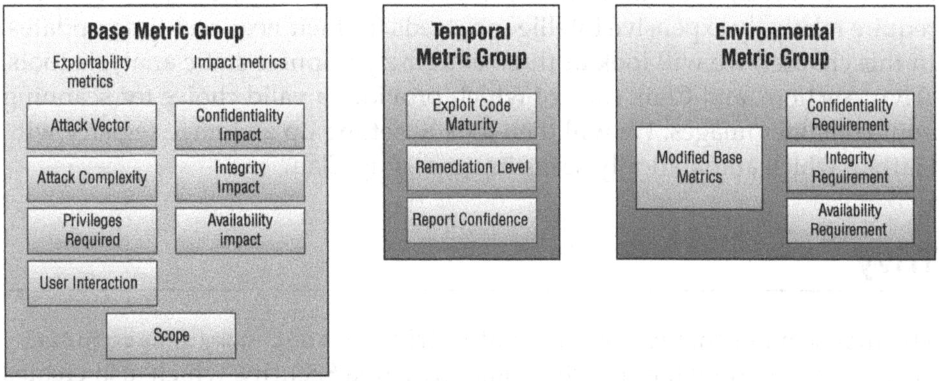

Figure 6.1: The Common Vulnerability Scoring System
Adapted from `https://www.first.org/cvss`.

Another useful resource for CVEs is the NVD database (`nvd.nist.gov`). The site is run by the U.S. government, and the data held is extremely helpful for automation purposes across a number of fields. You are encouraged to visit the home page and click one of the latest vulnerabilities to gain more insight into how the data is presented and how the common vulnerabilities lexicon is heavily abbreviated to include references such as "network" and "DoS" attack vectors for brevity. As you become more familiar with CVEs, you will see that this shorthand is extremely prevalent.

In addition, many vendors in the Cloud Native space use their own scoring methodologies; one popular vendor that does so is Red Hat. According to Red Hat, if Open Source software is shipped by multiple vendors, then CVSS Base Scores can differ from each vendor to account for different packaging methods. Combining, to name but a few, the security of built-in products, differences in configuration and software's intended use can make the scoring a moving target. To enable Red Hat's customers to make informed opinions about how serious a CVE might be, Red Hat assesses and aggregates the Base Scores to present its own scoring criteria that relates directly to its own products. This approach can be frustrating for some end users of software that operate their own in-house scoring system or strictly use the CVSS scoring directly, but it is a sane and logical approach you have to agree.

Let's continue now with less theory. There are a number of products that offer insight into what CVEs might be lurking within container images and image registries. It is safe to say, however, that not all CVE scanners are equal, and in fact even the best Open Source scanners on the market commonly report different results when scanning images. This can cause havoc if an agreed strategy is not in place and multiple scanners are used within one organization.

Note also that some CVE scanners also come with malware detection capabilities, in which patterns are matched after reverse-engineering a container's layers. However, this feature tends to be limited to proprietary tools, which require relatively expensive intelligence feeds for their near-real-time updates. In this chapter, we will look at three extremely popular static analysis tools, Trivy, Anchore, and Clair, each of which provides a valid choice for scanning your container images. We will then look at setting up an image registry with Harbor, which automatically scans images using Clair.

Trivy

The first scanner that we will look at is Trivy (`github.com/aquasecurity/trivy`), produced by the security company Aqua Security, which also creates `kube-hunter` that we looked at in Chapter 5, "Kubernetes Vulnerabilities." We will start by looking at the various ways that we can install Trivy and then use a container to run it for ease.

For the package installation of Trivy, you would follow the install commands shown here, ideally putting the long lines on one line each, on Debian derivatives as the `root` user:

```
$ apt-get install wget apt-transport-https gnupg lsb-release
$ wget -qO- https://aquasecurity.github.io/trivy-repo/deb/public.key \
| sudo apt-key add -
$ echo deb https://aquasecurity.github.io/trivy-repo/deb $(lsb-release \
-sc) main | sudo tee -a /etc/apt/sources.list.d/trivy.list
```

Then, having added the Trivy repository to your package manager's sources, you should update the local package lists and install the `trivy` package as so:

```
$ apt-get update
$ apt-get install trivy
```

There are also other installation methods, including Homebrew for Macs, compiling from source, and Arch Linux options. For Red Hat Enterprise Linux installations, you are encouraged to add the following content to this file:

```
$ cat /etc/yum.repos.d/trivy.repo
[trivy]
name=Trivy repository
baseurl= \
https://aquasecurity.github.io/trivy-repo/rpm/releases/$releasever/$basearch/
gpgcheck=0
enabled=1
```

Then, once that file is saved, update your local package lists in the same way, but using `yum` and not `apt` with this command before installing Trivy afterward:

```
$ yum update
$ yum -y install trivy
```

Getting Started

For our testing purposes we will use the containerized version to run Trivy in true Cloud Native style. In Listing 6.1, we can see the Dockerfile that creates the container image for reference so that, for security reasons, you can see the contents of the image.

Listing 6.1: The Innards of the Trivy Container Image

```
FROM alpine:3.12
RUN apk—no-cache add ca-certificates git rpm
COPY trivy /usr/local/bin/trivy
COPY contrib/gitlab.tpl contrib/gitlab.tpl
COPY contrib/junit.tpl contrib/junit.tpl
COPY contrib/sarif.tpl contrib/sarif.tpl
ENTRYPOINT ["trivy"]
```

It is possible to inspect all the files that comprise the image. We will just use the prebuilt container image for ease, however. To pull the image, run this command:

```
$ docker pull aquasec/trivy
```

We will run the next command to download the image from Docker Hub and spawn a container from it in order to scan the latest `nginx` for CVEs:

```
$ docker run --rm -v /var/run/docker.sock:/var/run/docker.sock \
    -v $HOME/Library/Caches:/root/.cache/ aquasec/trivy nginx:latest
```

Following some slightly unusual output, if you have not pulled down the Trivy container image before, you will notice a pause while Trivy accesses the target image and then analyzes it.

You are warned with this error that using the `latest` tag is a relatively lazy practice and that you will have to use the `--clear-cache` option to freshly scan images if you scan them more than once.

You will need a modicum of patience, but the sophisticated Trivy produces impressive results, as partly shown in Figure 6.2.

We can tell that Trivy has spotted that the base layer is Debian and there are a large number of CVEs. For comparison, a little later in this chapter, we will run our other scanning tools over the same image. The eagle-eyed will have spotted that the container `run` command sets up a local machine volume called `Library`. If we check the file sizes of that directory with the `du` command, it is clear that, potentially, the act of scanning a large number of images would mean that a nontrivial amount of local diskspace is required, as shown here:

```
$ du -h Library/Caches/trivy
153M    Library/Caches/trivy/db
76K    Library/Caches/trivy/fanal
153M    Library/Caches/trivy/
```

nginx:latest (debian 10.5)

Total: 146 (UNKNOWN: 0, LOW: 114, MEDIUM: 32, HIGH: 0, CRITICAL: 0)

LIBRARY	VULNERABILITY ID	SEVERITY	INSTALLED VERSION	FIXED VERSION	TITLE
apt	CVE-2011-3374	LOW	1.8.2.1		It was found that apt-key in apt, all versions, do not correctly...
bash	CVE-2019-18276		5.0-4		bash: when effective UID is not equal to its real UID the...
	TEMP-0841856-B18BAF				
coreutils	CVE-2016-2781		8.30-3		coreutils: Non-privileged session can escape to the parent session in chroot

Figure 6.2: Trivy's assessment of the latest `nginx` container image

Other scanning tools, those particularly focused on scanning image enterprise-sized registries, need efficient ways of processing potentially tens of terabytes of image files. A common approach is to pull each image (one at a time), process it (mostly by inspecting package versions), save the metadata (whose size should be relatively nominal) somewhere such as a database, and then delete the local image immediately afterward. This way a single worker can pull, scan, and process large volumes of image data without requiring extra CPU or disk capacity or indeed overly stressing the image registry to any great extent.

The help file can be accessed to display the functionality of Trivy, with this command:

```
$ docker run --rm -v /var/run/docker.sock:/var/run/docker.sock \
-v $HOME/Library/Caches:/root/.cache/ aquasec/trivy --help
```

If you type `i` for image, followed by **`--help`**, then you are greeted with a number of image scanning options. It is recommended to at least glance through these to become familiar with the tool. That command for clarity is as follows:

```
$ docker run --rm -v /var/run/docker.sock:/var/run/docker.sock \
-v $HOME/Library/Caches:/root/.cache/ aquasec/trivy i --help
```

From the help output we can also see that Trivy lets you scan using the `fs` option for some local files, but, possibly more usefully, the option also allows you to scan images from within a container. The documentation suggests an approach like this, starting with running a simple container from an image:

```
$ docker run --rm -it alpine:3.11
```

Then, once inside the container, you can execute this first command to pull the Trivy install script down, run it, and install it to the directory /usr/local/bin, having installed the curl package first:

```
$ apk add curl
$ curl -sfL
https://raw.githubusercontent.com/aquasecurity/trivy/master/contrib/install.sh \
| sh -s -- -b /usr/local/bin
```

The output from the install.sh script, inside the container, looks like this:

```
aquasecurity/trivy info checking GitHub for latest tag
aquasecurity/trivy info found version: 0.10.2 for v0.10.2/Linux/64bit
aquasecurity/trivy info installed /usr/local/bin/trivy
```

We can then run this command:

```
$ trivy fs /
```

This will ask Trivy to scan the container image, while it is running, from within the container itself. The Alpine container in our example offered these headline results, which is comforting:

```
705405408b39 (alpine 3.11.6)
============================
Total: 0 (UNKNOWN: 0, LOW: 0, MEDIUM: 0, HIGH: 0, CRITICAL: 0)
```

We can compare that to a Redis image, using the following command to get a prompt once the container is running:

```
$ docker run --rm -it redis bash
```

Using this command shows that Redis is based on Debian:

```
$ cat /etc/os-release
PRETTY_NAME="Debian GNU/Linux 10 (buster)"
[..snip]
```

In Debian we need to update the package list first as follows:

```
$ apt update
```

Then, we can install the curl package again:

```
$ apt install curl -y
```

After a little while, all the dependencies are installed for curl, and we can then run the install script command again:

```
$ curl -sfL
https://raw.githubusercontent.com/aquasecurity/trivy/master/contrib/install.sh \
| sh -s -- -b /usr/local/bin
```

Finally, execute the scan again:

```
$ trivy fs /
```

Such an approach would be useful if embedded as part of CI/CD pipeline tests (more on this in a moment) or if certain containers were used as utility containers, for example, to provide access to the AWS CLI. Or suppose a container is used to embed a specific binary, which was easy to containerize; it would then be prudent to check these containers for CVEs each time the latest version of the binary was upgraded in the upstream repository.

TIP **Maintaining the best security posture throughout the stages of the CI/CD software development pipeline is the focus of the chapters in Part II, "DevSecOps Tooling."**

Generally speaking, larger container images will be guilty of having more lines of code present, and that will therefore result in a greater risk and a higher number of CVEs. The secondary effect is therefore more admin time being required to remediate them. Smaller container images are always preferable for production workloads. The Redis scan's output is as follows:

```
bde86618030f (debian 10.7)
==========================
Total: 128 (UNKNOWN: 0, LOW: 90, MEDIUM: 6, HIGH: 30, CRITICAL: 2)
```

Note that this is the same operating system (OS) as the first test we ran against the `nginx` container image that we scanned. We can see that Redis totals 128 CVEs as opposed to `nginx` having 149 vulnerabilities that were discovered.

Besides the previous methodology, Trivy offers a simple approach for CI/CD automation. It is possible to embed a few lines within your Dockerfiles in order to run scans.

The code in Listing 6.2 shows how to do almost precisely what we did earlier when installing the `curl` package.

Listing 6.2: Embeddig Trivy Within Dockerfiles to Assist with Scanning

```
FROM alpine:3.7
RUN apk add curl \
    && curl -sfL
https://raw.githubusercontent.com/aquasecurity/trivy/master/contrib/install.sh \
| sh -s -- -b /usr/local/bin && trivy filesystem—exit-code 1—no-progress /
```

If we build an image from the Dockerfile (in this case using the `docker build` command), then we can scan images during the container image creation process effectively. Note, in Listing 6.2, that relative to the previous scan we are focusing on an older version of Alpine Linux on purpose for comparison.

In Figure 6.3 the results of the scan show that the older version of Alpine has a `high` vulnerability.

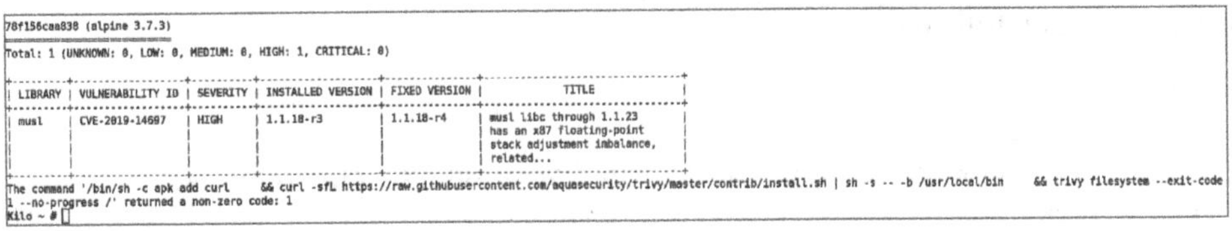
78f156caa838 (alpine 3.7.3)
Total: 1 (UNKNOWN: 0, LOW: 0, MEDIUM: 0, HIGH: 1, CRITICAL: 0)
| LIBRARY | VULNERABILITY ID | SEVERITY | INSTALLED VERSION | FIXED VERSION | TITLE |
| musl | CVE-2019-14697 | HIGH | 1.1.18-r3 | 1.1.18-r4 | musl libc through 1.1.23 has an x87 floating-point stack adjustment imbalance, related... |
The command '/bin/sh -c apk add curl && curl -sfL https://raw.githubusercontent.com/aquasecurity/trivy/master/contrib/install.sh | sh -s -- -b /usr/local/bin && trivy filesystem --exit-code 1 --no-progress /' returned a non-zero code: 1
Kilo ~ #

Figure 6.3: Older versions of images tend to flag more issues, as you'd expect.

By looking up the CVE mentioned here, CVE-2019–14697, we can see precisely what the problem is and ideally how to remediate that CVE. We can easily search for this CVE online. In this case, although the CVE website (`cve.mitre.org/cgi-bin/cvename.cgi?name=CVE-2019-14697`) also appeared near the top of the results, the first result using a popular online search tool is via NIST: `nvd.nist.gov/vuln/detail/CVE-2019-14697`. At the bottom of that NIST page, the "References to Advisories, Solutions, and Tools" section offers helpful suggestions for fixing the issues; it is worth a look to get used to how CVEs are reported and documented.

It is worth noting that not all vendors are equal when it comes to patching vulnerabilities and fixing issues within container images. There are some vendors that constantly iterate, adding and improving software using short development cycles. Others can take months and occasionally years to get around to it. When you are faced with mitigating an issue and make a change to an image in order to suit your own estate's security needs, be certain to carefully log the changes and check whether you have breached a vendor's license before doing so. Additionally, there is usually little point in remediating an issue if the vendor has done so already; you might just confuse the situation and cause other unforeseen security or stability issues in the future. Indeed, certain CVE scanners have clever insight, via intelligence feeds, into whether an upstream vendor fix is available to remedy a CVE and will only report CVEs when an upstream fix is made public by a vendor. This can be a risky business if you know some vendors only patch their images every few months or longer.

That said, when faced with having to remediate hundreds of CVEs on a containerized estate, spotting the note that an issue has been fixed already (upstream, by the vendor) can be a welcome relief. In Figure 6.3, such an entry is mentioned: it should be possible to remove this issue if you upgrade the package within your Dockerfile to version 1.1.18-r4.

For further automation methods, another nice addition to Trivy is being able to scan code repositories directly using the `repo` switch. The documentation provides you with an example repository to scan:

```
$ trivy repo https://github.com/knqyf263/trivy-ci-test
```

The output shows that the scanner looks for `.lock` files, which contain software versions that can be checked against for CVEs. Two such abbreviated outputs are as follows:

```
Pipfile.lock
============
Total: 17 (UNKNOWN: 2, LOW: 0, MEDIUM: 7, HIGH: 4, CRITICAL: 4)
Cargo.lock
==========
Total: 8 (UNKNOWN: 8, LOW: 0, MEDIUM: 0, HIGH: 0, CRITICAL: 0)
```

Note that the `repo` switch with Trivy applies only to public code repositories.

We have barely scratched the surface of the features that Trivy can support. The documentation contains a section on CI/CD and provides example Travis, GitLab CI, and CircleCI tests so that your build will fail if a vulnerability is discovered. Dependent on your preferred pipelining software it would be worth reading further about how to integrate the tool into your pipeline.

Exploring Anchore

The next tool we will look at is called Anchore (`anchore.com/opensource`). The Open Source version is designed for deep container image inspection and finding CVEs. In Anchore there is also functionality to enable the prevention of unwelcome, insecure images that are found with vulnerabilities being promoted into image registries. This is clearly the optimum way of dealing with scenarios where a registry exists in multiple environments, and CI/CD pipelines are used for testing prior to promotion of images into the production registry.

Anchore is clever enough to delve deeply into various types of files: from Ruby, Java, and Node. There is also the option to create custom policies so that pipelined builds will fail if policies are not complied with. Using such policies, it is also possible to prevent images being deployed into orchestrators such as Kubernetes, which is a valuable addition to Anchore's functionality.

The preferred installation method for Anchore is using Docker Compose. Created by Docker Inc., it is a tool that makes it possible to bundle multiple instructions into a single installation script to spawn multiple containers as interlinked services with relative ease. For clarity, you still have to create container images from Dockerfiles as usual. In other words, do not get this confused with a Dockerfile.

To download the `docker-compose.yaml`, which comes in at 146 lines in length, use this command:

```
$ curl https://engine.anchore.io/docs/quickstart/docker-compose.yaml \
> docker-compose.yaml
```

There are a few sections within the file whose purpose should become clearer when we create the containers noted within it. At the bottom of the file is a commented-out section that informs the user that removing the comments will fire up an instance of Prometheus to gather useful metrics from Anchore, some of which you may find useful.

To bring up the resources within the Compose file, once you have Docker Compose installed using these instructions `https://docs.docker.com/compose/install`, we run this simple command in the same directory:

```
$ docker-compose up -d
```

If you look closely during the process of services starting up, you will see that a PostgreSQL database and the Anchore Engine container images are pulled down locally, and then other resources are created. To check that the installation worked, try this command:

```
$ docker-compose ps
```

In Figure 6.4 we can see the names of the running containers on the left and other familiar information in the other column such as network ports being exposed on the right.

```
Kilo ~ # docker-compose ps
        Name                        Command                  State              Ports
------------------------------------------------------------------------------------------------
root_analyzer_1          /docker-entrypoint.sh anch ...   Up (healthy)   8228/tcp
root_api_1               /docker-entrypoint.sh anch ...   Up (healthy)   0.0.0.0:8228->8228/tcp
root_catalog_1           /docker-entrypoint.sh anch ...   Up (healthy)   8228/tcp
root_db_1                docker-entrypoint.sh postgres    Up (healthy)   5432/tcp
root_policy-engine_1     /docker-entrypoint.sh anch ...   Up (healthy)   8228/tcp
root_queue_1             /docker-entrypoint.sh anch ...   Up (healthy)   8228/tcp
Kilo ~ #
```

Figure 6.4: Anchore is up, courtesy of Docker Compose.

Another useful command that offers a sanity check on the status of the required Anchore Engine services is this:

```
$ docker-compose exec api anchore-cli system status
```

The output assures us that things are working as expected and provides version information, which is useful for troubleshooting:

```
Service apiext (anchore-quickstart, http://api:8228): up
Service catalog (anchore-quickstart, http://catalog:8228): up
Service simplequeue (anchore-quickstart, http://queue:8228): up
Service analyzer (anchore-quickstart, http://analyzer:8228): up
Service policy_engine
```

```
(anchore-quickstart, http://policy-engine:8228): up
Engine DB Version: 0.0.13
Engine Code Version: 0.8.0
```

One more command that you should familiarize yourself with is checking that the latest vulnerability data has been synced to your local machine. The documentation warns that the initial run of Anchore Engine will take a bit longer to complete this process. On a slow machine with very slow connectivity, it can take hours as opposed to minutes. Use this command to check the vulnerability status:

```
$ docker-compose exec api anchore-cli system feeds list
```

Expect the output from that command to be lengthy as the sophisticated Anchore updates all of its latest threat information. A successful update will have a timestamp of sorts, heavily abbreviated here:

```
Feed             Group          LastSync        RecordCount
[..snip. . .]
github           github:python  pending                None
nvdv2            nvdv2:cves     pending                None
vulnerabilities  alpine:3.10    2020-08-16[. . .snip. . .] 2016
```

We can see that Alpine Linux has updated its CVEs, but other syncs are still required.

You should wait until the rightmost column, depicting the number of records, is nonzero on each line of that command before proceeding. Thankfully, you will not have to wait for the initial period again as these records are cached and reused the next time Anchore is fired up.

The next command allows you to verify that the engine is ready to use; it will give feedback about the progress of the threat feed updates and stop you from proceeding if the threats have not synced yet:

```
$ docker-compose exec api anchore-cli system wait
```

After a little patience and CPU fan whirring, you can see lines of output further down the list completed as so:

```
vulnerabilities  debian:10  2020-08-16T13:19:58.223993  23334
```

The last command we ran, the `system wait` command, will output this when the process has finished:

```
Feed sync: Checking sync completion for feed set (vulnerabilities)..
Feed sync: Success.
```

It is easy to see why this process takes a while when you see that one OS alone has 23,334 issues to pay attention to.

We can now start using Anchore to scan the same `nginx` image that we tested using Trivy earlier, with this command:

```
$ docker-compose exec api anchore-cli image add \
docker.io/library/nginx:latest
```

The slightly abbreviated output from that `image add` command begins with the following, showing `not_analyzed`:

```
Image Digest: sha256:179412c42fe3336e7cdc253ad4a2e03d32f50e3037a860cf5
Parent Digest: sha256:b0ad43f7ee5edbc0effbc14645ae7055e21bc1973aee5150
Analysis Status: not_analyzed
Image Type: docker
```

We can pull the image for analysis and check the status of the process with the following command:

```
$ docker-compose exec api anchore-cli image get \
docker.io/library/nginx:latest | grep 'Analysis Status'
```

And, following the output showing `Analysis Status: analyzed`, we can then list its vulnerabilities this way:

```
$ docker-compose exec api anchore-cli image vuln \
docker.io/library/nginx:latest all
```

The output is too lengthy to display here. To sort through it to find the wheat in the chaff, we need to enter the next command, which shows us that the total number of unique CVEs is 61:

```
$ docker-compose exec api anchore-cli image vuln \
docker.io/library/nginx:latest all | awk '{print $1}' \
| sort -u | grep -v Vulnerability | wc
```

The following command demonstrates that we can list images with which we have run the `add` command. We can also show their scanning status:

```
$ docker-compose exec api anchore-cli image list
Full Tag                       Image Digest Analysis Status
docker.io/library/nginx:latest sha256:[..snip. . .] analyzed
```

In Figure 6.5 we can see the top of the output without counting the CVEs.

Of the findings related to the `nginx: latest` image, there are 4 CVEs with `Unknown` status, 52 `Negligible` (or `Low`) status, and the 2 `Medium` CVEs, as shown in Figure 6.5.

```
Kilo ~ # docker-compose exec api anchore-cli image vuln docker.io/library/nginx:latest all
Vulnerability ID    Package                          Severity     Fix     CVE Refs    Vulnerability URL                                                 Type    Feed
 Group              Package Path
CVE-2011-3389       libgnutls30-3.6.7-4+deb10u5      Medium       None                https://security-tracker.debian.org/tracker/CVE-2011-3389         dpkg    debi
an:10               pkgdb
CVE-2020-11724      nginx-1.19.2-1~buster            Medium       None                https://security-tracker.debian.org/tracker/CVE-2020-11724        dpkg    debi
an:10               pkgdb
CVE-2004-0971       libgssapi-krb5-2-1.17-3          Negligible   None                https://security-tracker.debian.org/tracker/CVE-2004-0971         dpkg    debi
an:10               pkgdb
CVE-2004-0971       libk5crypto3-1.17-3              Negligible   None                https://security-tracker.debian.org/tracker/CVE-2004-0971         dpkg    debi
an:10               pkgdb
```

Figure 6.5: Only 2 medium-ranked CVEs have been found by Anchore, but 52 low, or negligible, CVEs have been discovered.

If we compare that to the CVEs that Trivy discovered, which totaled `LOW: 107,MEDIUM: 7,HIGH: 32,CRITICAL: 3`, we can see the difference in results between Trivy and Anchore. As suspected, they differ in a nontrivial way. When scanning container images, it is worth repeating that as part of your strategy you should pin your colors to the mast of one variety of scanner, one that you trust will output reliable results. It does no harm to test images using other scanners periodically of course in order to test the performance of your scanner of choice. Using multiple scanners causes moving-goalposts syndrome, however, which can soak up time unnecessarily.

As a result of the blatant difference in vulnerability findings between tools, it is advisable that you employ multiple CVE scanning tools initially and really understand their output to help improve your image scanning strategy. Creating in-house policies is one way to track previous issues that you have resolved and additionally makes it quicker to respond, by adjusting or copying existing rules, when new issues arise.

Anchore describes how it goes about dealing with vulnerability scanning as the following process:

1. Pull the image down from the relevant image registry.
2. Delve deeply into the image using analysis techniques and save generated metadata for future reference in the database.
3. Check the results of the analysis against any custom policies.
4. Periodically synchronize the threat feeds and recalculate any pertinent changes in the vulnerabilities found from the upstream feeds.
5. Inform users of new findings and policy matches that might be useful.

The last two steps, in which Anchore updates threat feeds and informs users of changes, are periodically run on a schedule to keep results as fresh as possible. New CVEs are discovered over time, so regular updates are an important part of maintaining a robust security posture.

You are encouraged to use the noncommercial version of Anchore in either of two distinct ways. First, you can run it interactively, on an ad hoc, as-needed, basis, so that manual scans are performed by querying the APIs. Alternatively, you can use what is called *watch mode*. Here, you configure various registries, and any repositories (which can also be granularly separated by image tags) that receive new images are then automatically subject to the methodical querying process listed earlier.

By offering two such pieces of functionality, the vendor aims that all your image scanning needs are suitably met. You can have a constant, round-the-clock monitoring system running on image registries, with manual scans also available, which could potentially be incorporated into CI/CD pipelines.

The Open Source version is most easily accessed via the command line. Here you can extract any of the following information:

- Metadata from scanned images
- Files within the images
- Vulnerability data
- Historically discovered image information
- Whether images match any configured policies

Policies are an important part of preventing tainted images from being promoted upstream into production image registries. The key piece of information to expect from a policy's rules being tested is whether the status is `PASSED` or `FAILED`. The latter might involve a number of `STOP` errors, and both can equally show `WARN` findings. The intricate details of the tests that a policy comprises can be found here: `docs.anchore.com/current/docs/overview/concepts/policy/policy_checks`. The list is impressive and shows, for example, that reverse-engineered Docker files can sometimes be checked if the image layers can be inspected sufficiently. In Table 6.1, we can see some of the criteria that policies can be matched against.

Table 6.1: Policy Matching Criteria That Anchore Can Use Within Its Policies

CRITERIA	PURPOSE
Dockerfile inspection	Reverse engineered or supplied Dockerfile checking using checks such as FROM and exposed network port instructions
File checking	Searching within included files for regex, certificates, and loose, insecure file permissions
Password files	Inspects `/etc/passwd` for blacklisted users, groups, and shells
Packages	Tests whether a package must exist within the image or not, for example
Vulnerabilities	Matches certain packages, CVSS scores, or if a fix is available, for example
Licensing	Blacklists unwanted licenses being included
Ruby	Looks for Ruby Gems and if it is official, for example, or does not meet a specific version
Node and npm	Trusts various version and blacklist others amongst other criteria

Continues

Table 6.1 *(continued)*

CRITERIA	PURPOSE
Secrets	Hunts for sensitive data such as access and secret keys for AWS; checks using regular expressions on files and directories too
Metadata	Compares matches for OS, distribution or hardware, or image size
Always	Stops the processing in its tracks if certain unwanted images or other resources are found within an image
Retrieved Files	Looks for specific configuration files, for example, and if the file contains content, match against that
Malware	Flags any malware findings found within an image

As Table 6.1 demonstrates, the granular approach to policies that Anchore provides makes them exceptionally powerful. The features are certainly worthy of accolade when it comes to Open Source functionality, especially considering that functionality comes from a commercial vendor.

Finally, there is also a Jenkins plugin that has a dedicated page (`plugins.jenkins.io/anchore-container-scanner`) in the documentation. Note that older versions may suffer from storing the credentials (used to access the API) in plain text and should be deprecated in favor of the newer versions. The plugin looks useful and can be run within Freestyle or Pipeline jobs and, once run, provide the expected "pass" or "fail" status depending on whether the image meets preconfigured rules. You are encouraged to check this page for more information on the subject:

`www.jenkins.io/doc/book/managing/plugins/#from-the-web-ui`

You will need to run this command to get further help about the policies used in Anchore:

```
$ docker-compose exec api anchore-cli policy --help
```

Listing 6.3 displays what to expect from its output.

Listing 6.3: Help Output for Policy Options in Anchore

```
Usage: anchore-cli policy [OPTIONS] COMMAND [ARGS]..
Options:
  -h, --help  Show this message and exit.
Commands:
  activate  Activate a policyid
  add       Add a policy bundle
  del       Delete a policy bundle
  describe  Describes the policy gates and triggers available
  get       Get a policy bundle
  hub       Anchore Hub Operations
  list      List all policies
```

If we change the `--help` to `list` at the end of the previous command, then we can see which policies Anchore is aware of. The output is as so:

```
Policy ID              Active Created  Updated
2c53a13c-1765[..snip. . .] True    [. . .snip. . .] 2020-08-16T13:10:05Z
```

Another nice feature from Anchore is the Policy Hub. We can list what is available in the Policy Hub like this, with more detail displayed in Table 6.2:

```
$ docker-compose exec api anchore-cli policy hub list
```

Table 6.2: The Policies Available from the Policy Hub

POLICY NAME	PURPOSE
anchore_security_only	A single policy to help demonstrate whitelisting and blacklisting images' packages using their name
anchore_default_bundle	A stock policy bundle that is a mixture of checking Dockerfiles and best-practice warnings
anchore_cis_1.13.0_base	Based on parts of the CIS 1.13.0 benchmark where some customization is required by the user

TIP **You might need a look back at the options shown in Table 6.1 for more insight into what is included within the policies for a reminder.**

Using one of the policy names displayed within Table 6.2, we can now install the CIS Benchmark policy as so:

```
$ docker-compose exec api anchore-cli policy hub install \
anchore_cis_1.13.0_base
```

And, having done that, rerunning this command will confirm it installed as hoped:

```
$ docker-compose exec api anchore-cli policy list
```

The CIS policy is much more compliance-orientated and not CVE-related. It is an excellent addition to firming up your image scanning strategy.

Let's add another image to Anchore and run a scan against that using the CIS-based policy to check its compliance. Start with the `add` image command as we saw before:

```
$ docker-compose exec api anchore-cli image add \
docker.io/library/redis:latest
```

If we append `| grep Analysis Status` to the end of that command, we will see that the image has not been analyzed just yet.

Or, programmatically within a CI/CD pipeline, you can use this command to `wait` for the analysis to complete as mentioned earlier:

```
$ docker-compose exec api anchore-cli image wait \
docker.io/library/redis:latest
```

Once that command returns with an `analyzed` status, we can then run the scan against the CIS policy that we installed a moment ago:

```
$ docker-compose exec api anchore-cli evaluate check \
docker.io/library/redis:latest \
–policy anchore_cis_1.13.0_base–detail
```

And, unfortunately, for the example Redis image, the output is extensive and too much to list here, although `NEGLIGIBLE` results are by far the majority of the findings luckily.

The top of the output confirms that if that image was built within a CI/CD pipeline based on that policy it was checked against, it would have received a `fail` status.

```
Image Digest: sha256:cd28cf26cc2d9960c964917d2aa97ea2110a050dfed8c8
Full Tag: docker.io/library/redis:latest
Image ID: 1319b1eaa0b7bcebae63af321fa67559b9517e8494060403d083bb350
Status: fail
Last Eval: 2020-08-16T16:32:55Z
Policy ID: anchore_cis_1.13.0_base
Final Action: stop
Final Action Reason: policy_evaluation
```

Further down the output on the left side we can see that the `Gate` column relates to the criteria listed within Table 6.1. Examples within the CIS policy include `dockerfile`, `files`, and `vulnerabilities`.

It should be clear now how useful such policies can be when it comes to improving your image scanning. To add user-specific tweaks to policies, you can find the JSON file containing a policy, copy the bundle that includes the policy, and add the new policy bundle to suit your requirements.

Clair

Another popular Open Source scanner is Clair (`github.com/quay/clair`). Touted as a static analysis tool, its raison d'etre is entirely based around scanning container images.

Although it is a battle-hardened piece of software used within many CI/CD pipelines, at the time of writing, the tool is being repackaged. This is because the company that created it, CoreOS (`coreos.com`) was acquired by

Red Hat in 2018. CoreOS is famous for a number of products such as the `rkt` (`coreos.com/rkt`) runtime and the pervasive `etcd` (`etcd.io`), the distributed key:value store found in most Kubernetes distributions. As a result of this acquisition, CoreOS's product portfolio has been, and is apparently still, being integrated with Red Hat's, and Clair is being refactored as a result. To keep abreast of updates in this space, follow this page: `www.redhat.com/en/topics/containers/what-is-clair`.

As a stand-alone CVE scanner, Clair consists of three components, and it can be spun up using Docker and Docker Compose. The innards include a PostgreSQL database, the Clair server, and the Clairctl scanner. The scanner hooks into the server and has the ability to output reports in HTML after scanning has finished. If you are interested in exploring Clair further, this page will give you the route to do so using Docker Compose: `searchitoperations.techtarget.com/tutorial/How-to-scan-Docker-images-for-vulnerabilities-with-Clair`. If you compile components locally, then you are likely to need Go v1.11+ as a minimum. There are releases that you are encouraged to look at while Clair's integration continues in the meantime, here: `github.com/quay/clair/releases`.

Secure Registries

For completeness, to finish the `nginx` CVE scanning result comparisons, we will choose a different approach to seeing Clair in action. The approach that we will use also affords us the chance to look at an outstanding piece of Open Source software called Harbor (`goharbor.io`). The Harbor marketing strapline is as follows: "Our mission is to be the trusted Cloud Native repository for Kubernetes."

For any organization that does not want data to be stored publicly because of security concerns, a localized image registry is a key component in a container image strategy. The benefits include higher image-pull speeds, thanks to faster connectivity, and greater control over how the API and front end of a registry are made accessible.

Harbor is a fully functional, extensible, and aesthetically pleasing container image registry with a difference. Its features include fine-grained access control permissions per repository, repository quotas, tag retention policies, image signing capabilities, automated or manual vulnerability feed updates, and built-in CVE scanning, which can be scheduled or manually triggered. It also offers an API, a UI, and the ability to replicate images stored within other registries to assist when you migrate to using it as your main registry. We will look at some of those features in a little more detail shortly.

The installation process begins with two options. We will look at the Ubuntu 18.04 automated installation approach (the slightly older Long Time Support [LTS] version), as opposed to the piecemeal approach. Take note that, as you would expect for a self-hosted registry, disk space needs to be provisioned correctly (or be dynamically resized); and for Harbor to run smoothly, four CPU cores and 8GB of RAM are encouraged. Results gleaned from using less CPU and RAM suggest this is a sensible specification that should not be deviated from; otherwise, you risk unexpected results such as automated scanning not completing or out-of-memory errors showing up in the logs. We will go for 160GB of disk space, in addition to the suggested CPU and memory.

If you are using a cloud server with the suggested Ubuntu version installed, the process is as follows using the `root` user.

To begin, we will take a raw copy of this GitHub gist: `gist.githubusercontent.com/kacole2/95e83ac84fec950b1a70b0853d6594dc/raw/ad6d65d66134b3f40900fa30f5a884879c5ca5f9/harbor.sh`.

Then we will create a file named something like `install_harbor.sh`, save it in the `root` user's home directory, and make it executable:

```
$ chmod +x install_harbor.sh
```

The installation instructions (`https://goharbor.io`), which may change subtly over time, are not what to follow at this stage. Instead, you should first execute the script with this command:

```
$ ./install_harbor.sh
```

After you have waited patiently for a few minutes while watching Docker output, you will be dutifully informed that the installation is complete. However, we have not quite finished, and you should now enter the `harbor` directory and look for the `harbor.yml.tmpl` file. First, rename the file as follows:

```
$ cd harbor
$ mv harbor.yml.tmpl harbor.yml
```

Now we need to edit it a little. There is a relatively simple way of securing the Harbor installation using TLS certificates (under the `https` section within that file), but for our purposes we will continue with HTTP only. It should be obvious which three lines you need to comment out for HTTPS to be ignored at this point. The second and third lines just relate to certificate and private key paths. Look for the mention of `https`, and the lines are easy to spot.

Having made those edits, we will restart the installation script using these commands:

```
$ cd .
$ ./install_harbor.sh
```

Rather than stopping at the same point as before, you should be pleasantly surprised at how quickly the previous sections of the installation complete and then watch as more Docker output is displayed to help finalize the installation.

When it is completed, you are shown the following with either your IP address or server hostname, depending on your choice at the start of the installation:

```
Please log out and log in or run the command 'newgrp docker'
to use Docker without sudo
```

```
Login to your harbor instance:
docker login -u admin -p Harbor12345 123.123.123.123
```

We will ignore that instruction but instead go into the UI by visiting this address in a browser (replacing the IP address of hostname for the installation from here on in): `123.123.123.123`.

Using the login and password, we should be presented with an impressive-looking dashboard. Under Projects on the left side, we will choose + New Project on the right side, click it, and call our project **`cloudnativesecurity`**.

Then, from a different machine (as if we were developing on that machine and pushing images up to a registry remotely), we will run these commands to emulate a developer's experience:

```
$ docker login -u admin -p Harbor12345 123.123.123.123
Login Succeeded.
$ docker pull nginx:latest
$ docker tag nginx:latest \
123.123.123.123/cloudnativesecurity/nginx:latest
$ docker push 123.123.123.123/cloudnativesecurity/nginx:latest
```

After a few minutes, depending on your bandwidth, the pushed image should be available in our full-featured registry. Clearly, we need to avoid using the `admin` user and change its default password as soon as possible. Still under Projects on the left, if we enter the `cloudnativesecurity` repository and to see Clair in action, click the `nginx` image and then Scan, we can see the result shown in Figure 6.6.

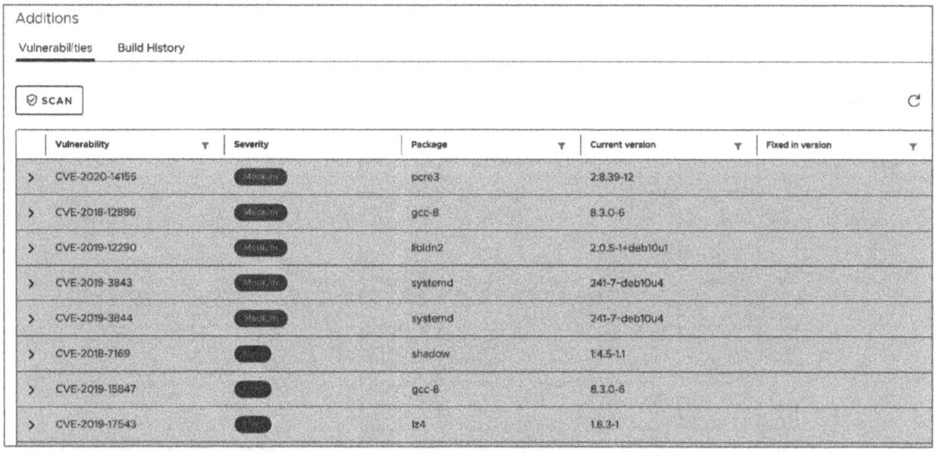

Figure 6.6: Harbor has the excellent Clair CVE scanner built-in.

As Figure 6.6 shows, Clair has determined that `nginx` has a number of CVEs, some of which are classed as Medium severity.

In Figure 6.7 we can see a suitable summary of the types of CVEs that were found.

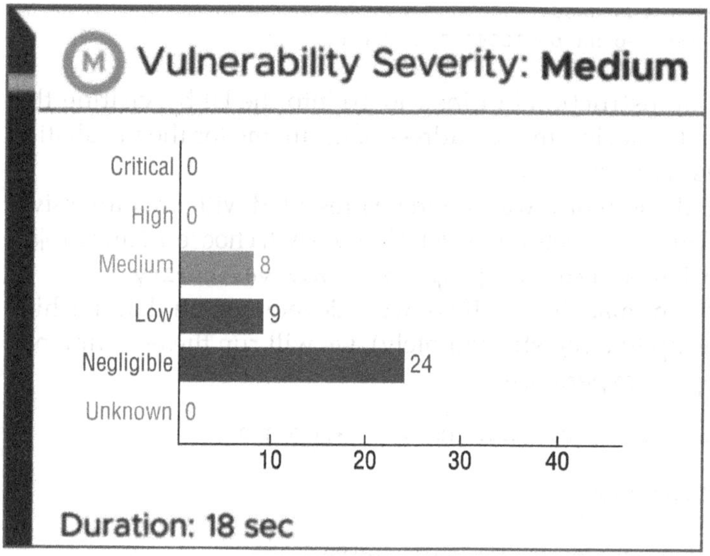

Figure 6.7: Different scanning results again for the `nginx` container image

As Figure 6.7 demonstrates, there are yet again differing results from our CVE scanners earlier in the chapter.

In addition to linking to the relevant CVE websites for each issue, another nice touch from Harbor is the ability to clearly inspect the layers of each image in the UI. In Figure 6.8 we can see a reverse-engineered Dockerfile, with various Dockerfile instructions such as COPY, ENV, and CMD.

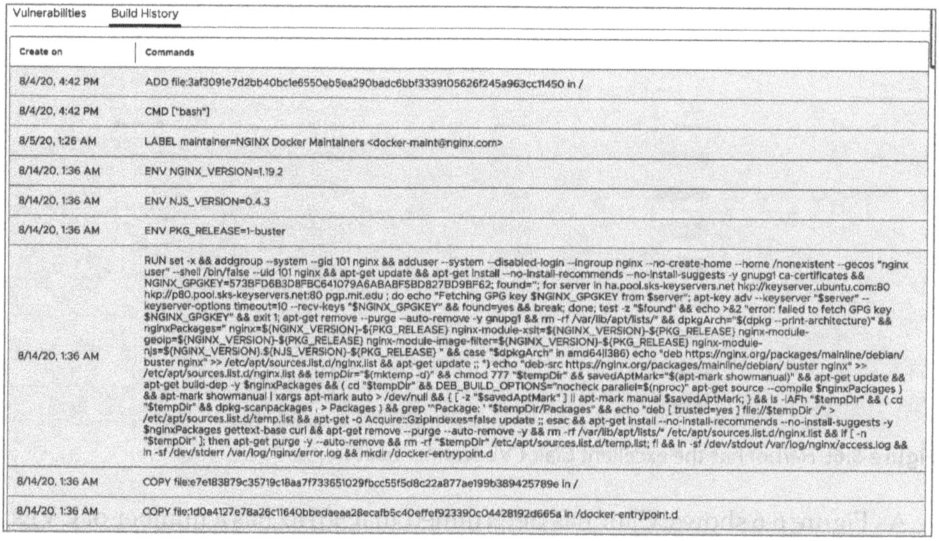

Vulnerabilities Build History

<table>
<tr><th>Create on</th><th>Commands</th></tr>
<tr><td>8/4/20, 4:42 PM</td><td>ADD file:3af3091e7d2bb40bc1e6550eb5ea290badc6bbf3339105626f245a963cc11450 in /</td></tr>
<tr><td>8/4/20, 4:42 PM</td><td>CMD ["bash"]</td></tr>
<tr><td>8/5/20, 1:26 AM</td><td>LABEL maintainer=NGINX Docker Maintainers <docker-maint@nginx.com></td></tr>
<tr><td>8/14/20, 1:36 AM</td><td>ENV NGINX_VERSION=1.19.2</td></tr>
<tr><td>8/14/20, 1:36 AM</td><td>ENV NJS_VERSION=0.4.3</td></tr>
<tr><td>8/14/20, 1:36 AM</td><td>ENV PKG_RELEASE=1~buster</td></tr>
<tr><td>8/14/20, 1:36 AM</td><td>RUN set -x && addgroup --system --gid 101 nginx && adduser --system --disabled-login --ingroup nginx --no-create-home --home /nonexistent --gecos "nginx user" --shell /bin/false --uid 101 nginx && apt-get update && apt-get install --no-install-recommends --no-install-suggests -y gnupg1 ca-certificates && NGINX_GPGKEY=573BFD6B3D8FBC641079A6ABABF5BD827BD9BF62; found=''; for server in ha.pool.sks-keyservers.net hkp://keyserver.ubuntu.com:80 hkp://p80.pool.sks-keyservers.net:80 pgp.mit.edu ; do echo "Fetching GPG key $NGINX_GPGKEY from $server"; apt-key adv --keyserver "$server" --keyserver-options timeout=10 --recv-keys "$NGINX_GPGKEY" && found=yes && break; done; test -z "$found" && echo >&2 "error: failed to fetch GPG key $NGINX_GPGKEY" && exit 1; apt-get remove --purge --auto-remove -y gnupg1 && rm -rf /var/lib/apt/lists/* && dpkgArch="$(dpkg --print-architecture)" && nginxPackages=" nginx=${NGINX_VERSION}-${PKG_RELEASE} nginx-module-xslt=${NGINX_VERSION}-${PKG_RELEASE} nginx-module-geoip=${NGINX_VERSION}-${PKG_RELEASE} nginx-module-image-filter=${NGINX_VERSION}-${PKG_RELEASE} nginx-module-njs=${NGINX_VERSION}.${NJS_VERSION}-${PKG_RELEASE} " && case "$dpkgArch" in amd64|i386) echo "deb https://nginx.org/packages/mainline/debian/ buster nginx" >> /etc/apt/sources.list.d/nginx.list && apt-get update ;; *) echo "deb-src https://nginx.org/packages/mainline/debian/ buster nginx" >> /etc/apt/sources.list.d/nginx.list && tempDir="$(mktemp -d)" && chmod 777 "$tempDir" && savedAptMark="$(apt-mark showmanual)" && apt-get update && apt-get build-dep -y $nginxPackages && (cd "$tempDir" && DEB_BUILD_OPTIONS="nocheck parallel=$(nproc)" apt-get source --compile $nginxPackages) && apt-mark showmanual | xargs apt-mark auto > /dev/null && { [-z "$savedAptMark"] || apt-mark manual $savedAptMark; } && ls -lAFh "$tempDir" && (cd "$tempDir" && dpkg-scanpackages . > Packages) && grep '^Package: ' "$tempDir/Packages" && echo "deb [trusted=yes] file://$tempDir ./" > /etc/apt/sources.list.d/temp.list && apt-get -o Acquire::GzipIndexes=false update ;; esac && apt-get install --no-install-recommends --no-install-suggests -y $nginxPackages gettext-base curl && apt-get remove --purge --auto-remove -y && rm -rf /var/lib/apt/lists/* /etc/apt/sources.list.d/nginx.list && if [-n "$tempDir"]; then apt-get purge -y --auto-remove && rm -rf "$tempDir" /etc/apt/sources.list.d/temp.list; fi && ln -sf /dev/stdout /var/log/nginx/access.log && ln -sf /dev/stderr /var/log/nginx/error.log && mkdir /docker-entrypoint.d</td></tr>
<tr><td>8/14/20, 1:36 AM</td><td>COPY file:e7e183879c35719c18aa7f733651029fbcc55f5d8c22a877ae199b389425789e in /</td></tr>
<tr><td>8/14/20, 1:36 AM</td><td>COPY file:1d0a4127e78a26c11640bbedaeaa28ecafb5c40effef923390c04428192d665a in /docker-entrypoint.d</td></tr>
</table>

Figure 6.8: Harbor lets you inspect the layers of your images with ease.

Thoroughly inspecting the layers of each image should make the remediation of CVE issues easier to understand. Focusing on a layer at a time means the resolution can be much more methodical. Although some images contain obfuscated binaries, this approach is time-saving; and with the `fixable` flag in the summary of CVEs, you can immediately see which CVEs the upstream vendor has made it much easier to fix by providing a package version upgrade in the container image.

You are encouraged to spend some more time with Harbor, not only for its built-in CVE scanning capabilities, which are extensible and can hook into other scanners with relative ease, but to get used to the other features that are plentiful.

Starting with a repository, such as the one we created called `cloudnativesecurity`, you could do worse than to create a less-privileged user and associate it with the repository. Having done that and allocated a specific quota to the repository, you could experiment with creating a custom label with a name such as `MustFix` and apply it to an image. And, having gotten more used to that functionality, you could look at automatically pruning certain image tags, after a specific retention period for the purposes of good housekeeping.

Summary

In this chapter, we looked at three particularly useful tools for scanning container images. The first, Trivy, is the newest of the three and appears to be gaining traction due to its simplicity. The second, Anchore, is well established and equally sophisticated.

With the third tool, Harbor, we took the functionality a little further and extolled the virtues of the type of features that you should look for within a secure image registry. Having the ability to store and scan container images automatically with such a well-refined Open Source tool means that Harbor is also well worth a closer look at. The considered features in addition should make the tool future-proof and a valuable asset to any Cloud Native estate.

As mentioned throughout the chapter, the tools each gave a different result when we scanned the same `nginx` image. And, no doubt, other scanning tools would also have a different perspective. For this reason, it is advisable to try different tools that suit your needs. As we have seen, Open Source tooling can be utilized within CI/CD pipelines for greater visibility into the vulnerability and compliance issues that your container images suffer from very effectively.

Part

II

DevSecOps Tooling

Having looked at container security in the preceding six chapters, we will now move on to DevSecOps tooling. The next six chapters walk through a series of security tools suitable for continuous integration/continuous deployment (CI/CD) software development pipelines. This pipeline concept is a widely used model for integrating security measures into every stage of development and deployment. A common DevSecOps expression is "shifting security to the left," a model in which developers become empowered to run their own security tests much earlier on in the development process. Although there is some debate, the term DevSecOps appears to have originated because the "Sec," or security, is intertwined within DevOps processes directly. SecOps, on the other hand, tends to refer to security operation staff and processes in a more traditional security setting, such as a Security Operations Center where live services are monitored.

While the DevSecOps tooling explored in these chapters can be used in specific sections of a pipeline, it should be noted that they are often deployed in different stages. For example, you would probably want to check that your initial build is not saving secrets to your code repositories very early on within a pipeline, but you could potentially check that your applications satisfy baseline compliance checks at the start of the build process and once again before the build is promoted to a new environment. As a result, make use of the security tooling in the most sensible way you see fit, and do not feel limited by certain conventions suggested by the tool authors. The quality of the tests in use is of paramount importance; however, more important is that builds fail when previously agreed conditions are not satisfied, and issues are resolved before builds are permitted to proceed.

In This Part

CHAPTER

7

Baseline Scanning (or, Zap Your Apps)

One of the most popular security tools for penetration testing heralds from the famous Open Web Application Security Project (OWASP) foundation (`owasp.org`) and boasts multiple facets within its toolset. OWASP has been around for many years and helps the security community with documentation and methodologies to include security posture among other things. One of the many tools within OWASP's arsenal (a full list of which can be found at `owasp.org/www-community/Free_for_Open_Source_Application_Security_Tools`) also slots neatly into CI/CD pipelines with ease and is called ZAP, shortened from Zed Attack Proxy (`www.zaproxy.org`). ZAP is suitably battle-hardened, having matured over the years with many developers improving or introducing features and removing bugs as they went. For the purposes of our use case for ZAP, unlike the broad mix of tools we will look at in subsequent DevSecOps tooling chapters, in this chapter we will look at what are known as *baseline* scans. Although the venerable ZAP comes with an excellent, easy to navigate user interface (UI), after a quick look at it, we are going to focus on a Cloud Native approach to using ZAP with containers and over the command line. You might think of baseline scans as like utilizing a spider, which is commonly used on the web in a different way to crawl across resources, taking note of them as it goes. In the same way, ZAP will traverse your assets, checking whether they are compliant. Before we try a baseline scan against a host, however, we will install ZAP and look at the excellent Webswing UI.

Where to Find ZAP

The documentation on the ZAP site is easy to understand, so if you get stuck, do not hesitate to visit the website.

The GitHub site (`github.com/zaproxy/zaproxy`) refers you back to the main Zaproxy website, where you can scrutinize the source code in detail if you want and potentially contribute. The splash page mentions that ZAP is one of the world's most popular free security tools, so you are definitely in good company if you choose to spend some time learning to use ZAP.

The Docker Hub page for ZAP (`hub.docker.com/r/owasp/zap2docker-stable`), in addition to having some more useful container image tags, also provides other useful pieces of information.

You are encouraged to consider how stable you want your ZAP build to be. There are multiple flavors to choose from, as described in Table 7.1.

Table 7.1: ZAP Builds Available via Docker

BUILD NAME	USAGE
zap2docker-stable	The build you'd most likely keep up-to-date and use, especially for deployments that need the desktop UI
zap2docker-weekly	A weekly build in which features and bug fixes are experimentally bundled
zap2docker-live	The release that contains every change to the ZAP project, so use with caution
zap2docker-bare	The minimal release, which produces the tiniest container image and should be used in CI/CD pipelines, especially in production environments

Without further ado, let's see how you might use ZAP. The WebSwing UI is so easy to use and fire up with Docker (as from v2.5.0) that it would be remiss not to quickly see how to use it. Even though you would always use the command-line interface version of ZAP within CI/CD pipelines, the UI is a great way to get to know the tool's functionality. If we run this command, it will download and then spawn a container:

```
$ docker run -u zap -p 8080:8080 -p 8090:8090 \
-i owasp/zap2docker-stable zap-webswing.sh
```

As mentioned, the "stable" container is much larger than the "bare" container and comes in at about 1.4GB. Once you have run that command, it is just a case of visiting this address within your browser: `localhost:8080/zap`.

There is no output from the previous command, but we can verify that the container is running by using the next command and noting the slightly abbreviated output below, noting the running time in the CREATED column:

```
$ docker ps
CONTAINER ID IMAGE                      COMMAND            CREATED
c0993694b5f7 owasp/zap2docker-stable zap-webswing.sh 37 seconds
```

In Figure 7.1 we can see what we're presented with when the UI is presented courtesy of the container.

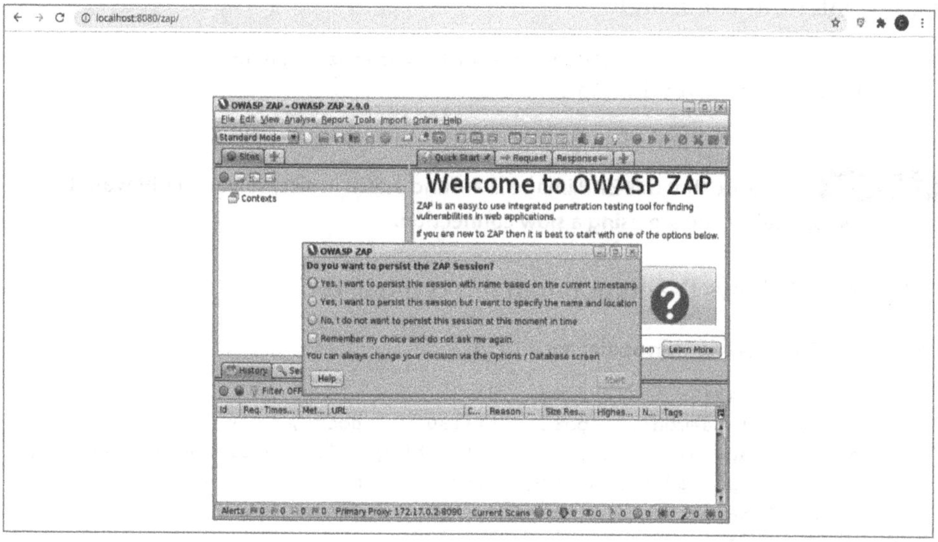

Figure 7.1: A combination of Docker and Webswing means that running ZAP with the UI is easy.

The venerable ZAP is multifaceted, as mentioned. It can be used for brute-forcing passwords, SQL injection, and cross-site scripting to name but a few tasks. It is highly recommended, and the UI appears within modern browsers using a single, simple command line, that you put it through its paces. There are not only video tutorials (`www.zaproxy.org/zap-in-ten`) on the main website, but YouTube has a wide-ranging library to assist you with navigating the UI (`www.youtube.com/channel/UC-3qyzm4f29C12KGp3-12bQ`).

Baseline Scanning

Let's now proceed with baseline scanning as it could be used within a CI/CD pipeline, as promised. To begin working with baseline scanning, press the Ctrl+C key combination on the previous ZAP container. If that doesn't stop your container, look up the container's ID with the `docker ps` command and stop it this way:

```
$ docker stop c0993694b5f7
```

The command we need to use to begin baseline scanning is shown in a moment, with the target redacted. The target in this case is one that is served by a web server over HTTPS (or HTTP), so it is assumed that your development environment presents your application as such. The command that follows calls the `zap-baseline.py` Python script. If you want to scrutinize it further, then use the `exec` command to enter a running ZAP container. To start a scan against a target, enter this command:

```
$ docker run -t owasp/zap2docker-weekly zap-baseline.py \
 -t https://chrisbinnie.tld
```

NOTE **Be aware that this ZAP image is around 1.6GB in size, so you might want to pull it separately if you are using a slow connection.**

Listing 7.1 shows the output from this command.

Listing 7.1: The Baseline Scan Spider Initializing

```
2020-08-02 15:47:23,132 Params:
['zap-x.sh', '-daemon', '-port', '43130', '-host', '0.0.0.0',
 '-config', 'api.disablekey=true', '-config', 'api.addrs.addr.name=.*',
 '-config', 'api.addrs.addr.regex=true', '-config',
'spider.maxDuration=1', '-addonupdate', '-addoninstall',
'pscanrulesBeta']
Aug 02, 2020 3:47:29 PM java.util.prefs.FileSystemPreferences$1 run
INFO: Created user preferences directory.
Total of 4 URLs
```

The baseline scan runs through a series of tests; they are too numerous to list, but we will briefly look further at some of them in a moment. For example, this section has shown that a number of tests have received a PASS status:

```
PASS: Directory Browsing [10033]
PASS: Heartbleed OpenSSL Vulnerability (Indicative) [10034]
PASS: HTTP Server Response Header [10036]
```

Here is another set of passed results, which are self-explanatory:

```
PASS: Modern Web Application [10109]
PASS: Absence of Anti-CSRF Tokens [10202]
PASS: Private IP Disclosure [2]
```

However, although 51 tests received a PASS, we did receive a WARN-NEW result for the following test: "Strict-Transport-Security Header Not Set [10035]."

We can easily look up the 10035 code at the following URL: `www.zaproxy.org/docs/alerts/10035`.

That web page offers the following advice: "Ensure that your web server, application server, load balancer, etc. is configured to enforce Strict-Transport-Security." It goes on to explain that HTTP Strict Transport Security (HSTS) is a mechanism for setting security policies and that it forces visitors to use HTTPS over HTTP, which the target on this occasion did not enforce.

The command to generate an HTML report of the results of a baseline scan is as follows:

```
$ docker run --user $(id -u):$(id -g) -v $(pwd):/zap/wrk/:rw—rm \
 -t owasp/zap2docker-stable zap-baseline.py \
 -t https://chrisbinnie.tld -g gen.conf -r report.html
```

For clarity, that command mounts a volume from our local machine's current directory (it is advised to create a new directory and change into it), where a `gen.conf` file exists, and we are hoping for an HTML report (called `report.html`, if you could not guess) to be generated following the scan, which should be recorded in the same place.

NOTE **Although it is uncommon, there might be a typo or two in the documentation for accomplishing this task. To be fair to the documentation writers, whether you see these typos depends on how, and where, you run the container. The syntax to use, with the correct user detail, is as shown here.**

The issue with the default documentation depends on which user you use to run the container, which sensibly is using a `zap` user in the Dockerfile and image. The options set after the `--user` flag force the container to run as UID zero and GID zero, `root` in other words. This means that the container can read from the `gen.conf` file and also output to the `report.html` if you are running the container from under the `/root` directory or within a directory with script permissions. You could create a user `zap` locally and move into a directory owned by that user and group potentially as a fix. Clearly, however, setting up something like nonprivileged user namespaces or rootless mode (which we looked at in Chapter 2, "Rootless Runtimes") would be a better solution as the container runtime does not need `root` permissions to execute.

Back to our baseline report, formatted into HTML, we can see a sample of the results in Figure 7.2.

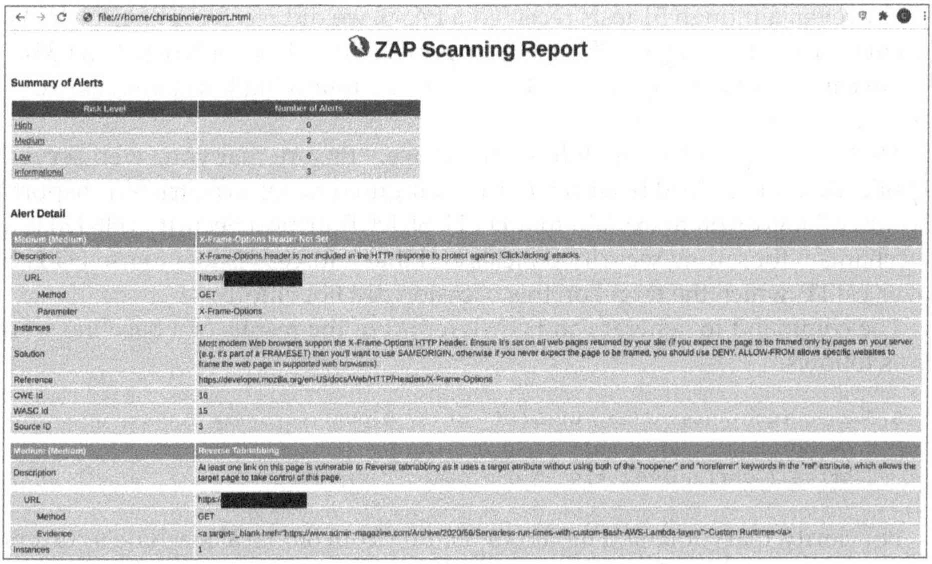

Figure 7.2: A redacted HTML report from a baseline scan

At the top of Figure 7.2 we can see which High, Medium, Low, and Informational results were captured. There is also particularly useful information related to each entry. The issue relating to Strict-Transport-Security Header Not Set [10035] from our nongraphical scan result earlier repeats much of the information that is mentioned earlier, but there are also useful links offered to help remediate and research the flagged issues:

```
owasp.org/www-project-cheat-sheets
cheatsheetseries.owasp.org/cheatsheets/HTTP_Strict_Transport_
Security_Cheat_Sheet.html
owasp.org/www-community/Security_Headers
en.wikipedia.org/wiki/HTTP_Strict_Transport_Security
caniuse.com/stricttransportsecurity
tools.ietf.org/html/rfc6797
```

You may be wondering what the `gen.conf` file option did in the previous command. It asked ZAP to generate a default configuration file for you to use that can be tweaked afterward to suit your needs. The contents should now be relatively familiar to you; a sample is as follows:

```
10098    WARN    (Cross-Domain Misconfiguration)
10105    WARN    (Weak Authentication Method)
10108    WARN    (Reverse Tabnabbing)
10109    WARN    (Modern Web Application)
50001    WARN    (Script Passive Scan Rules)
90001    WARN    (Insecure JSF ViewState)
```

```
90011   WARN   (Charset Mismatch)
90022   WARN   (Application Error Disclosure)
90033   WARN   (Loosely Scoped Cookie)
```

You can find all of the scanner codes for ZAP at `github.com/zaproxy/zaproxy/blob/develop/docs/scanners.md`. Let's try to set up our configuration file to fail a CI/CD pipeline build if "Strict-Transport-Security Header Not Set" is found during scanning tests.

If you get stuck with using ZAP from a container, you can output the help options using the same `entrypoint` as shown here, for the baseline scan:

```
$ docker run --user $(id -u):$(id -g) -v $(pwd):/zap/wrk/:rw --rm \
-t owasp/zap2docker-stable zap-baseline.py -h
```

Listing 7.2 shows the options for the baseline scan output.

Listing 7.2: ZAP's Baseline Scan Help Options

```
Usage: zap-baseline.py -t <target> [options]
    -t target         target URL including the protocol, e.g.
    https://www.example.com
Options:
    -h                print this help message
    -c config_file    config file to use to INFO, IGNORE or FAIL warnings
    -u config_url     URL of config file to use to INFO, IGNORE or FAIL
                      warnings
    -g gen_file       generate default config file (all rules set to WARN)
    -m mins           the number of minutes to spider for (default 1)
    -r report_html    file to write the full ZAP HTML report
    -w report_md      file to write the full ZAP Wiki (Markdown) report
    -x report_xml     file to write the full ZAP XML report
    -J report_json    file to write the full ZAP JSON document
    -a                include the alpha passive scan rules as well
    -d                show debug messages
    -P                specify listen port
    -D                delay in seconds to wait for passive scanning
    -i                default rules not in the config file to INFO
    -I                do not return failure on warning
    -j                use the Ajax spider in addition to the traditional
                      one
    -l level          minimum level to show: PASS, IGNORE, INFO, WARN or
                      FAIL, use with -s to hide example URLs
    -n context_file   context file which will be loaded prior to
                      spidering the target
    -p progress_file  progress file which specifies issues that are
                      being addressed
    -s                short output format—dont show PASSes or example
                      URLs
```

```
-T               max time in minutes to wait for ZAP to start and
                 the passive scan to run
-z zap_options   ZAP command line options e.g. -z "-config aaa=bbb
                 -config ccc=ddd"
—hook            path to python file that define your custom hooks
```

For more details see

`github.com/zaproxy/zaproxy/wiki/ZAP-Baseline-Scan`

Options from the help output offer you a URL to pull your config from (useful for automation), the duration of the Spider to run for, and whether to output JSON, XML, HTML and Markdown among many other execution options.

To get our build to fail with a specific issue, we will first take a copy of one of the generated lines in the `gen.conf` file and paste a copy of it to the end of the file on a new line. Next, we simply change PASS to FAIL on the new last line in the file, such as this example:

```
10035   FAIL    (Strict-Transport-Security Header Not Set)
```

Note that the comments in that file include these:

```
# Only the rule identifiers are used—the names are just for info
# You can add your own messages to each rule by appending them after
a tab on each line.
```

To prove that we can use a URL to retrieve our rules file, we will use the `-u` switch and upload our edited rules file to a web server.

The complete command we can use looks like this:

```
$ docker run --user $(id -u):$(id -g) -v $(pwd):/zap/wrk/:rw --rm \
-t owasp/zap2docker-weekly zap-baseline.py \
-t https://chrisbinnie.tld \
-u https://chrisbinnie.tld/custom-fail.conf -r fail-report.html
```

Pay close attention for a second. If you do not format the changes to your custom rules correctly, you will receive the following error, which could leave you with some head-scratching for a while:

```
Failed to read configs from https://chrisbinnie.tld/custom-fail.conf
not enough values to unpack (expected 3, got 1)
```

To avoid this error, ensure that you use tabs and not spaces to separate the columns within your rules file. In raw text terms, this mean that the line we added earlier as a FAIL rule should look like this, where the ^I entries stand for tabs:

```
10035^IFAIL^I(Strict-Transport-Security Header Not Set)
```

If you are ever unsure how a file is constructed, then use this command to check for the end of lines and tabs that might be otherwise hidden characters:

```
$ cat -ET custom-fail.conf
```

Let's run that command and see what happens. The end of the output from our command shows this:

```
FAIL-NEW: Strict-Transport-Security Header Not Set [10035]
```

Excellent. This means that in a pipeline we can monitor the status of the last line of the output and pass or fail our builds. The status line is as shown here:

```
FAIL-NEW: 1   FAIL-INPROG: 0   WARN-NEW: 0   WARN-INPROG: 0
INFO: 0   IGNORE: 0   PASS: 51
```

Scanning Nmap's Host

The generous people at Nmap offer a host for scans at `scanme.nmap.org`. They state that you are allowed to use other scanners but not to "scan 100 times a day or use this site to test your SSH brute-force password cracking tool." We will be respectful and run a single scan against that site now for comparison against our previous host. This will give us a better idea of what to expect when a vulnerable host, or at least one with more issues, is scanned using ZAP. As with all hosts used for penetration tests, it is impossible to predict what we may find; in addition, the exposed vulnerabilities might change periodically to keep scanning tools on their toes.

The status looks like this:

```
FAIL-NEW: 0   FAIL-INPROG: 0   WARN-NEW: 7   WARN-INPROG: 0   INFO: 0
IGNORE: 0   PASS: 45
```

Although there are a lot of passes, there are also a few more warnings that we can see here, abbreviated:

```
WARN-NEW: Cross-Domain JavaScript Source File Inclusion [10017]
WARN-NEW: X-Frame-Options Header Not Set [10020]
WARN-NEW: X-Content-Type-Options Header Missing [10021]
WARN-NEW: Server Leaks Version Information via "Server" HTTP
          Response Header Field [10036]
WARN-NEW: Content Security Policy (CSP) Header Not Set [10038]
WARN-NEW: HTTP to HTTPS Insecure Transition in Form Post [10041]
WARN-NEW: Absence of Anti-CSRF Tokens [10202]
```

Let's also look at the HTML report that we produced. Figure 7.3 shows the top of the results.

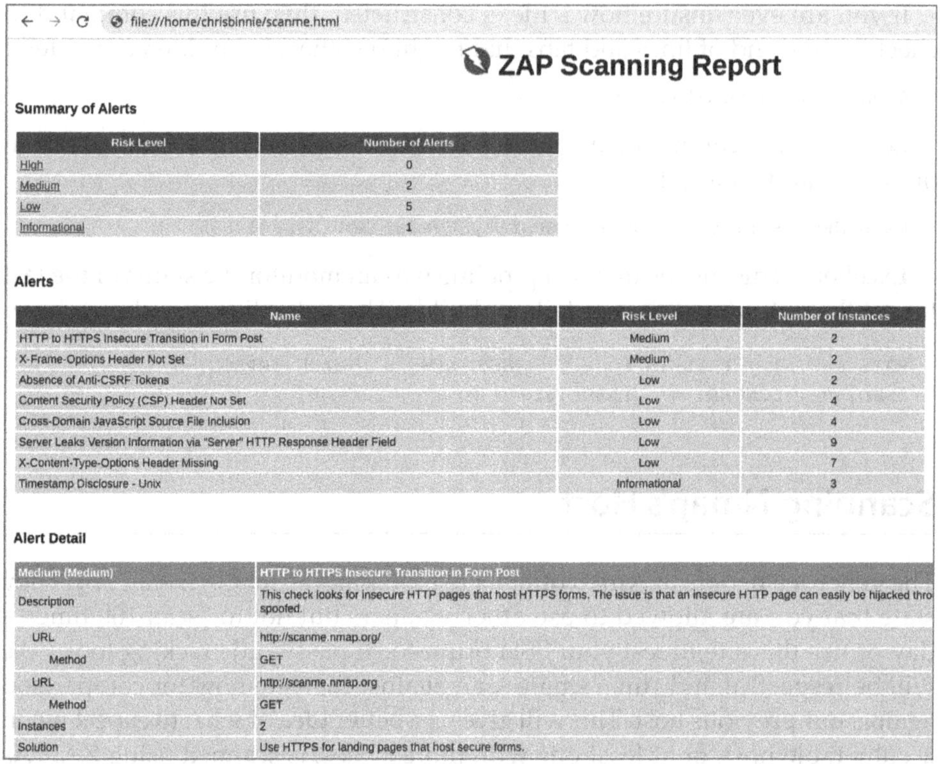

file:///home/chrisbinnie/scanme.html

ZAP Scanning Report

Summary of Alerts

Risk Level	Number of Alerts
High	0
Medium	2
Low	5
Informational	1

Alerts

Name	Risk Level	Number of Instances
HTTP to HTTPS Insecure Transition in Form Post	Medium	2
X-Frame-Options Header Not Set	Medium	2
Absence of Anti-CSRF Tokens	Low	2
Content Security Policy (CSP) Header Not Set	Low	4
Cross-Domain JavaScript Source File Inclusion	Low	4
Server Leaks Version Information via "Server" HTTP Response Header Field	Low	9
X-Content-Type-Options Header Missing	Low	7
Timestamp Disclosure - Unix	Informational	3

Alert Detail

Medium (Medium)	HTTP to HTTPS Insecure Transition in Form Post
Description	This check looks for insecure HTTP pages that host HTTPS forms. The issue is that an insecure HTTP page can easily be hijacked thro spoofed.
URL	http://scanme.nmap.org/
Method	GET
URL	http://scanme.nmap.org
Method	GET
Instances	2
Solution	Use HTTPS for landing pages that host secure forms.

Figure 7.3: A trimmed screenshot of the HTML report after scanning Nmap's host

There are a number of new issues with links to jump between the sections in our HTML report. As the attacks on web servers evolve continually, you would be advised to click each of the findings links and research what each issue involves and whether the issue is remediable. Generally, web server settings that are too permissive are commonly found, along with potential code injection vulnerabilities.

Adding Regular Expressions

You can also edit the rules file with regular expressions, as the documentation demonstrates. Here are some simple, adapted examples:

```
# Ignore the specified non-TLS/SSL HTTP intranet URL as it is internal
10012    OUTOFSCOPE    http://www.chrisbinnie.tld
```

As we can see, it is possible to completely ignore, and set as out of scope, certain URLs, potentially using only HTTP. This capability would suit ignoring an intranet URL running over HTTP, for example:

```
# Ignore URLS containing '.php' files
*    OUTOFSCOPE    .*\.php
```

Second, we can see that it is possible to ignore all rules with certain file extensions. In the example offered, we are ensuring that all PHP (`.php`) files are ignored and missed out of the scans. This might be because your intranet runs PHP, but your public website does not, for example.

There is also the ability to be able to scan multiple targets at once. The ZAP team has created a set of scripts to provide this functionality; it can be found at `github.com/zaproxy/community-scripts/tree/master/api/mass-baseline`.

The results of the scans are cleverly pushed up to the Wiki that the scripts belong to, which adds a nice level of welcome automation. To get started, you are encouraged to edit the `mass-baseline.sh` script with your targets, within this section:

```
# Replace these with your target URLs—these example ones will fail!
./mass-basewrapper.sh $repo.wiki www.fail.tld / https://example.tld
```

You then add your user and repository details to the same script and build a container image. As the container runs, you add your credentials for the prescribed user, and the results will be pushed to your wiki. All in all, that is a nice piece of functionality that saves you some scripting time.

Finally, a feature that more suits individual CI/CD pipeline tests is having the ability to add "in-progress" flags to certain issues during the scans. You begin with creating a progress file so that it is easier to mark certain results with the IN-PROGRESS tag. Listing 7.3 shows an example adapted from the documentation for our issue. As you can tell, it is in JSON format and is usefully extensible in nature, per the target website.

Listing 7.3: An Example IN-PROGRESS File

```
{
   "site": "chrisbinnie.tld",
   "issues": [
      {
         "id": "10035",
         "name": "Strict-Transport-Security Header Not Set",
         "state": "inprogress",
         "link": "https://chrisbinnie.tld/bugtracker/issue=1010"
      },
```

```
        {
          "id": "10999",
          "name": "Another error that's being fixed currently",
          "state": "inprogress",
          "link": "https://chrisbinnie.tld/bugtracker/issue=10999"
        }
      ]
    }
```

Summary

In this chapter, we looked at the intriguing graphical interface for OWASP ZAP that can now be run within a browser, using just a single command, thanks to the power of Docker and Webswing combined.

We then ran a simple text-only scan that generated some rules for a target and then, having found a WARN-NEW error, reran that scan and also created a nicely formatted HTML report afterward. Using that WARN-NEW error, we then configured a custom rules file and failed our scan successfully, just as a CI/CD pipeline test would, when issues were captured using the thorough ZAP scans.

Finally, we looked at scanning another target, courtesy of Nmap's `scanme` host, to get a better idea of what to expect when scanning a more vulnerable host using ZAP.

CHAPTER

8

Codifying Security

Having the ability to codify security controls using customized sets of rules means that your CI/CD pipelines produce repeatable, predictable results, ensuring that your applications follow a consistent path to release.

As we saw with ZAP in Chapter 7, "Baseline Scanning (or, Zap Your Apps)," and as we will see with tooling suggestions in other chapters within this section, there are a number of Open Source tools that can be used to offer return values that will pass or fail a build. In this chapter, we will look at a sophisticated tool called Gauntlt (`gauntlt.org`), which is perfect for creating extensible rulesets that will improve the security posture of your hosts.

Gauntlt describes itself as a "ruggedization framework that enables security testing that is usable by Devs, Ops and Security." The documentation notes that it provides hooks into a number of security tools and makes them accessible. The language that is used by Gauntlt is intuitive and should not be a barrier to getting started, even for inexperienced users. Gauntlt, used inside or out of pipelines, is flexible and can be configured to test many different use cases.

Security Tooling

We will start by looking at what we can expect from Gauntlt before installing it and running through some rules.

A key piece of terminology used by Gauntlt is that its tools are described as *attack adapters*. The website lists adapters for the following attack tools (among others, which we will look at a little later) as available for you to script rulesets around:

- curl
- nmap
- sslyze (github.com/iSECPartners/sslyze)
- sqlmap (sqlmap.org)
- Garmr (github.com/mozilla/Garmr)

As we can see, the vulnerable nmap is a welcome tool that Gauntlt can test with, as are the SSL inspection tool sslyze and the database hacking tool sqlmap.

In addition, having the ability to make simple requests for your tests using the sophisticated curl command is essential. Although some might not immediately think of curl as an attack tool per se, it is often used to reconnoiter by attackers and additionally download files along with wget. It is also commonly provided by default on Linux distributions.

Finally, if you are not familiar with Garmr, it heralds from the well-respected Mozilla security camp and focuses on checking the responses returned from websites.

Another nice feature is that Gauntlt uses standard exit codes for scripting (where 0 is good/success and 1 is bad/fail), so passing or failing a build does not involve lots of head-scratching. There is also a nice video demonstration of how to get up and running on the site that is referred to as the Gauntlt Starter Kit, which helps set up, in tandem with a Git repository (github.com/gauntlt/gauntlt-starter-kit), a preconfigured virtual machine using Vagrant (www.vagrantup.com) for you to run initial tests from. That repository should offer a suitable number of scripts and examples for you to cut your teeth on, in relation to the required components needed to use Gauntlt.

Installation

The website describes two ways to get started with Gauntlt. The simplest way to install it uses the Ruby package manager gem. On Debian derivatives, with the gem command available on your system, the syntax is as follows:

```
$ gem install gauntlt
```

If gem isn't already on your system, try installing it as follows:

```
$ apt install gem
```

NOTE There seems to be an issue on Ubuntu 18.04 with the error "Failed to build gem native extension." See `stackoverflow.com/questions/13767725/unable-to-install-gem-failed-to-build-gem-native-extension-cannot-load-such` for more information.

The Cloud Native approach to running Gauntlt is via a container, and we will use that method in this chapter. By opting to take the container route, you have a portable piece of prebuilt software that will not fill up your local machine with lots of small files, which can be difficult to find and delete post-installation. If you are determined to use `gem`, check the Dockerfile (`github.com/gauntlt/gauntlt-docker/blob/master/Dockerfile`) package version information for hints and tips that might potentially help you to install the correct versions. It can often be useful sifting through Dockerfiles for pointers from the developers.

To get started with the containerized version of Gauntlt, we will head over to its Docker repository (`github.com/gauntlt/gauntlt-docker`). Building the container will create a Docker image for you and also create a binary stub called `gauntlt-docker`, which will be written into the `bin/` directory once the Dockerfile has been processed. This allows two approaches to using the software. You can use a command to enter a running container and interact with the tools that way, or you can use the binary to interact with the container. Although there is also a prebuilt Gauntlt docker image you may be able to use, it is always better to build your own images, and this way you get the stub binary compiled for your system, too.

When you visit that page, you are told that the container is specifically tailored to get you up and running with Gauntlt and that you should look into tools such as Nikto (see Chapter 12, "Server Scanning with Nikto," for detailed information) and additionally Arachni to learn more.

The Dockerfile (`github.com/gauntlt/gauntlt-docker/blob/master/Dockerfile`), mentioned moments ago, provided in the repository is lengthy and, as you have probably guessed, references Ruby-related libraries and packages. You can also see Nikto, Arachni, `sqlmap`, `nmap`, `sslyze`, and `dirb` (`dirb.sourceforge.net`) being pulled into the container image. If you are not familiar with `dirb`, it's a penetration testing tool used in Kali Linux and used for web application testing. The documentation offers encouragement with the assertion that the container image is frequently used in CI/CD pipelines.

We will follow the documentation now to get started with the container and clone the Git repository using the following command so that we can build the image from scratch:

```
$ git clone https://github.com/gauntlt/gauntlt-docker.git
```

Although Gauntlt is still maintained by its developers, clearly not too regularly but when time permits, to fix the image build process, there were two changes that needed to be made to the Dockerfile to get the container image to build correctly.

These involved altering the base layer (on line 1 of the Dockerfile) from `ubuntu:16.04` to `ubuntu:18.04` and, second, on line 14, `libcurl3` to `libcurl4`. For clarity, `FROM ubuntu:16.04` is now `FROM ubuntu:18.04` and `libcurl3` is now `libcurl4`.

Do not be too concerned if the text during the output goes a slightly odd red color; it's just for effect.

Next, we will enter the repository and run `make`. You might want to experiment with rootless mode, as discussed in Chapter 2, "Rootless Runtimes," if you don't want to build and run Gauntlt's container as the `root` user.

```
$ cd gauntlt-docker
$ make build
```

In Listing 8.1 we can see the resulting, abbreviated output from the image creation process taking place. The process is relatively lengthy.

Listing 8.1: The Tail End of Output from Building Our Container Image for Gauntlt Using the Dockerfile

```
Installing collected packages: typing, nassl, tls-parser, sslyze
Successfully installed nassl-1.0.3 sslyze-1.3.4 tls-parser-1.2.2
typing-3.7.4.3
Removing intermediate container 568cfbaf2256
--> 562c08597f5b
Step 20/21: ENV SSLYZE_PATH /usr/local/bin/sslyze
--> Running in 0b6d560779e0
Removing intermediate container 0b6d560779e0
--> 92d5a1f1afab
Step 21/21: ENTRYPOINT [ "/usr/local/bin/gauntlt" ]
--> Running in e73e47ee9da2
Removing intermediate container e73e47ee9da2
--> 28055060be9f
Successfully built 28055060be9f
Successfully tagged gauntlt:latest
```

The success of a well-built binary can be checked by running the next command:

```
$ bin/gauntlt-docker—version
1.0.13
```

If you see an error relating to the `optimist` package, because it is now used instead of `trollop`, then fear not if your binary was created successfully and feeds back the version number. You could tweak the Dockerfile further if you saw fit. Some of the pull requests might be of interest, in the GitHub repository, as they potentially add some further excellent packages to the Gauntlt build.

There's a Makefile option to copy the binary into the `/usr/local/bin` directory so that it is in your current user's path. You can do just that if you run this command:

```
$ make install-stub
```

The output is shown here, as hoped:

```
installing gauntlt-docker to /usr/local/bin
```

Now that we have a container image built and also a working binary in our system path, let's put the software through its paces.

To verify that the binary is available to our user, run this command without the `bin/` part:

```
$ gauntlt-docker --help
```

In Listing 8.2 we can see the output, which we will bear in mind for the future.

Listing 8.2: The Help Output for Gauntlt

```
[DEPRECATION] The trollop gem has been renamed to optimist and
will no longer be supported. Please switch to optimist
as soon as possible.
gauntlt is a ruggedization framework that helps you be mean to your code
Usage:
       gauntlt <path>+ [–tags TAG_EXPRESSION] [–format FORMAT]
Options:
  -t,–tags=<s>        Only execute specified tags
  -l,–list            List defined attacks
  -s,–steps           List the gauntlt step definitions that can be
                        used inside of attack files
  -a,–allsteps        List all available step definitions including
                        aruba step definitions which help with file
                        and parsing operations
  -f,–format=<s>      Available formats: html, json, junit, progress
  -o,–outfile=<s>     Pipe run results to file
  -v,–version         Print version and exit
  -h,–help            Show this message
```

Our focus, however, will be on interacting with the container.

There is a `make interactive` command, executed again from inside the build directory, that the Makefile translates this way:

```
@docker run --rm -it–entrypoint /bin/bash gauntlt
```

Obviously, you can remove the prepended `@` sign and run that command yourself from anywhere on the system. We can see the image that we built is present locally as so:

```
$ docker images
REPOSITORY        TAG                  IMAGE ID           CREATED    SIZE
gauntlt         latest               28055060be9f       2 hours ago 1.38GB
```

For the next sections we will just use the previous command line directly (with the `@` sign) for ease and move out of the cloned repository's directory path.

Simple Tests

Let's try some simple examples now. To keep the processing of rules as fast as possible, Gauntlt uses the Gherkin language (`cucumber.io/docs/gherkin`). It is clear and logical, and the interpretation of that language is handled by software named Cucumber (`cucumber.io`). Think of the check that we will perform as simple, localized penetration-style testing, performed locally or remotely on assets that you own. Here's a note about some online examples, not just relating to Gauntlt: if you copy examples from websites, be careful not to automatically test against domain names such as `example.com`; although they are undoubtedly used to unwelcome traffic, it is not permitted to test against resources that you do not have permission to scan.

Listing 8.3: Using `nmap` as an Attack Adapter

```
# nmap-simple.attack
Feature: simple nmap attack to check for open ports
  Background:
    Given "nmap" is installed
    And the following profile:
      | name      | value           |
      | hostname  | chrisbinnie.tld |
      | tcp_ping_ports | 25,80,443 |
  Scenario: Check standard web ports
    When I launch an "nmap" attack with:
      """
      nmap -F <hostname>
      """
    Then the output should match:
      """
      80/tcp\s+open
      443/tcp\s+open
      """
    Then the output should not match:
      """
      25\/tcp\s+open
      """
```

In Listing 8.3, we can see some distinct sections within the rules file.

The start of the file contains a `Feature` entry, which provides a concise description of the rule's purpose. Within the next section, `Background`, you can see what you might almost call pseudocode. The logic is stating that `nmap` must be available and that a redacted hostname (replaced with `chrisbinnie.tld`) has been declared as the target for the attack adapter. Under the next section, `Scenario`, we can see which switches the `nmap` attack adapter will run with "fast mode" enabled, which is the reason for the `-F` option. To finish off, we are looking for an open TCP port 80 and TCP port 443 but not an open SMTP port (TCP port 25) because the target is just running a web server and should not be presenting a mail server port.

Inside our running container (accessed by the next command), a directory listing shows some of the build process results:

```
$ docker run --rm -it --entrypoint /bin/bash gauntlt
root@d469b6590ba7:/opt# ls
arachni-1.5.1-0.5.12-linux-x86_64.tar.gz  dirb222
dirb222.tar.gz  nikto  sqlmap
```

Additionally, using this command we can see where examples have been written within the container:

```
$ root@d469b6590ba7:~# find / -name attacks
/var/lib/gems/2.5.0/gems/gauntlt-1.0.13/features/attacks
```

And a directory listing of that directory shows the following:

```
arachni.broken  curl.feature  dirb.feature  garmr.feature
generic.feature  nmap.feature  sqlmap.broken  sslyze.feature
```

The examples are a great source for learning how to use Gauntlt more effectively, with the varying attack adapters that it supports.

Let's get back to our simple attack file. Let's exit the container and write the contents of that file to our local machine, into a new directory called `/root/attacks` for ease, with the filename `nmap-simple.attack`.

Next, we will point the container at the `/root/attacks` directory on our filesystem (with the same path inside the container) so that we can see the attack rule file, by mounting a volume with this command:

```
$ docker run --rm -it -v /root/attacks:/root/attacks \
—entrypoint gauntlt gauntlt /root/attacks/nmap-simple.attack
```

Clearly there are a few different ways of interacting with the container, but this way we can keep a copy of our custom attack rules on a local machine and start/stop containers as we want.

We could have just used the host-based binary to achieve the same scanning result, but it can be useful to understand the full commands, so we will continue to use the Docker command. For reference, if you wanted to use the binary we created during the build process, the command would simply look like this:

```
$ gauntlt-docker attacks/nmap-simple.attack
```

A useful way to understand how Gauntlt's engine works is to display all steps, as follows:

```
$ docker run --rm -it -v /root/attacks:/root/attacks \
—entrypoint gauntlt gauntlt—allsteps
```

In Listing 8.4 we can see abbreviated output from that command.

Listing 8.4: Displaying Abbreviated `allsteps` Including File Processing by Aruba

```
File and output parsing steps (using Aruba)
/I use (?:a|the) fixture(?: named)? "([^"]*)"/
/The default aruba timeout is (\d+) seconds/
/^(?:an|the) empty file(?: named)? "([^"]*)" with mode "([^"]*)"$/
/^(?:an|the) empty file(?: named)? "([^"]*)"$/
/^(?:a|the) (\d+) byte file(?: named)? "([^"]*)" should exist$/
/^(?:a|the) (\d+) byte file(?: named)? "([^"]*)"$/
/^(?:a|the) directory(?: named)? "([^"]*)" does not exist$/
/^(?:a|the) directory(?: named)? "([^"]*)" should (not )?exist$/
/^(?:a|the) directory(?: named)? "([^"]*)" with mode "([^"]*)"$/
[snip. . .]
Gauntlt Attack Steps
/^"(\w+)" is installed in my path$/
/^"Heartbleed" is installed$/
/^"arachni" is installed$/
/^"curl" is installed$/
/^"dirb" is installed$/
/^"garmr" is installed$/
/^"nmap" is installed$/
/^"sqlmap" is installed$/
/^"sslyze" is installed$/
/^I launch (?:a|an) "Heartbleed" attack with:$/
/^I launch (?:a|an) "arachni" attack with:$/
/^I launch (?:a|an) "arachni-(.*?)" attack$/
/^I launch (?:a|an) "curl" attack with:$/
```

Here we see the file processing, courtesy of a processor called Aruba in this case, that Gauntlt uses to approach the attack steps as it runs through them. Those of you familiar with regular expressions should be able to make some sense of the syntax used. It seems that there is not too much documentation about Aruba online, but it is worth seeing how the logic of Gauntlt works.

Example Attack Files

Let's look at another example now, using a different attack adapter. There are a number of examples online for you to tweak and finely tune; they tend to also be varied and complete.

Because `sqlmap` is a sophisticated tool, you should not feel confined to testing for SQL injections against only the most popular of databases, such as MySQL or Postgres. The `sqlmap` website (`sqlmap.org`) states in its compatibility advice that the following databases are fully supported: "MySQL, Oracle, PostgreSQL,

Microsoft SQL Server, Microsoft Access, IBM DB2, SQLite, Firebird, Sybase, SAP MaxDB, Informix, MariaDB, MemSQL, TiDB, CockroachDB, HSQLDB, H2, MonetDB, Apache Derby, Amazon Redshift, Vertica, Mckoi, Presto, Altibase, MimerSQL, CrateDB, Greenplum, Drizzle, Apache Ignite, Cubrid, InterSystems Cache, IRIS, eXtremeDB, FrontBase, Raima Database Manager, YugabyteDB and Virtuoso database management systems."

If you want to explore `sqlmap`'s multitudinous array of options, the website provides an exhaustive list of clearly written usage documentation. It can be found via GitHub here: `github.com/sqlmapproject/sqlmap/wiki/Usage`.

In Listing 8.5 we can see how Gauntlt might approach attacking a MySQL database using `sqlmap`.

Listing 8.5: Attacking a Database Using Gauntlt

```
@slow
Feature: Run sqlmap with Gauntlt
Scenario: Highlight SQLi vulnerabilities
  Given "sqlmap" is installed
  And the following profile:
    | name       | value                                          |
    | target_url | http://chrisbinnie.tld/splash-page?number_id=1 |
  When I launch a "sqlmap" attack with:
    """
    python <sqlmap> -u <target>—dbms mysql—batch -v 0—tables
    """
  Then the output should contain:
    """
    sqlmap identified the following injection points
    """
  And the output should contain:
    """
    [5 tables]
    +————————+
    | mysql_secure   |
    | database_users |
    | mysql_test     |
    | customers      |
    | accounting     |
    +————————+
    """
```

The main online examples directory, which is full of attack files that you should try, can be found on GitHub at `github.com/gauntlt/gauntlt/tree/master/examples`.

You may have noticed the `@slow` tag at the top of the `sqlmap` example. You have three speed options to choose from, as described in Table 8.1.

Table 8.1: Using Tags in Gauntlt to Get More or Less Results

TAG	PURPOSE
`<empty>`	Any scenarios found in the attack file will be executed for a period of three seconds.
`@slow`	Your scenarios will carry on going for up to 30 seconds per scenario.
`@reallyslow`	In this case, each scenario will continue, for up to 10 minutes.

It is worth taking a deeper look at Arachni (`www.arachni-scanner.com`). Apparently, it bundles with more than 40 "active" and "passive" modules, which can delve into SQLi and XSS issues of all varieties. In addition, you can test against NoSQL, code injection, and file-inclusion issues. According to Arachni, their tests are "unparalleled in reliability, accuracy and resiliency, even under unstable network conditions or when dealing with misbehaving web applications."

In Listing 8.6 we can see how `dirb` might be used in a test or attack scenario, when it trawls a website for visible and hidden objects that are of interest. The `dirb` website (`tools.kali.org/web-applications/dirb`) refers to itself as a *web content scanner* that runs through large word lists (also known as dictionary attacks) to find assets on a website that might be exploitable. If you ever check the web server logs after such a scan, logging is extremely noisy, containing thousands of hits with arbitrary strings trying to complete filenames.

Listing 8.6: The `dirb` Attack Adapter, Using Dictionary-Style Attacks

```
@reallyslow
Feature: Run a content scan with dirb on a target

Scenario: Scan a site with dirb—the DIRB_WORDLISTS variable must be set.
  Given "dirb" is installed
  And the following profile:
     | name                 | value |
     | url                  | chrisbinnie.tld |
     | dirb_wordlists_path  | $DIRB_WORDLISTS |
     | wordlist             | your_generated_wordlist.txt |
  When I launch a "dirb" attack with:
  """
  dirb <url> <path>/<wordlist> -f -N 404 -S
  """
  Then the output should contain:
  """
  FOUND: 0
  """
```

In Listing 8.6, we are referring to a word list that we created, and when dirb is run, it is told to ignore web server responses that give an error 404. The appended -S option also tells dirb not to output the potentially massive lists of words being used in the scan and instead be silent. It is not uncommon for such word lists to be in the hundreds of thousands of lines long, so for a pipeline test, such output is the last thing required. There are a number of ways to generate word lists of your own, as shown on the dirb website. The suggestions are to use a tool included with the dirb package called html2dic to generate a word list from a website (to act as a baseline for future scans presumably) or the gendict tool. Incidentally, if you were to run dirb directly, the command would look similar to this:

```
$ dirb https://chrisbinnie.tld/ /home/chris/your_generated_wordlist.txt
```

TIP **To get used to running Gauntlt yourself, also try the** sslyze.attack **example that is available. It will help you see in more detail how you can interact with results.**

Summary

In this chapter, we saw how you might install Gauntlt and looked at a few examples of deploying it to improve your application and host security. Having seen Gauntlt in action, you will recognize the syntax immediately if you visit the Cucumber website (cucumber.io).

The clever simplicity of Gauntlt makes it an excellent wrapper for automating a wide variety of attacks for assets that you have permission to do so. You can trust the attack adapters that it uses as they have almost universally been battle-hardened over many years. Therefore, the results are perfect for tests within a CI/CD pipeline to create a short feedback loop that informs you of any issues that might have otherwise been missed without automated checks.

CHAPTER

9

Kubernetes Compliance

This is the third DevSecOps tooling chapter and our first look at Kubernetes (`kubernetes.io`), the container orchestrator. Following an initial adoption of running containers to serve their applications, organizations soon realize, sometimes with horror, that it is almost impossible to pull together the many facets of a microservices architecture without some form of container orchestrator. And, while Kubernetes rises to that challenge and provides unparalleled levels of sophistication to herd multiple cat-like containers at once, there can be a steep learning curve for those who are new to it.

In hand with that complexity come a number of new and often unseen security challenges, which means that organizations quickly need to learn about the potential impact of the attack vectors that Kubernetes exposes. In early releases, for example, there were known attacks on the API Server component of Kubernetes. The API Server is the interface between the many components of a Kubernetes cluster, and being able to authenticate to it with privileges offered attackers a treasure trove. In this chapter, we look at the highlighting of potential security issues that industry experts consider might present your Kubernetes cluster issues.

Receiving regular reports about how secure your Kubernetes cluster is can be invaluable. And, running compliance tools within CI/CD pipelines is perfectly possible if they provide timely results and do not slow down your build processes.

Using such tools also means that you are armed with the ability to detect salient changes in your security posture after configuration changes and version upgrades. If you have the ability to test a cluster's compliance against a lengthy checklist, then you gain pertinent information about numerous components that require your attention. In some cases, for the unseasoned cluster operator, this applies to aspects of a cluster that you previously were not even aware of. By testing your security compliance against the widely respected, industry-consensus-based CIS Benchmarks, you can receive useful reports to help focus where to put your efforts in relation to Kubernetes security. There are many CIS Benchmarks available (`www.cisecurity.org/cis-benchmarks`) that can offer invaluable insight into operating systems, applications, and cloud platforms to name but a few. The website states that there are more than 100 configuration guidelines across more than 25 vendor product families to help improve their security posture. The detail the benchmarks provide is hard to match, and from a Cloud Native perspective, you are encouraged to look up your relevant Linux distribution, Docker, Kubernetes, and cloud platform benchmarks just to get you started.

In this chapter, we will install `kube-bench` (`github.com/aquasecurity/kube-bench`) and run it against a micro cluster to offer an insight into what you might expect on a fully blown Kubernetes installation.

Mini Kubernetes

We will install Kubernetes for our lab environment locally using the sophisticated Minikube (`github.com/kubernetes/minikube`).

The first step is to install a kernel-based virtual machine (VM) platform, KVM (`www.linux-kvm.org`), on our local machine so that we can then install Minikube within a VM.

The command to install the core KVM packages is as follows (some may already be installed):

```
$ apt install qemu-kvm libvirt-bin bridge-utils virtinst virt-manager
```

Note that you will need x86 hardware with CPU extensions enabled for the virtualization, namely, Intel VT or AMD-V, for KVM to work. KVM will create a kernel module called `kvm.ko`, which is loaded into the local system to enable it to interact with the system for virtualization. Then an Intel or AMD module (depending on your flavor of processor) is also loaded.

Listing 9.1 shows some of the packages and their dependencies installed with KVM, which total only approximately 30MB of installation footprint. Once all of them are installed, KVM should shortly become available to us.

Listing 9.1: Some of the Installation Packages for KVM

```
augeas-lenses bridge-utils gir1.2-gtk-vnc-2.0 gir1.2-libosinfo-1.0
gir1.2-libvirt-glib-1.0 libaugeas0 libnetcf1 libosinfo-1.0-0
libvirt-bin libvirt-clients libvirt-daemon libvirt-daemon-system
osinfo-db python-certifi python-chardet python-idna python-ipaddr
python-libvirt python-libxml2 python-pkg-resources python-requests
python-urllib3 qemu-kvm virt-manager virtinst
```

One of the main components is called `virsh`, which the manual describes as the program used as "the main interface for managing virsh guest domains." Running on an Ubuntu 18.04 laptop (using Linux Mint on top), we can see the output of the `nodeinfo` option in Listing 9.2.

Listing 9.2: The `virsh` Command Showing What Hardware Is Available to KVM

```
$ virsh nodeinfo
CPU model:           x86_64
CPU(s):              4
CPU frequency:       2226 MHz
CPU socket(s):       1
Core(s) per socket:  2
Thread(s) per core:  2
NUMA cell(s):        1
Memory size:         8071928 KiB
```

The installation of Minikube requires the following commands; at this point choose which directory you want to install your main Minkube file into and assume you will run your commands from this directory, too:

```
$ curl -O https://storage.googleapis.com/minikube/releases/latest/minikube_
latest_amd64.deb
$ dpkg -i minikube_latest_amd64.deb
$ ./minikube version
minikube version: v1.12.1
```

For other flavors of Linux, Mac, or Windows, choose the relevant installation option from this page: `minikube.sigs.k8s.io/docs/start`.

We need to start up Minikube next with this command, as the `root` user:

```
$ minikube start --driver=none
```

In Listing 9.3 we can see the execution process for Minikube.

Listing 9.3: The Abbreviated Installation Process for Our Kubernetes Lab Environment Courtesy of Minikube

```
minikube v1.12.1 on Linuxmint 19
Using the none driver based on user configuration
```

```
Starting control plane node minikube in cluster minikube
Running on localhost (CPUs=4, Memory=7882MB, Disk=230089MB) ..
OS release is Linux Mint 19
Preparing Kubernetes v1.18.3 on Docker 19.03.6 ..
  ■ kubelet.resolv-conf=/run/systemd/resolve/resolv.conf
  > kubeadm.sha256: 65 B / 65 B [————————-] 100.00% ? p/s 0s
  > kubectl.sha256: 65 B / 65 B [————————-] 100.00% ? p/s 0s
  > kubelet.sha256: 65 B / 65 B [————————-] 100.00% ? p/s 0s
  > kubeadm: 37.97 MiB / 37.97 MiB [—] 100.00% 1.00 MiB p/s 38s
  > kubectl: 41.99 MiB / 41.99 MiB [—] 100.00% 1.09 MiB p/s 38s
  > kubelet: 108.04 MiB / 108.04 MiB [-] 100.00% 1.60 MiB p/s 1m7s
Configuring local host environment ..
The 'none' driver is designed for experts who need to integrate
with an existing VM Most users should use the newer 'docker' driver
instead, which does not require root! For more information, see:
https://minikube.sigs.k8s.io/docs/reference/drivers/none/
```

Note the warning about the none driver. It appears because `root` level permissions are passed onto the Minikube environment if you install using this method. Be sure to tear down your virtual environment after running a lab like this.

We need a copy of `kubectl` installed now, which is the userland binary used to interact with the API Server in our Kubernetes cluster. We can query an online text file to see the latest stable release version:

```
$ curl -s \
https://storage.googleapis.com/kubernetes-release/release/stable.txt
# Get the latest version
V1.18.3
```

We can see that it is `v1.18.3`, so adjust the version in this next command to download the correct `kubectl` version (getting the version incorrect might mean that some features do not work and there's a higher risk of unexpected results):

```
$ curl -O https://storage.googleapis.com/kubernetes-
release/release/v1.18.3/bin/linux/amd64/kubectl
```

We now need to see if that download worked after adding the file to our user's path:

```
$ chmod +x kubectl # make the file executable
$ mv kubectl /usr/local/bin # put this file into our user's path
```

Verify that the versions match with the following command; in the slightly abbreviated output, look at both client and server versions:

```
$ kubectl version
Client Version: version.Info{Major:"1", Minor:"18", GitVersion:"v1.18.3"
GitCommit:"2e7996e3e2712684bc73f0dec0200d64eec7fe40",
GitTreeState:"clean", BuildDate:"2020-05-20T12:52:00Z",
```

```
GoVersion:"go1.13.9", Compiler:"gc", Platform:"linux/amd64"}
Server Version: version.Info{Major:"1", Minor:"18", GitVersion:"v1.18.3"
GitCommit:"2e7996e3e2712684bc73f0dec0200d64eec7fe40",
GitTreeState:"clean", BuildDate:"2020-05-20T12:43:34Z",
GoVersion:"go1.13.9", Compiler:"gc", Platform:"linux/amd64"}
```

Now for the moment of truth. Let's see if we have a local Kubernetes lab running, with this command:

```
$ kubectl get nodes
NAME   STATUS   ROLES    AGE   VERSION
kilo   Ready    master   3m    v1.18.3
```

That looks promising; we have a master node running.

Listing 9.4 shows the output from one more quick check to confirm that the cluster has all of its required components available.

Listing 9.4: All Looks Good from a Minikube Perspective

```
$ kubectl get pods --all-namespaces

NAMESPACE     NAME                              READY   STATUS   RESTARTS AGE
kube-system   coredns-66bff467f8-x8286          1/1     Running 0         14m
kube-system   etcd-kilo                         1/1     Running 0         14m
kube-system   kube-apiserver-kilo               1/1     Running 0         14m
kube-system   kube-controller-manager-kilo      1/1     Running 0         14m
kube-system   kube-proxy-tm765                  1/1     Running 0         14m
kube-system   kube-scheduler-kilo               1/1     Running 0         14m
kube-system   storage-provisioner               1/1     Running 0         14m
```

Let's turn to our Kubernetes compliance tool now and see if the cluster security can be improved.

Using *kube-bench*

Courtesy of the Cloud Native security company Aqua Security (`www.aquasec.com`), `kube-bench` is a piece of Open Source software that runs through the comprehensive CIS Benchmarks for Kubernetes. There is no direct correlation in terms of timelines between new releases of Kubernetes and the CIS Benchmarks, so bear that in mind if new features are not flagged as having issues by `kube-bench`. As an aside, any managed Kubernetes clusters—the likes of EKS on AWS (`aws.amazon.com/eks`)—that do not make their Control Plane visible obviously cannot be queried in quite the same way as other clusters by `kube-bench`. It is still worth trying such tools.

Let's see `kube-bench` in action now, using the Kubernetes lab that we built using Minikube.

To get started, we need to decide how to execute `kube-bench`. If we run it from inside a container, then it will have visibility of the process table of the host for its queries. Or we could install `kube-bench` via a container onto the host directly. The third choice (barring compiling it from source) is to use one of the provided, oven-ready binaries. You will need to ensure that your CI/CD pipeline security is in good shape, as `kube-bench` will require elevated privileges to have the ability to delve deeply into your Kubernetes cluster.

We will go down the second route and execute `kube-bench` from the host itself having installed a `kube-bench` container first. The command to do just that is as follows:

```
$ docker run --rm -v $(pwd):/host aquasec/kube-bench:latest install
```

In Listing 9.5 we can see what the installation process looks like via a container.

Listing 9.5: Installing `kube-bench` Directly onto a Host via a Container

```
Unable to find image 'aquasec/kube-bench:latest' locally
latest: Pulling from aquasec/kube-bench
df20fa9351a1: Pull complete
9c7b79b29816: Pull complete
267252e9f38f: Pull complete
4bf373814c8f: Pull complete
27fded220446: Pull complete
97978855d014: Pull complete
b0b3379a7f3c: Pull complete
Digest: sha256:c21b290f8708caa17[. . .snip. . .]9f2292b7d376f9cd0ebbc800e
Status: Downloaded newer image for aquasec/kube-bench:latest
===============================================
kube-bench is now installed on your host
Run ./kube-bench to perform a security check
===============================================
```

Having run that Docker command from within the `/root` directory, we can now see a binary waiting to be executed, located at `/root/kube-bench`. Also, in that directory we can see a `/cfg` directory with the following files and directory listed:

```
cis-1.3  cis-1.4  cis-1.5  config.yaml  eks-1.0  gke-1.0
node_only.yaml  rh-0.7
```

Following the advice offered in Listing 9.5, let's execute `kube-bench` now with autodetection enabled to see if it can determine the version of Kubernetes. As we saw with the earlier `get nodes` command, we are running version v1.18.3, which we can declare at this stage too if the autodetect feature fails.

For a single Minikube master node, that command might look like this:

```
$ ./kube-bench master --version 1.18
```

Equally, you can adjust which version of the CIS Benchmarks `kube-bench` refers to. Choose a framework that you want to run `kube-bench` against with a command like this one:

```
$ ./kube-bench node --benchmark cis-1.5
```

However, for a Minikube master node we will use this command instead:

```
$ ./kube-bench master
```

Success! The output from that command is exceptionally long, but the end displays the following:

```
== Summary ==
41 checks PASS
13 checks FAIL
11 checks WARN
0 checks INFO
```

Let's look through some of the other findings, a section at a time. It is recommended that you download the latest CIS Benchmarks PDF yourself at this stage from the CIS site (`www.cisecurity.org/benchmark/kubernetes`). That way you can compare and contrast the sometimes-concise output from compliance tools, and when researching an issue, you might be able to glean information from the PDF to use in combination with the compliance tool in order to help remediate any problems.

Listing 9.6 shows some of the benchmark-matching output entries, starting from the top. Although you cannot see color in this book, on your screen red text signifies a FAIL; orange text is a WARN; green, as you might have already guessed, is a PASS; and blue is INFO.

Listing 9.6: The Top of the Output from `kube-bench`

```
[INFO] 1 Master Node Security Configuration
[INFO] 1.1 Master Node Configuration Files
[PASS] 1.1.1 Ensure that the API server pod specification file
permissions are set to 644 or more restrictive (Scored)
[PASS] 1.1.2 Ensure that the API server pod specification file
ownership is set to root:root (Scored)
[PASS] 1.1.3 Ensure that the controller manager pod specification file
permissions are set to 644 or more restrictive (Scored)
[PASS] 1.1.4 Ensure that the controller manager pod specification file
ownership is set to root:root (Scored)
[PASS] 1.1.5 Ensure that the scheduler pod specification file
permissions are set to 644 or more restrictive (Scored)
[PASS] 1.1.6 Ensure that the scheduler pod specification file ownership
is set to root:root (Scored)
[PASS] 1.1.7 Ensure that the etcd pod specification file permissions
are set to 644 or more restrictive (Scored)
[PASS] 1.1.8 Ensure that the etcd pod specification file ownership
```

```
is set to root:root (Scored)
[WARN] 1.1.9 Ensure that the Container Network Interface file
permissions are set to 644 or more restrictive (Not Scored)
[WARN] 1.1.10 Ensure that the Container Network Interface file
ownership is set to root:root (Not Scored)
[PASS] 1.1.11 Ensure that the etcd data directory permissions are set
to 700 or more restrictive (Scored)
[FAIL] 1.1.12 Ensure that the etcd data directory ownership is set
to etcd:etcd (Scored)
```

As we can see within our Minikube installation, the `etcd` storage directory has come back with a FAIL. If we take note of that CIS Benchmark item number (1.1.12 in this case), then we can look further down the output and get the recommendations on how to remediate each issue.

In Listing 9.7 we can see what the clever `kube-bench` is reporting.

Listing 9.7: Item 1.1.12, `etcd` Data Directory Ownership Recommendations from `kube-bench`

```
1.1.12 On the etcd server node, get the etcd data directory,
passed as an argument—data-dir, from the below command:
ps -ef | grep etcd
Run the below command (based on the etcd data directory found above).
For example, chown etcd:etcd /var/lib/etcd
```

Let's look at another FAIL now. The layout of `kube-bench`'s output is by each Kubernetes component to keep things clearer. As a result, all items under 1.1 relate to master node configuration, items under 1.2 concern the API Server, 1.3 is for the Controller Manager, and 1.4 refers to the Scheduler.

Under 1.2.16 a FAIL relating to the API Server states the following:

```
[FAIL] 1.2.16 Ensure that the admission control plugin
PodSecurityPolicy is set (Scored)
```

In Listing 9.8 we can see how to remedy such an issue.

Listing 9.8: An API Server PodSecurityPolicy Error Has Been Flagged as a FAIL

```
1.2.16 Follow the documentation and create Pod Security Policy
objects as per your environment.
Then, edit the API server pod specification file
/etc/kubernetes/manifests/kube-apiserver.yaml
on the master node and set the—enable-admission-plugins parameter
to a value that includes PodSecurityPolicy:
—enable-admission-plugins=..,PodSecurityPolicy,..
Then restart the API Server
```

It looks like by default Minikube does not enable PodSecurityPolicies (PSPs), which are cluster-wide security controls to limit the permissions that pods are granted. Note that there is more information about pod security policies in Chapter 20, "Workload Hardening."

Moving on, under a Controller Manager FAIL (1.3.1) we can also see that a garbage collection issue has been raised:

```
[FAIL] 1.3.1 Ensure that the --terminated-pod-gc-threshold argument
is set as appropriate (Scored)
```

In Listing 9.9 we can see what might fix that.

Listing 9.9: Garbage Collection Is Important for Kubernetes Too

```
1.3.1 Edit the Controller Manager pod specification file /etc/
kubernetes/manifests/kube-controller-manager.yaml
on the master node and set the --terminated-pod-gc-threshold
to an appropriate threshold,
for example:
--terminated-pod-gc-threshold=10
```

As mentioned, if you are not sure about a certain issue, then there is usually enough information offered between the PDF of the CIS Benchmark and the compliance tool. Failing that, a quick search for `--terminated-pod-gc-threshold` online offered the following information for clarity from the Kubernetes site (`kubernetes.io/docs/reference/command-line-tools-reference/kube-controller-manager`):

```
--terminated-pod-gc-threshold int32      Default: 12500
```

As we can see, the default setting is to run 12,500 pods at the most. Underneath that the Kubernetes site explains:

```
"Number of terminated pods that can exist before the terminated pod
garbage collector starts deleting terminated pods. If <= 0, the
terminated pod garbage collector is disabled."
```

Settings such as these are not only good housekeeping but can also potentially enable your Kubernetes cluster to survive certain types of stress events such as a misconfiguration, a race condition, or a denial-of-service attack of some description.

In Listing 9.10 we can see an issue that was flagged about the Scheduler, namely, the `--profiling` argument, item 1.4.1, which should be disabled for production use. This is followed by the `kube-bench` recommendations on a fix for this issue.

Listing 9.10: Profiling Needs to Be Switched Off Within Our Cluster

```
[FAIL] 1.4.1 Ensure that the --profiling argument is set to false
(Scored)
1.4.1 Edit the Scheduler pod specification file
/etc/kubernetes/manifests/kube-scheduler.yaml file
on the master node and set the below parameter.
--profiling=false
```

According to an online search, `--profiling` is now deprecated as per this comment from the Kubernetes site (`kubernetes.io/docs/reference/command-line-tools-reference/kube-scheduler`):

```
DEPRECATED: enable profiling via web interface host:port/debug/pprof/
```

This option is really only for troubleshooting issues that can expose system and software versions unnecessarily, so it can be safely switched off.

Troubleshooting

If for some reason your Kubernetes cluster does not play nicely with `kube-bench`, you can increase logging verbosity this way:

```
$ ./kube-bench master -v 3 --logtostderr
```

To assist further with the research of the recommendations provided by `kube-bench` if necessary, you can turn on debugging to provide full visibility of the compliance tool's testing methods. For example, Listing 9.11 shows one such set of tests that were run with debugging enabled.

Listing 9.11: Under the Bonnet of `kube-bench`'s Tests

```
"permissions=600\n"
- Error Messages:""
I0726 18:52:49.337928   20899 check.go:187] Check.ID: 1.1.1
Command:
"/bin/sh -c 'if test -e /etc/kubernetes/manifests/kube-apiserver.yaml;
then
stat -c permissions=%a /etc/kubernetes/manifests/kube-apiserver.yaml;
 fi'" TestResult: true State: "PASS"
I0726 18:52:49.341432   20899 check.go:225]
Command
"/bin/sh -c 'if test -e /etc/kubernetes/manifests/kube-apiserver.yaml;
then
stat -c %U:%G /etc/kubernetes/manifests/kube-apiserver.yaml; fi'"
- Output
```

As Listing 9.11 demonstrates, a nontrivial number of tests and lines of code are whirring away internally when `kube-bench` is executed. The following output shows it checking for specification file permissions; here a more restrictive 600 is preferred over the looser 644:

```
[PASS] 1.1.1 Ensure that the API server pod specification file
permissions are set to 644 or more restrictive (Scored)
```

Automation

If you have automated the execution of `kube-bench` but want to omit certain tests to reduce alarms being triggered and therefore the level of report noise, you can enter the `cfg/` directory mentioned earlier and tweak rulesets. Within that directory there are YAML files containing detailed information about each compliance test performed. In Listing 9.12 you can see an example for the `etcd` server.

Listing 9.12: An Item Relating to `etcd` That Can Be Disabled

```
–id: 2.2
   text: "Ensure that the–client-cert-auth argument is set to
          true (Scored)"
   audit: "/bin/ps -ef | /bin/grep $etcdbin | /bin/grep -v grep"
   tests:
      test_items:
      –flag: "–client-cert-auth"
          compare:
            op: eq
            value: true
          set: true
    remediation: |
      Edit the etcd pod specification file $etcdconf on the master
      node and set the below parameter.
     –client-cert-auth="true"
    scored: true
```

Within Listing 9.12 if the line `skip: true` was added to the YAML file under the entry stating `text:`, then this test would not be run, and any output would just be shown as INFO, meaning it is for informational purposes only.

Summary

In this chapter, we set up a temporary Kubernetes lab using the clever Minikube, and then we ran a highly respected compliance checking tool, `kube-bench`, over its live, running config.

The speedy and comprehensive output provided by `kube-bench` is perfect for CI/CD pipeline tests. Even if tools like this are run only after each version upgrade or are executed daily on a schedule, with output containing FAILs being forwarded to human eyes for evaluation, then this type of approach to mitigating potentially serious issues before they occur is not to be ignored.

CHAPTER 10

Securing Your Git Repositories

The familiar process of writing code, pushing it to a code repository, and waiting patiently for a peer review became increasingly popular at the start of the adoption of DevOps methodologies. Raising a pull request (PR) for the code changes you want to be merged before code is pulled into the master branch and set live in your applications meant that more than one set of eyes approved those changes before they could potentially cause issues with the applications.

Of course, the code repositories in which you store your application code are another attack surface that are often overlooked on modern Cloud Native estates, and one that can offer hackers the keys to your kingdom.

When using code repositories with AWS, for example, developers often accidentally push access keys and secret keys to the likes of GitHub, BitBucket, or GitLab (services based on the `git` repository search query software written by the venerable Linus Torvalds, who brought us Linux). Certificates and plain-text passwords are also common residents of online repositories. If you do not think that the storing of precious secrets is a massive problem for today's developers, visit this link: `github.com/search?q=PRIVATE+KEY&type=Code`.

The search engine on GitHub allows any registered user to hunt for the string `PRIVATE KEY` via their web interface. At the time of writing, there are a staggering 85,955,849 search results returned from that string. Of course, the vast majority will be correctly programmed code with references to where a key might be stored, but what are the bets that, with some patience, there are a few results that could really benefit an attacker?

There are a few ways of monitoring the storage of such secrets in code repositories, including tokens, certificates, and access keys. In this chapter, we will explore two Open Source tools that can help you automate their discovery.

Things to Consider

There are a few prerequisites to consider when setting up your code repositories for security. The first is that you need to make sure the hosting of your code repository is secure and suitable for your needs. Even some exceptionally large enterprises trust their intellectual property to GitHub's infrastructure, the most popular online `git` repository service. Microsoft bought GitHub at the end of 2018 in an attempt to increase its reach further into the Open Source community, which now puts some organizations off. For obvious reasons, the majority of larger organizations simply cannot risk an information leak of any variety and instead opt to host their code repositories either within Atlassian's BitBucket (formerly known as Stash) and GitLab on-premises, locked away within their own cloud infrastructure.

To follow best practices for the basic security principle of privilege separation, it is important for your repositories to offer users only a minimal set of permissions. GitHub and the likes have matured significantly over the years and now provide granular permissions to achieve such levels of separation. Try the following for a hands-on demonstration of generating permission-based access tokens within GitHub:

1. Sign into the web interface and click Settings, under the top-right menu for your user, and then choose Developer Settings at the bottom of the navigation menu on the left.
2. Then click Personal Access Tokens, and you are presented with the ability to generate an access token. GitHub says this about these tokens, which are effectively ordinary OAuth tokens: "They can be used instead of a password for Git over HTTPS or can be used to authenticate to the API over Basic Authentication." In other words, you should treat your access token in the same way as your GitHub password.

In Figure 10.1 we can see an abbreviated list of permissions that you might want to fine-tune on a per-user basis.

Aside from the permissions shown in Figure 10.1, privileged users, who can merge code from user-generated pull requests so that changes will be added to the master branch, should obviously be limited in number. In addition, you will also need a way of quickly revoking users that become persona non grata for one reason or another.

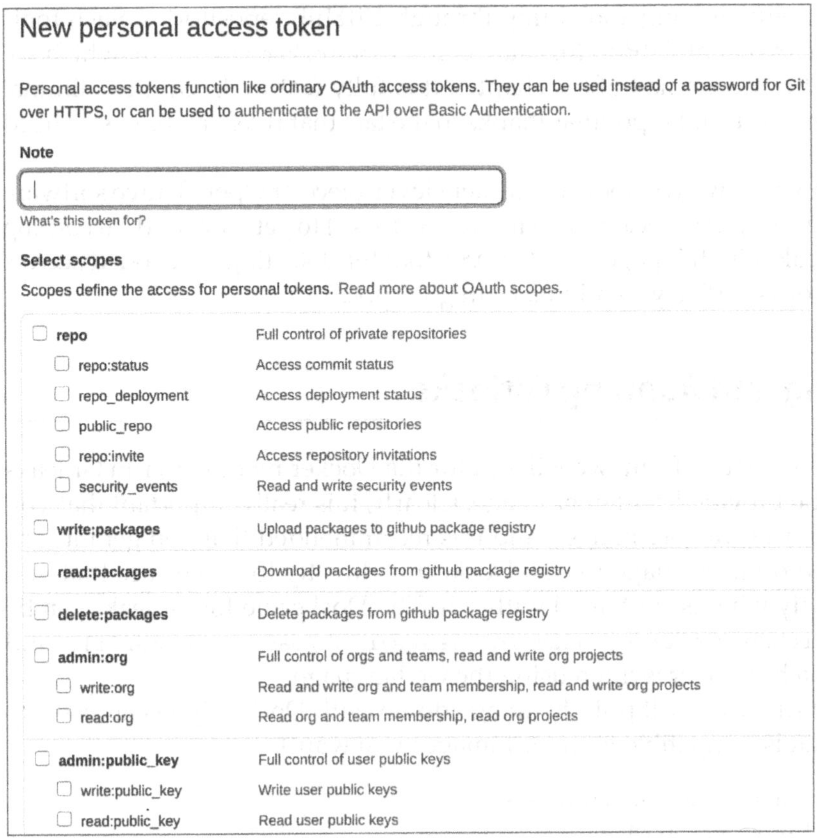

Figure 10.1: Fine-grained permissions from GitHub via personal access tokens
Source: `github.com/settings/tokens/new`

You might have many private repositories and also a handful of public ones, especially if you are Open Sourcing some of your software. As a result, it is essential to enforce public/private classifications carefully to avoid potentially devastating mistakes.

And, to prevent data leaks, it is imperative that you avoid giving too much information away in public repositories. An attacker who learns a developer's real name, username, company, department, and email address might feel empowered to conduct targeted phishing attacks.

If you are concerned about information that needs to be secret and how to integrate it securely in your code repositories, there is an interesting page on GitHub (`docs.github.com/en/actions/configuring-and-managing-workflows/creating-and-storing-encrypted-secrets`) that explains how to store and encrypt secrets.

Let's look at installing and configuring tools that can automatically assist with some of the issues that we have looked at. There are a number of popular options for enumerating and sifting through GitHub repositories. Such tools include the excellent GitRob (`github.com/michenriksen/gitrob`), which we will try in the second half of the chapter. It is fully featured, requires minimal installation effort, and is popular thanks to the fact that rules can be customized with relative ease.

First, however, we will look at another clever piece of Open Source software called Gitleaks (`github.com/zricethezav/gitleaks`) to get us started. According to the Gitleaks GitHub page, it is "a SAST tool for detecting hardcoded secrets like passwords, API keys, and tokens in git repos."

Installing and Running Gitleaks

In true Cloud Native form, we will opt for the Docker method to run Gitleaks by using the provided container image. Clearly, it is really important that you explicitly trust container images, and it is recommended that you get into the habit of building an image from a Dockerfile directly to make sure that you know exactly what is contained within it. The Dockerfile for Gitleaks can be found at `github.com/zricethezav/gitleaks/blob/master/Dockerfile`, and it contains a base layer written using the Go language.

To get started, we will pull the image down with Docker (you can use any runtime that is compatible with OCI images you want):

```
$ docker pull zricethezav/gitleaks
Using default tag: latest
latest: Pulling from zricethezav/gitleaks
aad63a933944: Pull complete
02ab6908a836: Pull complete
1b175b4469a1: Pull complete
Digest: sha256:8207101097bf84f3ed[. . .snip. . .]98012f5e447bc16256a7ca3ac7
Status: Downloaded newer image for zricethezav/gitleaks:latest
docker.io/zricethezav/gitleaks:latest
```

There are also installation options for `brew` on Macs and the Go language, shown respectively within the documentation as the following commands:

```
$ brew install gitleaks
$ GO111MODULE=on go get github.com/zricethezav/gitleaks/v4
```

There is a bundled configuration file full of useful default settings that can be found at (`github.com/zricethezav/gitleaks/blob/master/config/default.go` and then finely tuned afterward as you see fit. Let's look at an example now. From the top, the second rule down within that file is looking for regular expressions (regex) relating to secret keys from AWS.

```
[[rules]]
        description = "AWS Secret Key"
        regex = '''(?i)aws(.{0,20})?(?-i)['\"][0-9a-zA-Z\/+]{40}['\"]'''
        tags = ["key", "AWS"]
```

As you can see, the rule uses a regular expression (regex) that is used to catch the format of a typical AWS secret key. This is how Gitleaks spots information leakage within a repository, and you will find this is the common approach of such tools—just as we will see with GitRob in a moment. Using regex means that the rulesets are extensible and relatively easy to alter and fine-tune to suit your needs (although admittedly sometimes regex can have an arcane syntax). Let's take a look at Gitleaks in action next.

To show off its abilities, we will point Gitleaks at a file created in GitHub with some bogus AWS credentials called `secret_key.txt`. It can be found at `github.com/chrisbinnie/CloudNativeSecurity/blob/master/secret_key.txt`.

The file is just a replica of what you would expect to see in a `~/.aws/credentials` file, which stores your AWS credentials locally if you do not use the preferred environment variables approach, and its contents are shown here:

```
[default]
aws_access_key_id = AKIAYEKNPWXOCW4YDEWX
aws_secret_access_key = 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
```

Let's try a simple scan using this command to run Gitleaks along with the required options:

```
$ docker run zricethezav/gitleaks \
--repourl=https://github.com/chrisbinnie/CloudNativeSecurity --redact

time="2020-07-20T20:12:04Z" level=info msg="cloning..
https://github.com/chrisbinnie/CloudNativeSecurity"
time="2020-07-20T20:12:04Z" level=info msg="scan time:
2 milliseconds 167 microseconds"
time="2020-07-20T20:12:04Z" level=info
msg="commits scanned: 3"
time="2020-07-20T20:12:04Z" level=warning
msg="leaks found: 2"
```

As we can see from the output, there have been two leaks detected in that repository.

We can get more output for further clarity on what content was highlighted as an issue by using the -v switch at the end of the previous command for verbosity:

```
$ docker run zricethezav/gitleaks \
--repourl=https://github.com/chrisbinnie/CloudNativeSecurity -v
```

Using that switch, the abbreviated output is visible in Listing 10.1, which really helps get to the core of the issues highlighted by the tool.

Listing 10.1: Offending Content Was Flagged More Than Once Across Different Commits

```
{"line":"aws_access_key_id = AKIAYEKNPWXOCW4YDEWX",
"offender":"AKIAYEKNPWXOCW4YDEWX",
"comit":"3c7c6639b9b7c34d5c192ef017e3047d2ac671d0",
"repo":"CloudNativeSecurity","rule":"AWS Manager ID",
"commitMessage":"Add bad creds\n",
"author":"Chris Binnie",
"email":"chris@chrisbinnie.tld",
"file":"secret_key.txt",
"date":"2020-07-19T14:33:57+01:00","tags":"key, AWS"}
{"line":"aws_access_key_id = AKIAYSRHAVXOCW4YFK26",
"offender":"AKIAYSRHAVXOCW4YFK26",
"commit":"3c7c6639b9b7c34d5c192ef017e3047d2ac671d0",
"repo":"CloudNativeSecurity","rule":"AWS Manager ID",
"commitMessage":"Add bad creds\n",
"author":"Chris Binie",
"email":"chris@chrisbinnie.tld",
"file":"secret_key.txt",
"date":"2020-07-19T14:33:57+01:00","tags":"key, AWS"}
```

If you get stuck at any point with Gitleaks, you can use the following command, with the appended `--help` switch as you would expect:

```
$ docker run zricethezav/gitleaks --help
```

Additionally, you can check the version as so:

```
$ docker run zricethezav/gitleaks --version
v4.3.1
```

To prevent your logs from being populated with potentially sensitive credentials simply add `--redact` to the end of the command:

```
docker run zricethezav/gitleaks \
--repourl=https://github.com/chrisbinnie/CloudNativeSecurity --redact

Enumerating objects: 9, done.
Counting objects: 100% (9/9), done.
Compressing objects: 100% (7/7), done.
Total 9 (delta 0), reused 9 (delta 0), pack-reused 0
{
      "line": "aws_access_key_id = REDACTED",
      "lineNumber": 2,
      "offender": "REDACTED",
      "commit": "3c7c6639b9b7c34d5c192ef017e3047d2ac671d0",
      "repo": "CloudNativeSecurity",
      "repoURL":
        "https://github.com/chrisbinnie/CloudNativeSecurity",
      "leakURL": "https://github.com/chrisbinnie/
```

```
        CloudNativeSecurity/blob/[. . .snip. . .]/secret_key.txt#L2",
      "rule": "AWS Access Key",
      "commitMessage": "Add bad creds\n",
      "author": "Chris Binnie",
      "email": "chris@binnie.tld",
      "file": "secret_key.txt",
      "date": "2020-07-19T14:33:57+01:00",
      "tags": "key, AWS"
}
```

Another useful option is `-pretty`. If any leaks are found, this will output nicely formatted JSON, which is probably easier to parse than the other output with a CI/CD pipeline test. In Listing 10.2, you can see an abbreviated output for the leaks found.

Listing 10.2: Prettified JSON Output of a Detected Leak

```
{
    "line": "aws_access_key_id = AKIAYEKNPWXOCW4YDEWX",
    "offender": "AKIAYEKNPWXOCW4YDEWX",
    "commit": "3c7c6639b9b7c34d5c192ef017e3047d2ac671d0",
    "repo": "CloudNativeSecurity",
    "rule": "AWS Manager ID",
    "commitMessage": "Add bad creds\n",
    "author": "Chris Binnie",
    "email": "chris@chrisbinnie.tld",
    "file": "secret_key.txt",
    "date": "2020-07-19T14:33:57+01:00",
    "tags": "key, AWS"
}
```

Within a pipeline you could add a tool like Gitleaks to your unit tests, to your integration tests, or as a pre-commit hook. Equally, even in tandem, you could run a tool such as this on a schedule of some description, sweeping all of your repositories overnight at quiet times, for example, and then reporting back. Note that AWS actually performs tests like these itself on GitHub (or at least did in the past) to ensure that user accounts are not compromised by a moment of cut-and-paste madness. Should AWS get in touch about such an issue, you will see a warning at the top of the AWS Console under Alerts/Notifications, and potentially the `root` user of the AWS account or AWS organization might also receive an email or a similar notification.

We will look at another similar tool in a moment, GitRob, but let's quickly look at some other alert types from Gitleaks. The Gitleaks GitHub repository itself holds some treasure to plunder for testing purposes, so we will run the tool against that next. Using the first command shown earlier, it is possible to find `811 leaks detected` and `584 commits audited`; in Listing 10.3 you can see an abbreviated output in verbose mode.

Listing 10.3: A Heavily Abbreviated Output of the Findings When Run Against Gitleaks' Own GitHub Repository


```
{"line":"\t\t\"SSH\":
regexp.MustCompile(\"-----BEGIN OPENSSH PRIVATE KEY-----\"),
","offender":"-----BEGIN OPENSSH PRIVATE KEY-----
","commit":"1f80d14f3f069118a2e578d83bbc8440495fc906",
"repo":"gitleaks","rule":"Asymmetric Private Key",
"commitMessage":"Gitleaks v1.0.0 (#75)\n\nmajor bump",
"author":"Zachary Rice","email":"zricezrice@gmail.com",
"file":"main.go","date":"2018-07-20T20:02:52-05:00",
"tags":"key, AsymmetricPrivateKey"}
{"line":"regex = '''-----BEGIN RSA PRIVATE KEY-----'''",
"offender":"-----BEGIN RSA PRIVATE KEY-----
","commit":"2a6bd1636fcc2cf41722d67a2bd2cbe2ec9ec123",
"repo":"gitleaks","rule":"Asymmetric Private Key",
"commitMessage":"Merge pull request #189 from zricethezav/debt/
breakout\n\nDebt/breakout",
"author":"Zachary Rice","email":"zricezrice@gmail.com",
"file":"main.go","date":"2019-03-29T19:27:54-05:00",
"tags":"key, AsymmetricPrivateKey"}
{"line":"regex = '''-----BEGIN PGP PRIVATE KEY BLOCK-----'''",
"offender":"-----BEGIN PGP PRIVATE KEY BLOCK-----
","commit":"86737955deb80fb966a25a295727ef1e30ee9a35",
"repo":"gitleaks","rule":"Asymmetric Private Key",
"commitMessage":"Merge pull request #281 from
zricethezav/v3\n\nV3","author":"Zachary Rice",
"email":"zricer@protonmail.com",
"file":"src/constants.go",
"date":"2019-11-14T07:38:34-05:00",
"tags":"key, AsymmetricPrivateKey"}
{"line":"  \"line\": \"Here's an AWS secret:
\\\"AKIALALEMEL33243OLIAE\\\"\",",
"offender":"AKIALALEMEL33243OLIA",
"commit":"b7438011b4522b295660a6cd5b16af18a22787b6",
"repo":"gitleaks","rule":"AWS Manager ID",
"commitMessage":"Rm generic from default (#379)\n\n*
fixing commit latest bug\r\n\r\n* remove generic rule
from default to reduce false positives","author":"Zachary
Rice","email":"zricer@protonmail.com",
"file":"test_data/test_local_repo_two_leaks_commit_to.json",
"date":"2020-05-09T11:21:17-04:00","tags":"key, AWS"}
```


There are lots of other options that Gitleaks can support, and you are encouraged to fine-tune the output to your needs.

Installing and Running GitRob

Now let's take a look at a similar tool, called GitRob, which can be found in GitHub as you'd expect (`github.com/michenriksen/gitrob`). GitRob is possibly the first Open Source tool that springs to mind when people think about scanning code repositories. As we will see, there are some alternative features available, relative to Gitleaks.

To get started, you are offered the choice of compiling the tool from source code using the Go language or using a precompiled binary (`github.com/michenriksen/gitrob/releases/tag/v2.0.0-beta`). Assuming you trust the provenance of the binary (and that it is not a security threat), you can download Linux, Mac, and Windows versions to suit your needs. One way to test the provenance is by using a checksum. Let's download the Linux Zip file and validate its checksum using these commands where the long URLs are executed on one line each:

```
$ wget
https://github.com/michenriksen/gitrob/releases/download/v2.0.0-
beta/gitrob_linux_amd64_2.0.0-beta.zip
$ wget
https://github.com/michenriksen/gitrob/releases/download/v2.0.0-
beta/checksums.txt
```

Next, view the checksums of the downloaded ZIP file:

```
$ cat checksums.txt
1ec57a99c9a4c7fde9041077f6007330873b6710ccc45ce77814410b5289ad7c
gitrob_linux_amd64_2.0.0-beta.zip
f8e429a1a7f36877b9691a473d4b0a053eac2ce26d12cdfc1b7c57a3504bbb7c
gitrob_macos_amd64_2.0.0-beta.zip
51608bcdb7dfd2446379678b792c266a9fdb649d0296db2b130f12c587d962e7
gitrob_windows_amd64_2.0.0-beta.zip
```

You can then verify that the result of this next command matches the previous output for the same filename:

```
$ sha256sum gitrob_linux_amd64_2.0.0-beta.zip
1ec57a99c9a4c7fde9041077f6007330873b6710ccc45ce77814410b5289ad7c
gitrob_linux_amd64_2.0.0-beta.zip
```

Excellent. As we can see from the top line in the `checksums.txt` file, our `SHA256sum` command's output matches, which means our file has not been tampered with en route during its download. This offers a little comfort, but of course if the code repository had been compromised, a precompiled binary might contain unknown threats.

Next, we will unzip the ZIP file:

```
$ unzip gitrob_linux_amd64_2.0.0-beta.zip
Archive:  gitrob_linux_amd64_2.0.0-beta.zip
  inflating: gitrob
  inflating: README.md
```

The `README.md` file is the same as the one found in the GitHub repository for GitRob. You can find more useful information by executing the `gitrob` binary to check the contents of its `--help` output. In Listing 10.4 we can see some of the tool's options, which are not too dissimilar to Gitleaks' options.

Listing 10.4: The GitRob Help Output Contents

```
$ ./gitrob --help
Usage of ./gitrob:
  -bind-address string
        Address to bind web server to (default "127.0.0.1")
  -commit-depth int
        Number of repository commits to process (default 500)
  -debug
        Print debugging information
  -github-access-token string
        GitHub access token to use for API requests
  -load string
        Load session file
  -no-expand-orgs
        Don't add members to targets when processing organizations
  -port int
        Port to run web server on (default 9393)
  -save string
        Save session to file
  -silent
        Suppress all output except for errors
  -threads int
        Number of concurrent threads (default number of logical CPUs)
```

Let's see what GitRob makes of our `secret_key.txt` file, hosted in the GitHub repository. A little earlier in this chapter, we walked through creating an access token in GitHub, instead of using a password. We will need to add an environment variable with an access token to scan the repository as follows:

```
$ export GITROB_ACCESS_TOKEN=9e3b27d7c382XXXXXXXXXXXX96b1a45ea351c24
```

Next, we will run GitRob against the entire GitHub user account for `chrisbinnie` (to scan all of its repositories in one go) with this command:

```
$ ./gitrob chrisbinnie
```

In Figure 10.2 you can see what the aesthetically pleasing output looks like.

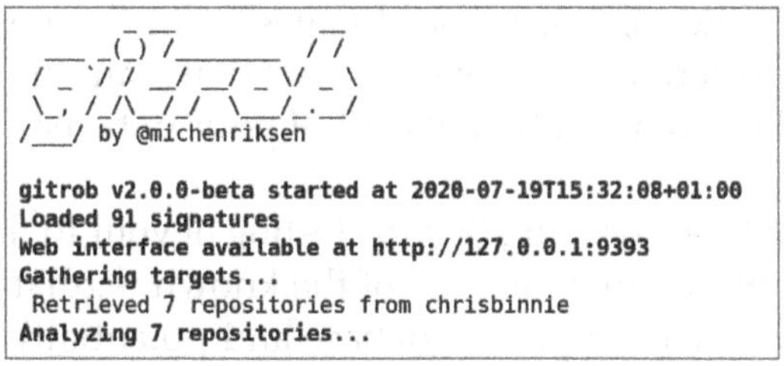

by @michenriksen
gitrob v2.0.0-beta started at 2020-07-19T15:32:08+01:00
Loaded 91 signatures
Web interface available at http://127.0.0.1:9393
Gathering targets...
Retrieved 7 repositories from chrisbinnie
Analyzing 7 repositories...

Figure 10.2: GitRob initializing and beginning to scan all repositories belonging to `chrisbinnie` in GitHub

It is worrying that this tool, using the default settings, failed to spot the `secret_key.txt` file secret as found by Gitleaks. However, it instead found another purposely placed file in a separate repository:

```
Analyzing 7 repositories..
 INSERT: AWS CLI credentials file
  Path....: .aws/credentials
```

It is important to note that Gitleaks missed this second file using its default configuration.

This would suggest that GitRob has cloned the repositories but not pattern-matched the contents of the `secret_key.txt` file with its default regex. It is possible that the tool may have only captured the actual path and filename `aws/credentials` using regular expressions. An investigation into its bundled rules configuration would reveal exactly what was caught, what was missed, and why. Those craving some eye strain might start here: `github.com/michenriksen/gitrob/blob/master/core/signatures.go`.

An important note from an operational perspective is that as a standard, and apparently for security reasons, when GitRob is run against a repository, the contents of the tool's output are only stored in memory for that session. This means that when GitRob is stopped, the results are lost completely. You can use the `-save` option to create a report of your findings to analyze later if you are sure that you want to save a scan's results.

Summary

In this chapter, we discussed the likelihood of developers accidentally pushing sensitive tokens, certificates, access keys, and passwords into code repositories and why monitoring your repositories is critically important to avoid unwelcome compromises.

We also looked at two popular Open Source tools, which appear, using default settings, to have differing scanning abilities. Along the same lines as the CVE scanning, which we looked at in Chapter 6, "Container Images CVEs," from the simple examples shown, it is important to remember the fact that scanning code repositories with one tool will not magically make all of your data leak worries go away.

It would be prudent to spend some time ensuring that the testing of your tool of choice is working exactly as you intend, matching all of the known regular expression patterns that you deal with within your codebase and potentially taking a belt and braces approach to guarding your highly valuable secrets with more than one tool. It should be clear that how you test for secrets is as equally important as just testing for the sake of it.

CHAPTER

11

Automated Host Security

One area often overlooked in today's modern DevSecOps world is the underlying host's operating system (OS). For enterprise-ready Cloud Native applications, it is often not enough to simply focus on the updating of the packages on a host. When it comes to securing your Linux servers, there are a surprising number of facets that it is possible to improve upon relative to a default installation.

It should go without saying that even with multiple layers of network protection (from Web Application Firewalls sifting through visitor traffic looking for malicious payloads to Content Devilvery Networks (CDNs) preventing denial-of-service attacks) on a containerized estate, ultimately it is the containers themselves that are actually serving the application. And, having walked through what a container actually is in Chapter 1, "What Is A Container?," it should be clear that your containers are simply an extension of the underlying host's OS. As a result, without a robust security posture for your hosts, your containers and therefore your applications are at risk.

A popular approach to helping customize the security of your Linux builds is focusing on the correct flavor of CIS Benchmark for your Linux distribution of choice from the CIS site (`www.cisecurity.org/cis-benchmarks`). Running through the recommendations found in these benchmarks unquestionably helps you achieve a better security posture, and there is little doubt that because the benchmarks are industry-consensus based, they can be relied upon. Be warned, however, that many of the changes recommended will almost definitely cause outages to host-based services or even cause issues for the entire host if applied without fully understanding their implications. You should therefore methodically test any changes for a prolonged period of time before putting them into production. Some alterations to your operating system might only become a problem a few months after a server has gone live when a certain type of network packet is received by a tweaked kernel, for example.

There are some custom-created Ansible playbooks, written to follow CIS benchmarks exactly, that can be downloaded from GitHub such as this example for Red Hat Enterprise Linux 7: `github.com/radsec/RHEL7-CIS`. However, if you opt to apply such rules verbatim, be warned that you may experience unpredictable results. Using a one-size-fits-all playbook can cause outages and other issues that take a lot of time to diagnose. As such, this approach does not sit well with some admins when they know how onerous middle-of-the-night callouts can be.

Remember that there are various "levels" to meet within CIS benchmarks. They offer differing levels of comfort and compliance. For example, according to CIS (`www.cisecurity.org/blog/everything-you-need-to-know-about-cis-hardened-images/`), if you configured your hardening settings to meet Level 1, then you might be considered to have taken a "practical and prudent" approach that may not "inhibit the utility of the technology beyond acceptable means." If, however, you followed Level 2 to the letter, you would have potentially added defense-in-depth improvements to your configuration, but you may "negatively inhibit the utility or performance of the technology" as a result.

For obvious reasons, be certain that you are only applying those rules that you are comfortable with and that you expect a security improvement from.

In the Cloud Native world, the long life of servers is usually not a familiar problem because in cloud environments we should aim to build cattle and not pets. In other words, we are looking to create disposable hosts that can be reproduced almost immediately, with predictable consistency, which are not individual, uniquely configured "pets" that we need to nurture. These pets are also known as *snowflakes*—they are unique and beautiful. To prevent such hosts from existing, we want to cycle our Linux servers frequently (aiming for the life of a host to be days or weeks, not years), and because we are automating their build, we should be able to programmatically make universal changes to remedy any issues across all hosts once we have identified the root cause of an issue.

In this chapter, we will look at some of the security details that you might focus on when hardening a machine image. We will automate using an Ansible playbook, narrowed down into tasks that you can construct a playbook with later, to ensure that our servers are hardened. We will also look at one-off hardening exercises using a concept called *idempotency*, a server's ability to be returned to precisely its previous or original state. The contents of the following Ansible tasks can be considered as a mixture of compliance, governance, and hardening.

How you structure the Ansible task content and to what extent you decide to follow the likes of the CIS Benchmarks largely depends on these three factors:

- How much value you put on your online services (remember that a compromise can be exceptionally costly not only in downtime but in brand reputation, too) should you not earn revenue directly from your online presence, for example.
- How much time you have to focus on improving the security posture of your Linux servers.
- Your appetite for risk (if you favor a weaker security posture over usability and/or making changes to the operating system that you do not fully understand or cannot sufficiently test).

Machine Images

A moment ago, we mentioned that the following examples are what Ansible calls *tasks*. By collecting a number of tasks, it is possible to create a "playbook," which is how Ansible code is more commonly referred to. How many tasks you include in a playbook, which hosts they will run against, and what the content of the tasks is will depend entirely on your requirements. Let's take the dominant cloud provider AWS as our first example of how you might make use of an Ansible playbook and think about AWS EC2, the service that runs Linux servers on AWS, known as *instances*.

Using the suggestions within the benchmarks, we can create our Ansible playbook to run over an Amazon Machine Image (AMI) to create a machine image that is used throughout our estate. It might be based on Red Hat Enterprise Linux, CentOS, Debian, or Ubuntu, for example. The flavor of Linux is of no consequence (but the finer details of how you write your playbooks will be OS dependent as they are subtle differences that appear to be designed to trip you up!).

It is also of benefit to encrypt the Elastic Block Storage (EBS) volume that you attach to your instances in AWS EC2. There is a relatively imperceptible cost of latency when accessing your encrypted volumes thankfully. You can also encrypt then with any Key Management Service (KMS) key that you want to use within your AWS account. The result of doing so provides you with "data at rest" encryption, which means that intercepted images cannot be read without your KMS keys. As of May 2019, AWS now permits you to opt into encryption being enabled for all EBS volumes. There are some limitations with this feature as the AWS blog notes (`aws.amazon.com/blogs/aws/new-opt-in-to-default-encryption-for-new-ebs-volumes/`), such as certain EC2 instance types not being available to use with this feature.

Before opt-in EBS encryption, the workflow required to encrypt an AWS EBS volume for your Linux servers consisted of the following steps:

1. Choose a trustworthy, vanilla Amazon Marketplace AMI and create an EC2 instance with it.
2. Update all the Linux packages, reboot, and create a snapshot of that running instance to create a new AMI of your own.
3. Copy the snapshot and encrypt it using a KMS key of your choice (ideally not the AWS account's default key for good practice but one of your own newly created keys with an expiration set).
4. Create a new EBS volume from your encrypted snapshot.

There is more information in the AWS documentation (`docs.aws.amazon.com/AWSEC2/latest/UserGuide/AMIEncryption.html`) relating to the encryption of EBS volumes.

Idempotency

Rather than securing a machine image once that can be disseminated throughout Amazon Elastic Compute Cloud (Amazon EC2), another way to use the Ansible playbook in this chapter would be to repeatedly execute the playbook over running servers. This is where the term *idempotency* comes in.

Put simply, it means returning something to its original state, in every sense of the definition, after it has changed in some way. In the case of the Ansible playbooks, that means configuring them to suit our organization's requirements and then rerunning the playbooks every 20 or 30 minutes over the top of existing EC2 instances to destroy any changes to the server that a CI/CD pipeline has made, or, of course, equally an attacker. Clearly, changes occur accidentally or intentionally, and to maintain predictable infrastructure, some form of enforcement is sensible. This offers us a cattle-not-pet model but also, as has been observed, offers a nuanced contradiction at the same time.

Consider that by using idempotency, we are in some ways treating servers more like pets and tweaking them as they run. The obvious solution might be destroying servers and re-creating them, rather than tweaking them. Think, however, that idempotency is actually dealing with running configuration as opposed to static configuration. In other words, when a machine image becomes a server, it behaves differently than the static image file that created it. There are temporary files written to running memory and disk, and in addition various configuration files are populated with data such as an IP address or hostname that previously were just placeholder variables. For this reason, you can think of the benefits of idempotency applying to servers that run for a few weeks and aren't just destroyed within a day or two. After all, although we have disposable servers (worker nodes in the case of Kubernetes), we want their shelf life to meet reasonable expectations, and by doing so we also avoid stressing other components of our infrastructure unnecessarily.

As a result, you can consider the type of Ansible tasks that follow as being geared up to compliance. Our aim is that we want to be able to predict how running machines behave, not only as an afterthought but through enforcement.

The benefits of enforcement include predictable behavior, identically configured and better managed systems, easier patching, a more secure security posture, and predictable lifecycles for your servers. Any attacker trying to take a foothold might be kicked off a server if your security controls reset frequently via compliance enforcement. Therefore, advanced persistent threat (APT) attacks might also be mitigated to a degree, dependent on the quality of your security controls.

If you have not used Ansible much, then fret not because the structure of operating a playbook is straightforward and the syntax is relatively logical. Let's look at the directory structure that we will use to secure our servers. In Figure 11.1 you can see the output of the `tree` command, which shows how to structure the content.

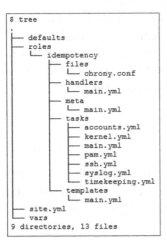

```
$ tree
.
├── defaults
├── roles
│   └── idempotency
│       ├── files
│       │   └── chrony.conf
│       ├── handlers
│       │   └── main.yml
│       ├── meta
│       │   └── main.yml
│       ├── tasks
│       │   ├── accounts.yml
│       │   ├── kernel.yml
│       │   ├── main.yml
│       │   ├── pam.yml
│       │   ├── ssh.yml
│       │   ├── syslog.yml
│       │   └── timekeeping.yml
│       └── templates
│           └── main.yml
├── site.yml
└── vars
9 directories, 13 files
```

Figure 11.1: The Ansible directory structure, courtesy of the `tree` command

Within the structure shown in Figure 11.1, we can have multiple templated variables (using variables from the Jinja language) in our configuration files. Under the `tasks/` directory, we can have a variety of executable tasks that will make changes to a remote or local server. As an example, we can fill up our `network.yml` file with a large number of tasks that we want to run through in order to harden our network stack.

For more clarity you should refer to the latest CIS Benchmark and methodically choose which areas you want to harden. There are varying levels of compliance in CIS, and achieving certain levels of compliance is time-consuming; additionally, it may be disruptive to the operation of your hosts. There is more on the CIS levels later in this chapter. As mentioned, before hardening a distribution, it is vitally important to consider your risk appetite when it comes to potentially invasive changes.

The default Linux kernel includes a number of tunable aspects that can be tweaked, but bear in mind that we do not just want to switch on or disable various features. Instead, we want to make sure these features are set precisely as we intend in order that our server configuration is entirely predictable.

Configuration management tools such as Ansible are best suited to this task. Although you can write similar processes in Bash or other languages, Ansible has the inherent functionality available to be able to test whether a setting is currently present or not, without having to write extra logic into your scripts.

A quiet word of warning about Pluggable Authentication Modules (PAMs), which sit with most Linux distributions as a key part of the login process: make sure you have an alternative way into your servers when testing this aspect. With PAM you can set up sophisticated rate limiting login options when passwords are incorrectly entered multiple times. You might also want to secure users in a more subtle way if you are concerned with locking users out of servers during an emergency; carefully consider which options suit your needs.

Probably the most common entry point for modern servers is via the SSH daemon. Hence, there is a good chance that you will benefit from hardening the default options it is shipped with on your Linux distribution. Generally, this is a relatively safe component to harden, but, as with PAM, make sure that you have sufficient out-of-band console access for testing, just in case.

Secure Shell Example

Let's look at an Ansible task relating to hardening your SSH daemon. We will choose the stoic OpenSSH, which runs as `sshd`, for our example because it's the most popular SSH daemon in use on Linux. Within our `ssh.yaml` file, you might expect to see changes such as the following:

- An enforced idle logout time being set.
- Prevent empty passwords from being accepted (via PAM).
- A legal warning banner to help with the prosecution of attackers for compliance.
- No remote superuser access to the daemon for the `root` user.
- Enforce one distinct user group of admins access to the server for granular user management.
- Increase the amount of logging that the daemon produces.

Inside our Ansible file, the contents might look like Listing 11.1.

NOTE **Remember that your OS of choice might be subtly different, so cutting and pasting the code is not sensible without lots of testing.**

Listing 11.1: Example Contents from the `ssh.yaml` File

```
---
- name: Display a legal banner for compliance reasons
  copy: src=iss.txt dest=/etc/issue.net owner=root group=root mode=0644

- name: Make sure the permissions on the main sshd dir are set
  file: path=/etc/ssh owner=root group=root mode=0755

- name: Explicitly set permissions on the main SSH daemon config file
  file: path=/etc/ssh/sshd_config owner=root group=root mode=0600

- name: Insist that SSH is always running after a reboot
  service: name=sshd state=started enabled=yes
```

Bundled into all of the task files, along with templated replacement configuration files, it is possible to make subtle changes, numbering into the hundreds, if you have enough time to get it right. There is obviously some ongoing tweaking required if software upgrades deprecate or introduce new features. For such tasks it would be wise to pay attention to the latest releases of CIS benchmarks, if that is what you used to select your changes.

Another area worth considering is your time-keeping and use of the Network Time Protocol (NTP). A question you might ask is: Does each of your workhorse servers need a fully fledged time server running 24/7? If the answer is "no," then you are reducing the external attack surface, perhaps massively.

Over the years, there have been numerous software bugs found (with security holes) in the standard `ntpd` implementation due to the significant number of lines of code it contains.

A few years ago AWS improved its internal time service (`aws.amazon.com/blogs/aws/keeping-time-with-amazon-time-sync-service`) using a "a fleet of redundant satellite-connected and atomic clocks in each region" so that AWS resources could synchronize their clocks more efficiently and, most importantly, more accurately. Within AWS local networks you can access this service via the 169.254.169.123 IP address, if you set it as your upstream time server.

To avoid using the time-honored `ntpd` time server package, which we might consider a founding father of internet services, the highly recommended lightweight alternative is called `chrony`. In the `timekeeping.yaml` file, your Ansible tasks might look like those shown in Listing 11.2.

Listing 11.2: Example Contents of the `timekeeping.yaml` File

```
---
- name: Remove the old NTP package
  package: name=ntp state=absent

- name: Ensure that the chrony package is installed
  package: name=chrony state=present

- name: Copy the custom config file over /etc/chrony.conf
  copy: src=cust.cfg dest=/etc/chrony.conf owner=root group=root

- name: Explicitly make sure that chrony always run
  service: name=chrony state=started enabled=yes
```

One caveat with `chrony` is that there are likely to be subtly differing package names and services between operating systems, so check these precisely if it causes frustration.

Inside the `chrony.conf` file, customized to our needs, few changes are required, and it would be possible to make some text pattern search-and-replace changes using Ansible rather than copy the whole file over if you wanted. A search and replace entry in Ansible might look like this one:

```
- name: Generic search and replace in Ansible, similar to sed
  replace: path="{{path}}" regexp='^found-text' replace='target'
```

Inside `chrony.conf`, it is really only the bottom of the file that you might want to adjust, relative to the default file. Using the `cmdport` option is sensible, as you will see in a moment. Useful comments that you might want to add to the changes in the default Chrony file can be used to help remind you about what setting `cmdport` to zero achieves:

```
# Setting cmdport to zero means no network ports are accessible but
# sources still sync
# If you don't need to use chronyc at all or you need to run chronyc
# only under the root
# or chrony user (which can access chronyd through a Unix domain socket
# since version 2.2),
# you can disable the internet command sockets completely by adding
# cmdport 0 to the configuration file.
# Taken from here: https://chrony.tuxfamily.org/faq.html
```

As you can see, Chrony will sit dutifully running in the background, taking up little-to-no system resources, and keep track of your configured time servers. But with `cmdport` set to zero, it will not open up any network ports for attackers to attempt to compromise.

The other adjustment you might need to make within that file is to add your own preferred NTP servers to synchronize with. What follows are some example time servers that you could place within that file, written in the Chrony format:

```
pool clock.redhat.com iburst
pool 1.debian.pool.ntp.org iburst
pool 1.rhel.pool.ntp.org iburst
pool 1.uk.pool.ntp.org iburst
```

In Chapter 4, "Forensic Logging," we looked at creating the capability to monitor every single action of a running system using the kernel's built-in auditing tool, `auditd`. We can use Ansible to set this up for us. Listing 11.3 offers some of the Ansible syntax.

Listing 11.3: Ansible Setting Up `auditd` with Our Custom Rules

```
---
- name: If it is not present on the system, install auditd
  package: name=auditd state=latest

- name: Make sure that we start up auditd after a reboot
  service: name=auditd state=started enabled=yes

- name: Do a search and replace to affect the number of log files
  replace:
    dest: /etc/audit/auditd.conf
    regexp: 'num_logs = 5$'
    replace: 'num_logs = 50'

- name: Keep each log file small so they're easier to manage at 100MB
  replace:
    dest: /etc/audit/auditd.conf
    regexp: 'max_log_file = 8'
    replace: 'max_log_file = 100'

- name: Install our custom rules (copy: is all on one line)
  copy: src=audit.rules dest=/etc/audit/rules.d/audit.rules
        owner=root group=root mode=0600

- name: Reload rules before a reboot using the augenrules command
  command: /sbin/augenrules—load
```

The content of Listing 11.3 is quite logical and easy to follow. Be aware that different operating systems may treat `auditd` slightly differently in terms of the file paths that are mentioned too.

Kernel Changes

Tweaking the kernel is quite possible, but make sure you know what you are affecting. The CIS benchmarks go to great lengths to describe why they recommend changes, using a problem-solution approach, but as with all things related to information technology, there are simply too many scenarios to cover within such a document, so it is quite possible to get caught out if you are not careful.

The Ansible code shown in Listing 11.4 offers some insight into what you might consider fine-tuning in the `kernel.yaml` file.

Listing 11.4: Kernel Tweaks Using Ansible

```
---
- name: Switch off the IPv6 networking stack entirely if not used
  lineinfile: dest="{{old-var}}" line="{{item.line}}" state=present
  with_items:
    - { line: 'net.ipv6.conf.all.disable_ipv6 = 1' }
    - { line: 'net.ipv6.conf.default.disable_ipv6 = 1' }

- name: Ignore packets to our interfaces for IPs we don't know
  lineinfile: dest="{{old-var}}" line="{{item.line}}" state=present
  with_items:
    - { line: 'net.ipv4.conf.all.log_martians = 1' }
    - { line: 'net.ipv4.conf.default.log_martians = 1' }

- name: Mitigate spoofing attacks (lineinfile: all on one line)
  lineinfile: dest="{{old-var}}"
              line='net.ipv4.tcp_syncookies = 1' state=present

- name: Prevent broadcasting over ICMP(lineinfile: all on one line)
  lineinfile: dest="{{old-var}}"
              line='net.ipv4.icmp_echo_ignore_broadcasts = 1'
              state=present
```

As with all the entries in the example tasks in this chapter, in Listing 11.4 there is a mixture of compliance and hardening. In many cases, the action of a task may not be needed as the system defaults to that setting, but if you followed the idempotency route and rewrote these changes using Ansible tasks repeatedly, then you would be certain that these settings were as you intended them to be should something or someone change them. The next example will confirm this more clearly. It pertains to the user account management files on a Linux server as we can see in Listing 11.5. As mentioned, PAM can be a more complex area but can certainly be set up securely using Ansible too.

Listing 11.5: User and Group Account Management via `account.yaml`

```
---
- name: Set up permissions /etc/passwd
  file: path=/etc/passwd owner=root group=root mode=0644

- name: Set up the permissions for /etc/passwd-
  file: path=/etc/passwd- owner=root group=root mode=0644

- name: Configure permissions on the file /etc/group
  file: path=/etc/group owner=root group=root mode=0644

- name: Configure the permissions for /etc/group-
  file: path=/etc/group- owner=root group=root mode=0644

- name: Set up permissions on the file /etc/shadow
  file: path=/etc/shadow owner=root group=root

- name: Set up permissions on the file /etc/shadow-
  file: path=/etc/shadow- owner=root group=root

- name: Configure permissions on the file /etc/gshadow
  file: path=/etc/gshadow owner=root group=root

- name: Configure permissions on the file /etc/gshadow-
  file: path=/etc/gshadow- owner=root group=root
```

As a final example, let's make sure that SElinux is set to "enforcing" mode on Red Hat Enterprise Linux. The venerable SElinux package is used in other Linux distributions but is not always installed by default. The snippet for Ansible could look something like Listing 11.6.

Listing 11.6: Ensuring SElinux Is Set Up in "Enforcing" Mode

```
- name: Switch permissive mode to enforcing (replace: all on one line)
  replace: path=/etc/selinux/config regexp='SELINUX=permissive'
           replace='SELINUX=enforcing'
```

Summary

In this chapter, we learned about two ways of securing your underlying Linux servers and discussed why host security should never be an afterthought.

First, we looked at applying such a configuration once on a trusted machine image. Then, we considered the strategy of repeatedly applying rules to potentially help prevent attackers gain a foothold if a minor compromise was successful.

In addition to the suggested approaches, you can of course apply such running-configuration settings just once as the server goes live, as opposed to repeatedly, with the aim of achieving idempotency. There are lots of options and different use cases for how you might harden servers, and you should carefully consider the best operational approach for your needs. It is an extremely worthwhile task, adding further defense in depth to your security model, and with just some effort you can reap the rewards and become much more confident in your infrastructure's security posture as a whole.

CHAPTER

12

Server Scanning With Nikto

There are a handful of Open Source security tools that always deserve a mention with CI/CD pipelines. One such tool is the sophisticated Nikto (`cirt.net/Nikto2`), which is a web server scanner that can hunt for a staggering 6,700+ specific files and programs that may cause security issues. It also has a historical function that can test for 1,250 out-of-date servers and can highlight version-specific issues on 270 different servers. In other words, to say that Nikto is comprehensive is an understatement. It can be used with the latter parts of your CI/CD pipeline tests, once your hosts are configured and live, to offer an invaluable insight into potential issues with your hosts.

In this chapter, we will look through the installation and configuration of the excellent Nikto.

Things to Consider

It should be noted that Nikto flies through its tests at a rate of knots. It is not going to sit quietly in stealth mode and suddenly appear with a coup d'état; instead, it will fill your servers' logs up dramatically and cause a flurry of activity in every corner of your host's intrusion detection system (IDS).

Also, because it is so powerful, you need to be sure only to run Nikto on hosts that you own or have explicitly received permission to scan. You have been suitably warned!

One final thing to note is that issues Nikto identifies are not always security problems but can be used for informational purposes to improve operational functionality among other things.

Installation

Let's dive straight into installing and running Nikto by looking at its GitHub repository (`github.com/sullo/nikto`). The documentation recommends getting started with cloning the repository first, as follows:

```
$ git clone https://github.com/sullo/nikto
Cloning into 'nikto'..
remote: Enumerating objects: 66, done.
remote: Counting objects: 100% (66/66), done.
remote: Compressing objects: 100% (49/49), done.
remote: Total 6077 (delta 30), reused 46 (delta 15), pack-reused 6011
Receiving objects: 100% (6077/6077), 3.81 MiB | 897.00 KiB/s, done.
Resolving deltas: 100% (4401/4401), done.
```

It looks like the whole repository sits at a very respectable 7MB in size. Let's enter the correct directory to find the Perl scripts that comprise Nikto:

```
$ cd nikto/program
```

Running an `ls` command inside that directory offers the following content:

```
databases  docs  nikto.conf.default  nikto.pl
plugins  replay.pl  templates
```

Let's begin by running Nikto against our localhost just to see that the main script is working:

```
$ ./nikto.pl -h http://127.0.0.1
- Nikto v2.1.6
---------------------------------------------------------------------------
+ No web server found on 127.0.0.1:80
---------------------------------------------------------------------------
+ 0 host(s) tested
```

As suspected, because there is no web server running, Nikto completes its run successfully but without offering any results. We will put it through its paces in a moment.

As an alternative to using Perl scripts, a more Cloud Native approach to using Nikto is via a container. This time we will move up a directory level (into the `nikto/` directory) and then build a container image from scratch, using Docker, as follows:

```
$ cd ..; docker build -t sullo/nikto .
```

Listing 12.1 shows the Dockerfile that creates that image. If you use this file to create an image, then make sure you use the latest version.

Listing 12.1: The Dockerfile for Nikto, as Found in GitHub

```
FROM alpine:3.10.0

LABEL version="2.1.6" \
      author="Author Paul Sec (https://github.com/PaulSec),
Nikto User https://github.com/drwetter" \
      docker_build="docker build -t sullo/nikto:2.1.6 ." \
      docker_run_basic="docker run --rm sullo/nikto:2.1.6 \
      -h http://www.example.com" \
      docker_run_advanced="docker run --rm \
      -v $(pwd):/tmp sullo/nikto:2.1.6 \
      -h http://www.example.com -o /tmp/out.json"

COPY ["program/", "/nikto"]
ENV  PATH=${PATH}:/nikto
RUN echo 'Selecting packages to Nikto.' \
&& apk update \
&& apk add --no-cache --virtual .build-deps \
   perl \
   perl-net-ssleay \
&& echo 'Cleaning cache from APK.' \
&& rm -rf /var/cache/apk/* \
&& echo 'Creating the nikto group.' \
&& addgroup nikto \
&& echo 'Creating the user nikto.' \
&& adduser -G nikto -g "Nikto user" -s /bin/sh -D nikto \
&& echo 'Changing the ownership.' \
&& chown -R nikto.nikto /nikto \
&& echo 'Creating a random password for root.' \
&& export RANDOM_PASSWORD=`tr -dc A-Za-z0-9 < /dev/urandom|head -c44` \
&& echo "root:$RANDOM_PASSWORD" | chpasswd \
&& unset RANDOM_PASSWORD \
&& echo 'Locking root account.' \
&& passwd -l root \
&& echo 'Finishing image.'

USER nikto
ENTRYPOINT ["nikto.pl"]
```

Source: `github.com/sullo/nikto/blob/master/Dockerfile`

As we can see, the Dockerfile uses Alpine Linux and creates a suitable Nikto group and user. Next, it cleverly generates a random password for the `root` user before then locking the `root` account so that operations run via the less-privileged `nikto` user.

Using our freshly baked local container image, let's try running the Docker container against our `localhost`, and save its report to the current directory onto our local machine, to verify that it is working:

```
$ docker run --rm sullo/nikto -h http://localhost
- Nikto v2.1.6
---------------------------------------------------------------
+ No web server found on localhost:80
---------------------------------------------------------------
+ 0 host(s) tested
```

That looks promising, even with no results, just as before.

The next task is to try to run Nikto over the network against a remote `nginx` server - one that shall remain nameless in this case. If you do not have access to a web server, then you could create one as a container to test against. You can refer to Apache's Docker Hub page for instructions on how to do that (`hub.docker.com/_/httpd`). Change the following commands to suit your needs. The first command should create an Apache container, and then the second should return the container's IP address for you to scan against as a target with Nikto using TCP port 8080.

```
$ docker run -dit --name my-apache-app -p 8080:80 \
  -v "$PWD":/usr/local/apache2/htdocs/ httpd:2.4
$ docker inspect my-apache-app | grep -i "IPAddress"
```

Use the container image to spawn a container and then run the same basic scan command:

```
$ docker run --rm sullo/nikto -h http://remotehost.tld
```

In Listing 12.2 we can see some of the output, heavily abbreviated. The host in question is running a web server, but it is heavily firewalled with `iptables`. That said, there is no blocking when ports are scanned. The web server root is password-protected using `htaccess`.

Listing 12.2: Our First Target, Heavily Firewalled

```
- Nikto v2.1.6
---------------------------------------------------------------
+ Target IP:          123.123.123.123
+ Target Hostname:    remotehost.tld
+ Target Port:        80
+ Start Time:         2020-07-29 18:45:11 (GMT0)
---------------------------------------------------------------
+ Server: nginx/1.14.2
+ The anti-clickjacking X-Frame-Options header is not present.
+ The X-XSS-Protection header is not defined.
  This header can hint to the user agent to protect
  against some forms of XSS
+ The X-Content-Type-Options header is not set.
```

```
  This could allow the user agent to render the
  content of the site in a different fashion to
  the MIME type.
+ Root page / redirects to: https://remotehost.tld/
+ No CGI Directories found
  (use '-C all' to force check all possible dirs)
```

In Listing 12.2 Nikto offers up a few pieces of relatively innocuous information that are nonetheless potentially useful. For clarity, these findings are not revealing any gaping security holes but instead offer advice on room for improvement with both the web server scanning by Nikto and also the target web server's configuration. And, that is precisely why we are using the comprehensive Nikto for within our pipelines: to see what we have missed that an attacker might make use of. The information revealed might be as simple as a software package version or directory listing being enabled, but it is all potentially valuable information to an attacker.

To incorporate such a tool in your pipeline, you can create a step to trigger Nikto and filter its response. If you are familiar with Jenkins (`www.jenkins.io`), an example of how that might look in both the Freestyle and Pipeline projects can be found here: `blog.probely.com/how-to-configure-jenkins-to-integrate-security-into-ci-cd-2b340728de56`.

Having waited patiently for a little while (250 seconds in total) the scan completes as follows:

```
8037 requests: 0 error(s) and 3 item(s) reported on remote host
```

The three items that Nikto is referring to in Listing 12.2 are relatively standard issues, but knowing that you should make improvements is valuable. From the host's logs, we can see in Listing 12.3 how Nikto has been viewed from our host's perspective. The heavily abbreviated sample output is what you might expect to see in server logs after a host has been scanned.

Listing 12.3: The Host's Perspective of a Nikto Scan

```
123.123.123.123-- [29/Jul/2020:19:48:18 +0100] "GET /snort/base_stat_
common.php?BASE_path=http://cirt.net/rfiinc.txt?
HTTP/1.1" 301 185 "-" "Mozilla/5.0 (Windows NT 10.0; Win64; x64)
AppleWebKit/537.36 (KHTML, like Gecko)
Chrome/74.0.3729.169 Safari/537.36"
123.123.123.123-- [29/Jul/2020:19:49:17 +0100] "GET /passwords.xml
HTTP/1.1" 301 185 "-" "Mozilla/5.0 (Windows NT 10.0; Win64; x64)
AppleWebKit/537.36 (KHTML, like Gecko)
Chrome/74.0.3729.169 Safari/537.36"
123.123.123.123-- [29/Jul/2020:19:48:49 +0100]
"GET /horde/util/barcode.php
?type=./././././././././././etc/./passwd%00
HTTP/1.1" 301 185 "-" "Mozilla/5.0
(Windows NT 10.0;Win64; x64) AppleWebKit/537.36
(KHTML, like Gecko) Chrome/74.0.3729.169 Safari/537.36"
```

It is safe to say that any respectable admin is not going to miss a fully fledged Nikto scan. As we can see, the logging entries are plentiful. In Listing 12.3, we can see just a sample of some of the several thousands of tests that Nikto has performed against our remote host.

Scanning a Second Host

Let's now take a look at scanning a different host, also one with a web server. This time, it is an Apache web server and not `nginx`. The difference here is that this host is not particularly well firewalled, although it does have a reduced number of open ports with some IP address restrictions on certain ports. Let's see how Nikto performs against these challenging conditions.

We will move onto other options shortly, but in this instance, the command line that we will run is as follows:

```
$ docker run --rm sullo/nikto -h https://remotehost-2.tld
```

Along with those items discovered with the previous host, initially Nikto picks up these additional issues from the second host:

```
+ Server may leak inodes via ETags, header found
  with file /, inode: 28f, size: 5777821f0e558, mtime: gzip
+ Allowed HTTP Methods: POST, OPTIONS, HEAD, GET
```

According to an online forum, the "inodes via ETags" issue is a false positive and can be ignored. The next piece of output is as follows:

```
OSVDB-3233: /icons/README: Apache default file found.
```

That result is a little surprising, because this is a production server of sorts (on a small estate), and Apache is set up not to reveal its version numbers or fingerprint and not to present a revealing salutation when it is connected to. This shows how valuable a tool Nikto is.

The final piece of pertinent information found by Nikto can be verified manually. The finding from Nikto was as follows:

```
+ /server-status: Apache server-status interface found
  (protected/forbidden)
```

We can see that Nikto would have been clever enough to spot that it was an Apache server within a few more seconds of tests after all. This result means that the web server was password-protecting access.

We can prove this response with the following `curl` command:

```
$ curl -I http://remotehost-2.tld/server-status
HTTP/1.1 403 Forbidden
```

```
Date: Wed, 29 Jul 2020 19:16:26 GMT
Server: Apache
Content-Type: text/html; charset=iso-8859-1
```

Figure 12.1 shows the response from the command line as shown in a browser. You can see that the signature on the error page was generated by an Apache server; this a common source of information and identifies which application an attacker will prepare to attack with vendor-specific attacks.

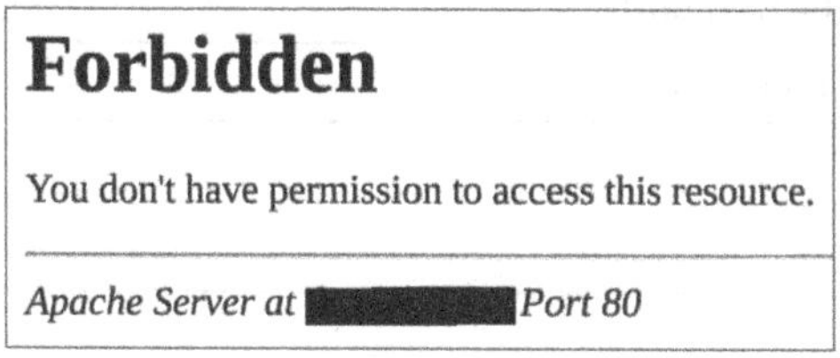

Figure 12.1: Even an HTTP 403 is revealing.

Running Options

We do not have to scan just one host, of course. Nikto will let you scan multiple hosts using the `-h` switch. To do this, as opposed to distinctly specifying individual targets, we can populate a file brimming with targets. The file can contain entries such as IP addresses or URLs (with the protocol and port number explicitly stated). Here's an example:

```
https://firsthost.com:1111
http://172.16.12.31:8080
```

Also note that if no port is listed in each entry, then HTTP is assumed, so make sure, especially on today's internet, that you explicitly state HTTPS if you mean to do so.

Table 12.1 shows some of the interactive options that can be requested even in midflow, during a running scan.

Table 12.1: Interactive Options for Nikto While It's Running

KEYSTROKE	ACTION
Spacebar	Shows current status
v	Enables verbosity
d	Toggles debugging
p	Toggles progress reporting
r	Toggles redirect display

Continues

Table 12.1 *(continued)*

KEYSTROKE	ACTION
c	Toggles cookies display
o	Toggles OK display
a	Toggles auth display
q	Quits
N	Moves onto the next host
P	Suspends current scan

Command-Line Options

Nikto also comes armed with an impressive set of command-line options at execution time. These can be found at `cirt.net/nikto2-docs/options.html`. One of the options includes specifying a configuration file path or filename instead of using the default `nikto.conf` file in the installation directory with the `-config` switch. You can also use the `-Display` option that allows a number of changes to the output displayed by Nikto, such as debugging verbosity. Or, for greater visibility into which plugins Nikto can use in its scan, the `-list-plugins` option exists. It is recommended that you read that web page to gain further insight, as you begin to use Nikto in a more focused way.

Evasion Techniques

Take a look at a sophisticated extra that Nikto incorporates, named Libwhisker. Run from a Perl module, Libwhisker is used for much of Nikto's internal functionality. As part of its feature set, there is an `-evasion` option. This functionality allows attackers to disguise their intentions and fool intrusion detection systems (IDSs). That might include throttling packets that might fool an IDS into thinking a standard flow of traffic is taking place or encrypting packets in a way that means deep inspection becomes near impossible. Tools such as `sslproxy` and `nmap` can provide this type of functionality if you want to test such an approach. Another obfuscation technique that is used by scanners is to completely overload logs with valid requests with the intention of hiding illegitimate ones. The result is that admins have little chance of finding the proverbial needle in a haystack. As seasoned firewall operators will be aware, it tends to be proprietary enterprise-level security devices that can flag such attacks, and they are provided at significant cost.

In Nikto terms, such evasion means using some of the options shown in Table 12.2, direct from the documentation. You can use multiple options in the same request.

Table 12.2: IDS Evasion Capabilities Courtesy of Libwhisker

OPTION	EVASION DESCRIPTION
1	Random URI encoding (non-UTF8)
2	Directory self-reference (/ . /)
3	Premature URL ending
4	Prepend long random string
5	Fake parameter
6	Tab as request spacer
7	Change the case of the URL
8	Use Windows directory separator (\)
A	Use a carriage return (0x0d) as a request spacer
B	Use binary value 0x0b as a request spacer

You are encouraged to check the Libwhisker documentation (tarballs of Libwhisker can be found here: `sourceforge.net/projects/whisker`) to supplement these options. As stated, it is unlikely that modern, enterprise-grade IDS functionality will be fooled by employing these options, but you can certainly run tests with them potentially to become more familiar with how they work or prove their efficacy against older systems.

Another handy set of options in Nikto come in the form of "mutate" options. Mutation techniques involve mixing and matching a multitude of tests based on educated guessing. Each test might differ slightly from the last to put the target system through its paces. If you go down this route, be aware that you may end up firing an even higher volume of tests at your destination host. In Table 12.3 we can see the mutate options.

Table 12.3: Nikto Offers "Mutation" Technique Options, Too

OPTION	MUTATION TECHNIQUE
1	Test the contents of the `root` directories.
2	Hunt for common password files.
3	Work out usernames via Apache.
4	Find usernames from the contents of scripts in the `cgi-bin/` directory.
5	Figure out if subdomains exist.
6	Search for directory names.

There is a plethora of other options that you can explore with Nikto. Some miscellaneous options follow, but it is worth looking at the documentation yourself to fine-tune the suitable options to reduce the length of time that a scan might take.

A useful feature that is worth considering is the `-no404` option. This means that HTTP 404s error checks will not be performed, which can significantly reduce the number of probes if scanning with limited bandwidth, for example. Note that a greater number of false positives might be found enabling this feature, however. Certain websites use slightly counterintuitive responses for "not found" errors, such as HTTP 302 redirects, so neither approach is necessarily an exact science.

You can also set up "tuning" options with Nikto. In Table 12.4 we can see what is available. You can select these options, and Nikto will just focus on just this specific set of options during the scan. The `x` option excludes any options that you wish to avoid using. For clarity, in this example we are asking Nikto to scan for XSS injection issues (among others), SQL injection, and remote command execution, denoted by "498" for their categories:

```
$ perl nikto.pl -h 10.10.10.10 -T 498
```

However, if we wanted to do the same scan but purposely avoid flagging any interesting files or information found in log files, we could explicitly exclude that type of scan, listing its category after the `x` with a numeral 1 in this case.

```
$ perl nikto.pl -h 10.10.10.10 -T 498x1
```

Table 12.4: Tuning Options Within Nikto

OPTION	TUNING OPTION
1	File uploads tests.
2	Focus on things of interest in logs or filenames.
3	Test for misconfigurations and known filenames.
4	Check for XSS, HTML, and script injections.
5	Try to retrieve web `root` files.
6	Focus on denial-of-service possibilities.
7	Look for all files that are possible to retrieve.
8	Test for remote shell access or command executions.
9	Check for SQLi.
a	Focus on Auth bypass.
b	Try to identify software.
c	Look for remote source.
x	Exclude other options shown and don't include them.

When you list the tuning options, they are parsed from left to right, and if there's an `x`, for excluding options, then anything to the right side of the `x` is ignored, and the other tests are performed instead.

The Main Nikto Configuration File

If you clone the Nikto GitHub repository, you can immediately see the main configuration file, which resides at `nikto/program/nikto.conf.default`. This file exists so that once you have made changes you can revert to it afterward if required. The name is to prevent a `git pull` command from losing your changes. The comments at the top of the file state the following:

```
If you want to change it, we strongly suggest you copy it to nikto.conf
# This will stop it being over-ridden when you git pull
```

Let's look at some of the options that you might want to change.

There's the ability to miss some network ports completely with the `SKIPPORTS=` option.

As mentioned, when Nikto runs, it is populating the destination host's logs with multiple entries. You can alter the user agent that an admin might find in those logs by using the `USERAGENT=` option (which should sit on one line) within the configuration file:

```
# User-Agent variables:
# @VERSION    - Nikto version
# @TESTID    - Test identifier
# @EVASIONS    - List of active evasions
# Example:
# USERAGENT=Mozilla/5.00(Nikto/@VERSION)(Evasions:@EVASIONS)
# (Test:@TESTID)
USERAGENT=Mozilla/5.0 (Windows NT 10.0; Win64; x64)
AppleWebKit/537.36(KHTML, like Gecko)Chrome/74.0.3729.169
Safari/537.36
```

By default, anonymous updates are sent back to Nikto's website (`www.cirt.net`), which helps the hardworking developers improve the product with newly found version strings. You can switch off this option by changing the `UPDATES=no` option so that now data is sent back.

There is also a useful CI/CD option where you will not be asked to confirm anything before proceeding. Simply set `PROMPTS=no`.

And, if necessary, you can also generate cookies for each of your requests. Available cookies options look like this:

```
# Cookies: send cookies with all requests
# Multiple can be set by separating with a semi-colon, e.g.:
```

```
# "cookie1"="cookie value";"cookie2"="cookie val"
#STATIC-COOKIE="name=value";"something=nothing";
```

To make changes to any of Nikto's filesystem paths, there is the ability to repoint to a different path for plugins, for example, nearer the end of the file.

There is also the ability to change the SSL library that Nikto uses, as shown here:

```
# Choose SSL libs:
# SSLeay        - use Net::SSLeay
# SSL           - use Net::SSL
# auto          - automatically choose what's available
#                 (SSLeay wins if both are available)
LW_SSL_ENGINE=auto
```

Finally, there is the option to stop scanning altogether if a number of failed scans occur. This is handy for backing out of a scan when something is not quite right. The default is `FAILURES=20`. If you change this setting to zero, then no matter how many failures are spotted, Nikto will keep going relentlessly.

Summary

In this chapter, we looked at scanning hosts for issues once your application software is installed and running upon them. Commonly the web server scanner of choice, Nikto has an impressive and extensible feature set including mutation techniques and evasion options.

You can precisely configure the tool for your needs and gain confidence in how secure your applications are from an external attacker's perspective.

To make the best use of Nikto, it is important to keep an eye on the scope of your scans. The output can be a little daunting at first, not to mention the footprint left inside a target's web server logs. However, continually fine-tuning the scope of the scans that you are interested in will keep your CI/CD pipeline scan results quick and ultimately provide much more valuable security information that is useful to the security posture of your application.

Part

III

Cloud Security

In This Part

In this section, we deviate almost entirely from the workload aspects of Cloud Native security, which involve our containerized applications, and focus on what has commonly been referred to recently as *cloud security posture management* (CSPM). In other words, these chapters pay close attention to the cloud platform that applications will run upon, often in parts referred to as *infrastructure as a service* (IaaS). The key facets explored include the operational perspective of running cloud infrastructure, monitoring what resources are running, and noting how they are interacting both internally and publicly.

Additionally, because it soon becomes clear that there are simply too many static configuration options and running configuration options to tweak for compliance manually, this section looks at sophisticated automation around policies that you can customize to meet your own requirements.

And, once your policies are set live, we continue to look at examining, in detail, precisely what the status of your cloud infrastructure is from an auditing perspective.

Finally, this section looks at an all-too-common area that allows for data leaks to take place from organizations and examines permissions around cloud storage. Although AWS is used throughout this section, there are common operational, configuration, and storage concerns within Azure and Google Cloud, so knowledge can be transposed with relative ease in many cases.

CHAPTER

13

Monitoring Cloud Operations

Once you've containerized your applications and configured your orchestrators, clearly you need somewhere to host your workloads. Thanks to a decade and a half of cloud platform maturity, it is now possible to integrate your workloads tightly with dynamic cloud services. Keeping them running and limiting downtime requires effort, and much depends on how securely they are configured. In this chapter, however, we look at the Ops side of the cloud and how to navigate confidently through the challenges involved.

There are a number of reliable open source cloud monitoring tools that can greatly improve the visibility of your cloud estate and improve your cloud security posture management (CSPM) as a result.

Having a large screen in an office with dashboards offering useful and continuous, real-time updates about cloud infrastructure gained popularity as screens became cheaper, but being able to quickly interrogate varying cloud resources using specific criteria through a browser or API can mean that issues are spotted before they cause headaches. And do not forget that a welcome side effect of keeping a close eye on your cloud resources is also significant cost savings. For example, what if a race condition caused endless EC2 instances to be spawned unnecessarily? Or suppose repeated API calls push AWS account limits to their maximum, causing downtime after AWS directly rate-limited API calls in your account.

In this chapter, we will look at two excellent tools that offer varied operational dashboard functionality: Netdata and Komiser. The first deals with nodes, and the second sits at the cloud platform level. Although both offer a lens into different parts of a cloud estate, between them they provide comprehensive coverage and offer an exceptional open source capability that is well worth exploring further.

Host Dashboarding with NetData

Netdata is focused on providing per-host feedback, but it is far from a run-of-the-mill, 1970s-style reporting system when the tools-of-old struggled to create any graphical representation of statistics. According to its website, Netdata (`netdata.cloud`) is one of the most starred projects on the Cloud Native Computing Foundation (CNCF, `www.cncf.io`) site, which makes it a hard act to follow. As well as sponsoring the CNCF, Netdata is a member and sponsor of the Linux Foundation. The versatility of the software is worth mentioning, and the developers describe it as suited for all types of deployments including physical, virtual, container, IoT, and edge applications.

The dashboarding is completely reactive, which means that on a touchscreen you can pinch and zoom and rewind logging timelines with ease. Two impressive aspects of Netdata that are immediately obvious are first its ease of installation (which is both painless and efficient and gives you confidence in the maturity and maintenance of the product) and the unquestionably impressive levels of effort that have been put into the product's aesthetics. Those users familiar with Kibana and the like will no doubt have seen some impressive dashboards, but Netdata is quite simply beautifully presented and is hard to beat.

Installing Netdata

Like other tools that we have examined in this book, Netdata can be installed in two different ways, either as a host installation or simply running as a container. As always, the second will be our preference from a Cloud Native perspective.

Host Installation

If you choose to go down the host installation route for Netdata, be prepared for a few different steps to be displayed on your terminal as the installation completes but with little interaction thankfully. The process throws no errors (at least on modern Debian derivatives) and communicates well throughout. You might want to use this form of installation if you are not running containers on specific hosts, for example, and do not want to install a container runtime specifically for Netdata.

We will begin by downloading the installation script, which we will use to install Netdata from source directly onto our machine. We can do just that by running this command:

```
$ curl https://my-netdata.io/kickstart.sh
```

If you scrutinize the `kickstart.sh` script, you can see that a few host directories will be used for files, and in addition a number of packages will be installed. At the least you might expect the following packages to be installed, for example:

```
autoconf autoconf-archive autogen automake autotools-dev cmake
cmake-data libc-dev-bin libc6-dev libelf-dev libjson-c-dev
libjsoncpp1 libjudy-dev libjudydebian1 liblz4-dev libmnl-dev
libopts25 libopts25-dev librhash0 libssl-dev python3-bson
python3-pymongo uuid-dev zlib1g-dev
```

Note that Netdata does expect elevated permissions to run; in this case we will use the `root` user directly.

For installation use the following command, which will pull in the script that we just downloaded at and then execute it rather than just allowing you to inspect it beforehand. You will need to be running the Bash shell for this, or with another shell you might be able to run `chmod +x` on the script and alter the way your shell interacts with the script.

```
$ bash <(curl -Ss https://my-netdata.io/kickstart.sh)
```

In Figure 13.1 we can see the start of the process spawned by that install script; even the ASCII output is well-presented. As mentioned, the process does not take long to complete, but there are a few interactions along the way. Figure 13.2 shows the end of the installation process as it completes successfully.

```
--- Installing netdata... ---
[/tmp/netdata-kickstart-Fagr80/netdata-v1.23.2-151-g0e5f2e38]# ./netdata-installer.sh --auto-update
 ^
 |.-.   .-.   .-.   .-.   .  netdata
 |   '-'   '-'   '-'   '-'   real-time performance monitoring, done right!
 +----+-----+-----+-----+-----+-----+-----+-----+-----+-----+-----+--->


 You are about to build and install netdata to your system.

 It will be installed at these locations:

  - the daemon     at /usr/sbin/netdata
  - config files   in /etc/netdata
  - web files      in /usr/share/netdata
  - plugins        in /usr/libexec/netdata
  - cache files    in /var/cache/netdata
  - db files       in /var/lib/netdata
  - log files      in /var/log/netdata
  - pid file       at /var/run/netdata.pid
  - logrotate file at /etc/logrotate.d/netdata

 This installer allows you to change the installation path.
 Press Control-C and run the same command with --help for help.
```

Figure 13.1: The start of the Netdata installation process

```
 --- Wrap up environment set up ---
Preparing .environment file
[/tmp/netdata-kickstart-Fagr80/netdata-v1.23.2-151-g0e5f2e38]# chmod 0644 /etc/netdata/.environment


Setting netdata.tarball.checksum to 'new_installation'

 --- We are done! ---

  ^
  |.-.   .-.   .-.   .-.   .-.   .  netdata                          .-.   .-
  |   '-'   '-'   '-'   '-'   '-'   is installed and running now!  -'   '-'
  +----+-----+-----+-----+-----+-----+-----+-----+-----+-----+-----+-----+--->

  enjoy real-time performance and health monitoring...



Kilo ~ #
```

Figure 13.2: Netdata has completed its installation successfully.

The promise of real-time performance and health monitoring here is just the start of the story. If we navigate within a browser to `http://localhost:19999`, we are presented with Netdata's crystal-clear user interface. In Figure 13.3 we can see the top of the long, scrollable, and detailed dashboard.

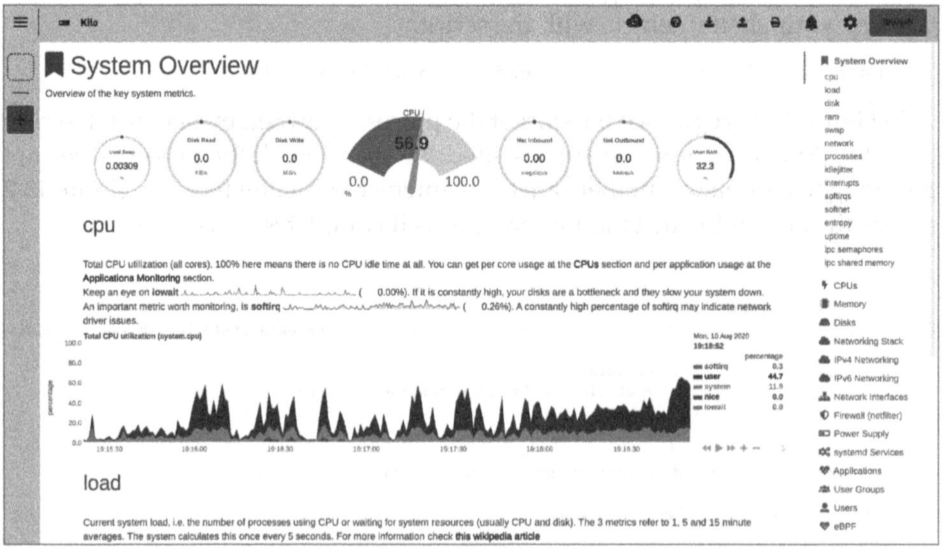

Figure 13.3: The top of the dashboard

Here we are presented with real-time updates of the present state of our system. On the right side of the screen, the navigation panel offers around 30 options, covering every aspect you can think of on your system. And they do not simply create a snapshot of what is happening right now but instead offer a scrollable, historical view that provides visibility of all things salient to your running host, whether that host is a local laptop or a remote cloud server.

Container Installation

We will look at more of the dashboard content in a moment, but first we need to install Netdata via a container installation, without adding any extra packages to our host at all.

The command, as shown in Listing 13.1, is relatively lengthy but easy to cut and paste into a script for later use if you prefer.

Listing 13.1: The Simple Container Installation Version of Running Netdata

```
docker run -d --name=netdata \
  -p 19999:19999 \
  -v netdatalib:/var/lib/netdata \
  -v netdatacache:/var/cache/netdata \
  -v /etc/passwd:/host/etc/passwd:ro \
  -v /etc/group:/host/etc/group:ro \
  -v /proc:/host/proc:ro \
  -v /sys:/host/sys:ro \
  -v /etc/os-release:/host/etc/os-release:ro \
  --restart unless-stopped \
  --cap-add SYS_PTRACE \
  --security-opt apparmor=unconfined \
  netdata/netdata
```

As you can see in Listing 13.1, this code offers the container the `SYS_PTRACE` kernel capability, which allows the container to make changes to other processes in the host's process table. Additionally, on Ubuntu in particular, and other derivatives, we are relinquishing the protections afforded to the system by `AppArmor` for this container. Make sure you are willing to run a container under these conditions with these permissions on all of your hosts before proceeding.

Also, in Listing 13.1 you can see the ability to quickly alter which network port is visible; this capability is a useful addition when multiple network interfaces are in use.

The resulting output from the long command in Listing 13.1 simply shows a container starting up with its own hash ID. There are extremely detailed instructions for getting the most out of your containerized version of Netdata available on the GitHub site (`github.com/netdata/netdata/blob/master/packaging/docker/README.md`), which is definitely well worth a read. Key points include recommendations to use Docker Compose, give Netdata containers a specific name, inspect specific storage volumes, and integrate with the Travis CI/CD tool.

In Figure 13.4 we can see other features and the utilization percentages of our network interfaces.

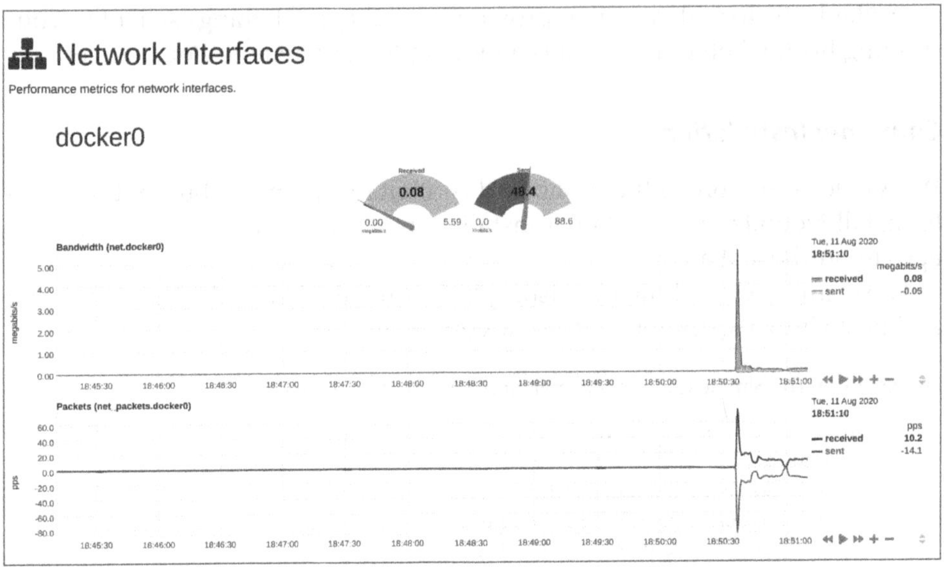

Figure 13.4: Networking information showing the `docker0` network interface

Here we are able to monitor traffic closely across any of our network interfaces, historic and current; this can show us spikes in traffic for DDoS attacks, potential trends for future use (think about applications that are being used once a year and nearing resource capacity), and the like. The view that we can see is just after starting up the container that is running Netdata itself. Having clicked `cpuidle` on the right then, in Figure 13.5, we are able to see when energy-saving kicks in and a CPU core is sitting idle.

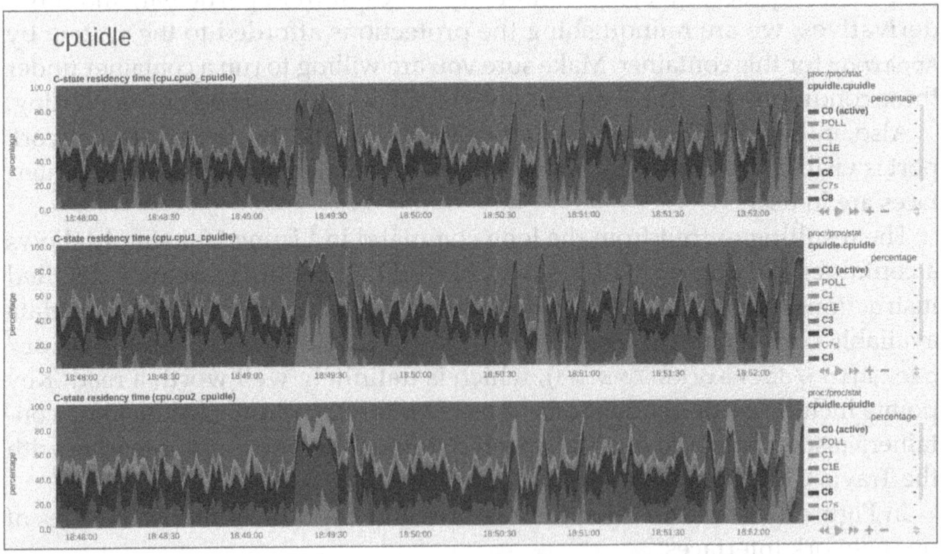

Figure 13.5: The `cpuidle` dashboard to show how quiet your CPU cores are

Figure 13.6 presents sample output from the sensor readings that provide temperature telemetry.

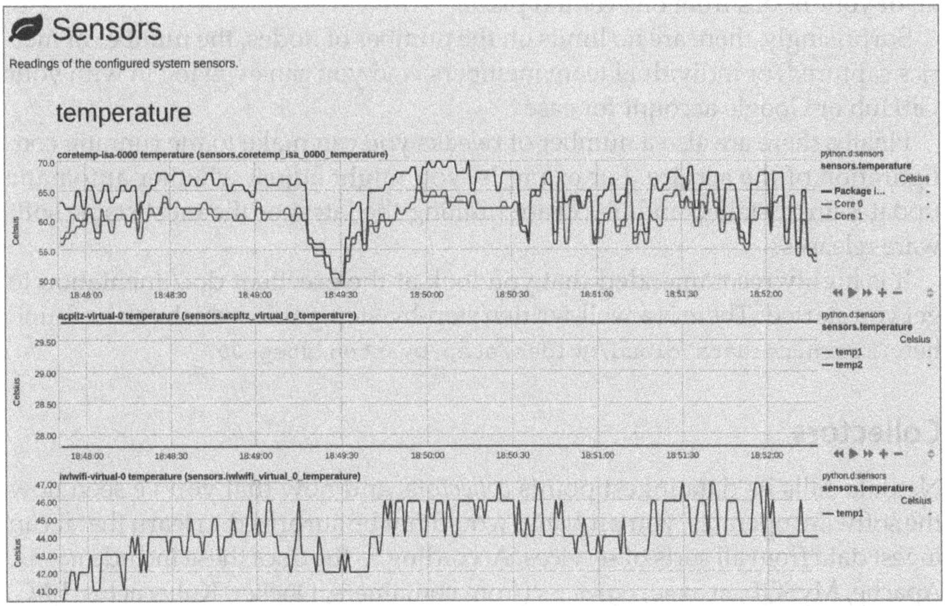

Figure 13.6: Temperature metrics can be useful for on-premises hosts that have data center heat cooling issues.

On this screen are some useful temperature statistics for hardware components. A reminder again that if the dashboard is viewed on touchscreen devices, the ability to inspect a particular set of graphs makes it far easier to pinpoint, and then pinch, a certain timeline or to change the displayed measure of statistics.

We have looked at only a handful of the criteria that Netdata monitors. There are apparently thousands of metrics available, and standard Netdata is equipped with insightful alarms when health checks do not pass tests as expected. This section of the documentation offers insight into what is possible with Netdata: `learn.netdata.cloud/docs/collect/how-collectors-work`. The left navigation menu under Collect lists the types of metrics.

Coupled with the fact that there is no registration required to use Netdata and that commercial-grade software is available as open source software, there is little reason not to try deploying Netdata on your hosts. Just be certain that you are aware of any security considerations and that you pay attention to accidentally exposing the dashboard's network port to unwanted visitors.

To centralize your many hosts, again without a fee, Netdata comes with an additional service called Netdata Cloud (`app.netdata.cloud`). This service allows you to register your Netdata host agents so that you can then manage all of your nodes from one central place.

Surprisingly, there are no limits on the number of nodes, the number of metrics captured, or individual team members, and you can even log in with your GitHub or Google account for ease.

Finally, there are also a number of tweaks you can make to the running configuration of the service. For example, you might adjust whether automatic updates are installed and if you are running the latest or the most stable software releases.

It is highly recommended that you look at the excellent documentation to get you started. There is a well-written step-by-step guide, which can be found here: `learn.netdata.cloud/guides/step-by-step/step-00`.

Collectors

Netdata calls its data ingest points *collectors*, and now that you've seen how the software operates, you probably would not be surprised to learn that it can ingest data from all sorts of services. According to the docs these include `nginx`, Apache, MySQL, `statsd`, `cgroups` (from containers, Docker, Kubernetes, LXC, and so on), Traefik, and web server `access.log` files. From a Cloud Native perspective, the Kubernetes collector is extremely welcome to automate multiple containers in a cluster being monitored (`learn.netdata.cloud/docs/agent/collectors/collectors#kubernetes`). Visiting that page offers the welcome knowledge that the Kubernetes collector allows kubelet monitoring, kube-proxy monitoring, and additionally service discovery monitoring.

Uninstalling Host Packages

Incidentally, if you want to uninstall the host package installation of Netdata, there are instructions on this page: `learn.netdata.cloud/docs/agent/packaging/installer/uninstall`. As discussed earlier, the installation uses a number of host directories, so cleanly uninstalling packages is a sensible approach.

Cloud Platform Interrogation with Komiser

As mentioned in the introduction to this chapter, to maintain a robust cloud security posture on modern server estates, it is really important to have exceptional levels of visibility on your resources.

Another sophisticated tool that is designed to assist with that requirement is called Komiser (`github.com/mlabouardy/komiser`). It offers some welcome functionality to assist with improving the cost analysis and hardening of your Amazon Web Services accounts. The tool will run through a number of your AWS services to offer the security insight that is required on a per-region basis. Our discussion of Komiser will assume that you have an AWS account available to you (and that you have run the `aws configure` command to set up your credentials; see `docs.aws.amazon.com/cli/latest/userguide/install-cliv2.html` if you do not know how).

Let's look at installing it now. The process is incredibly simple, but we will need AWS credentials (access and secret keys) copied into the environment variables to help populate a container's environment. To interact with the authentication role-based access control (RBAC) components of AWS, we will use an Identity and Access Management (IAM) policy as provided by `raw.githubusercontent.com/mlabouardy/komiser/master/policy.json`. You will need to create as a custom policy that is not designed to give excessive permissions to change resources but instead just read, list, and describe AWS services. If you are new to IAM users, roles, and policies, then you can find the official AWS documentation at `docs.aws.amazon.com/IAM/latest/UserGuide/access.html`.

Once you have attached that policy to your user or role, you do not even need to clone a repository to run Komiser. Just run this Docker command in a script or as one line if it fails to run (displayed with the credentials redacted):

```
$ docker run -d -p 3000:3000 -e "AWS_ACCESS_KEY_ID=AKXXXXXXXXXXXGN4" \
-e AWS_SECRET_ACCESS_KEY="GLXXXXXXXXXXXXXXXXKY" \
-e AWS_DEFAULT_REGION="eu-west-1" \
--name komiser mlabouardy/komiser:2.4.0
```

To confirm that the container spawned as we hoped, use this heavily redacted `ps` command:

```
$ docker ps
IMAGE                    COMMAND          PORTS
mlabouardy/komiser:2.4.0 "komiser start" 0.0.0.0:3000->3000/tcp
```

That looks great, as if it spun up as hoped, using TCP port 3000. We can now use our browser to navigate to that on our localhost:

```
http://localhost:3000
```

The test AWS account is not giving too much information away on the splash screen, but the dashboard is well-designed and intuitive, as we can see in Figure 13.7.

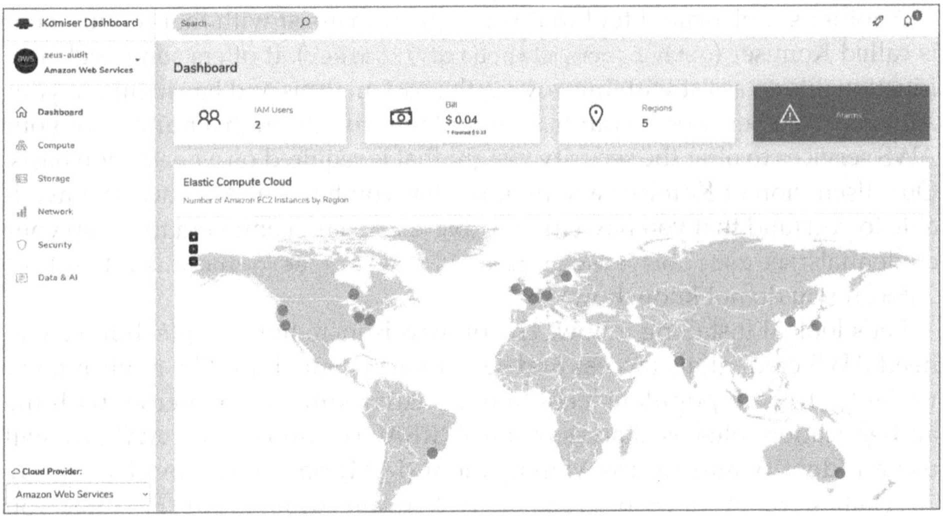

Figure 13.7: The splash screen for Komiser made available by our container

In Figure 13.7 we can see that there are two IAM users in our default region and a minuscule AWS bill of a few US cents due, forecasted to rise because it is the beginning of the billing period. We can see that there are five regions listed as areas of interest, and in the map, we can see the AWS regions that have been discovered. If we hover over them, we immediately see how many EC2 instances are live and running.

In Figure 13.8, we can see a summary of our support tickets for this region, having scrolled down on the splash screen and our tiny billing forecast. The instant snapshot of per-service billing costs is a welcome addition.

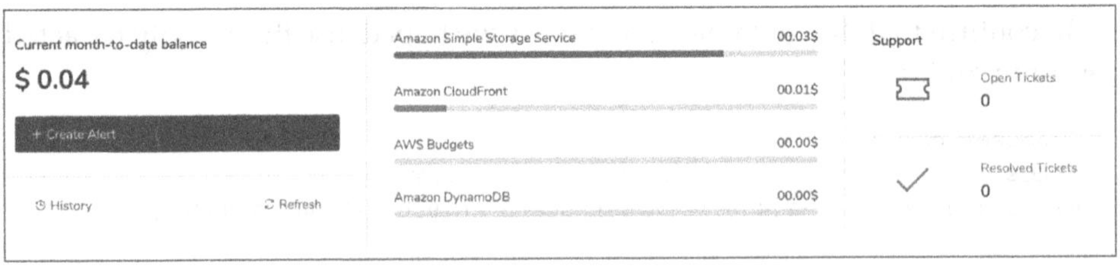

Figure 13.8: A billing summary per-service plus outstanding support tickets

Hidden away at the top right of the screen is a rocket-shaped icon to list any service limit checks, a feature that could be useful if you are nearing API call limits or EC2 instance limits due to stress events, such as an attack or a runaway race condition due to a misconfiguration.

If you have ever worked with hundreds of EC2 instances, you will know how important it is to be able to quickly check how many are running and how many have been terminated recently. In Figure 13.9 we can see that the considerate Komiser offers this information in a timely fashion.

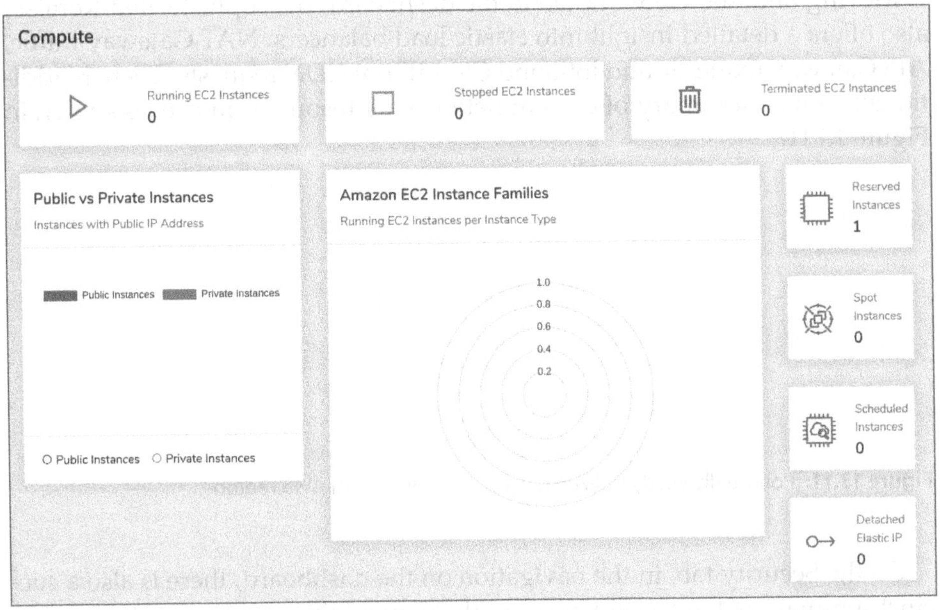

Figure 13.9: Checking running instances is useful not just for costs but stress events too.

Another valuable addition relates to Serverless functions in AWS. Komiser presents a must-have, critically important view of any Lambda function execution errors. If your functions are running security tasks and they fail to run, or equally fail to complete their execution without errors, then this is an extremely important metric to pay attention to for obvious reasons. We can see this metric in Figure 13.10.

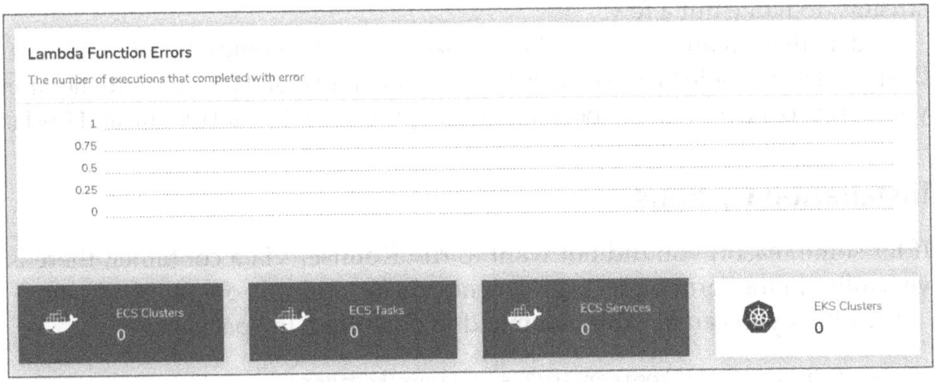

Figure 13.10: Lambda functions aren't forgotten about in Komiser.

Additionally, there is a section regarding AWS S3 and a useful aggregator of the size of all combined S3 buckets and their total number, which will of course affect your billing.

Moving onto the Network tab in the dashboard, the sophisticated Komiser also offers a detailed insight into elastic load balancers, NAT Gateway traffic, API Gateway requests, and inbound CloudFront CDN requests. There is additionally a nice summary of current networking resources in use, as shown in Figure 13.11.

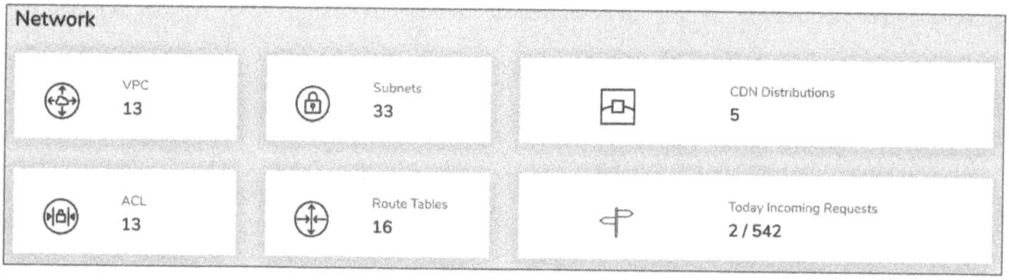

Figure 13.11: Potentially costly utilized network resource in an AWS region

On the Security tab, in the navigation on the dashboard, there is also a succinct summary of the security services that you might want to pay attention to. Among others that are shown, there are recent sign-in events in graph form, how many KMS keys from the Key Management Service are in use, the number of keypairs, and a count of the number of security groups in use. You can see a live login map of where current users are logged in from currently on a global map, and additionally you can see a list of unrestricted security groups in the region, plus the top IP addresses accessing the AWS API currently, which is a nice touch.

The final section of the dashboard offers a large number of metrics on data and AI. Within that section, you will find SQS, SNS, Active MQ, and Kinesis streams, to name but a few.

And, if all the features that we have looked at are not comprehensive enough, then you are also able to move freely between different cloud platforms to monitor your resources within them too, namely, Google Cloud, Digital Ocean, and OVH.

Installation Options

If for some reason you did not want to run Komiser via a container, there is versatility in the form of package downloads for multiple operating systems.

For Linux you can use this command to download the package:

```
$ wget https://cli.komiser.io/2.4.0/linux/komiser
$ chmod +x komiser
```

Also available are packages for Windows and macOS X in addition.

If you take this installation route, then you will still be required to provide authenticated access to the AWS platform. If you need assistance, then refer to the IAM instructions earlier in the chapter to create a user or role with this IAM policy: `komiser.s3.amazonaws.com/policy.json`.

Once it is installed, you can just run this command to start the service up for Komiser:

```
$ ./komiser start --port 3000
```

Finally, if you want to do so, then it is possible to also use Redis as a caching server as follows (this is apparently only for preexisting Redis installations on the system, so install it first):

```
$ ./komiser start --port 3000 --redis localhost:6379 --duration 30
```

Listing 13.2 shows the startup options available for Komiser to complement the previous command.

Listing 13.2: Options to Use When Starting Up Komiser

```
--port value, -p value      Server port (default: 3000)
--duration value,
  -d value  Cache expiration time (default: 30 minutes)
--redis value, -r value     Redis server (localhost:6379)
--dataset value,
  -ds value  BigQuery dataset name
  (project-id.dataset-name.table-name)
--multiple, -m              Enable multiple AWS accounts feature
```

Summary

In this chapter, we looked at two exceptional monitoring tools. Even a daily check of issues from such tools can greatly improve your chances against unwelcome attacks or misconfigurations and tangible cost issues that affect your cloud estate.

First we saw Netdata in action that provided a centralized location to monitor the health of all your cloud and on-premises hosts. The clarity provided by its dashboards is a sight to behold. And, running Netdata as a container is a painless exercise. You would be wise to change the configuration to your needs and ensure that your security requirements are satisfied when deploying it to multiple hosts.

Next we looked at real-time checks against resources in AWS that are currently in use, with a dashboarding system called Komiser. Although both tools provide quite different perspectives, both play a critical role in how you approach cloud security posture management and the health of your cloud estate. You are encouraged to look at the paid-for enterprise edition for further features if you make extensive use of Komiser via its website: `www.komiser.io`. There is some well-written and nicely formatted documentation available for Komiser on the docs site: `docs.komiser.io`. Adopting the paid-for version means that you will be able to declare credentials in different ways among other benefits. And, with the right version, you can output alerts to Slack so that critical issues are not missed. There is also an online service which is still in private beta at `cloud.komiser.io`, which is worth keeping an eye on and signing up for when it goes live.

CHAPTER

14

Cloud Guardianship

There are times when innovation is the result of having dealt with a crisis. At other times innovation takes place when individuals and businesses have spare capacity and the need for a solution.

One now extremely popular tool was developed because of an organization's increasing security challenges; it offers sophisticated security advantages that can be fully automated and in addition help with cost savings.

In this chapter we will look at a tool open sourced from a UK bank called Cloud Custodian (`https://github.com/cloud-custodian/cloud-custodian`), which we will use to set up AWS policies and additionally automate the enforcement of those policies. Tried and tested, with a thorough understanding of such policies, you can trust the tool with the guardianship of your cloud platform infrastructure.

Installing Cloud Custodian

Cloud Custodian was developed by Capital One and has gained deserved popularity over the years. Let's get straight into the process of installing it and look at some of the policies it offers that might help you.

The policies are written in YAML (`https://yaml.org`), which is the most popular coding language in today's Cloud Native world and is used in several chapters of this book. Cloud Custodian can run from scheduled scripts (using cron jobs, for example) or equally from serverless functions (such as AWS Lambda and other cloud platform serverless equivalents) on the AWS, Azure, and GCP cloud platforms. How you execute the policing of your cloud estate using its policies is up to you; choose an appropriate approach for your needs.

The impetus for Cloud Custodian's Open Source distribution was reportedly its achievement of impressive cost savings. Apparently, the bank discovered that using a rules engine to define AWS policies meant a reduction of around 25 percent of AWS resources, which was clearly a big deal in terms of the running costs in a large financial institution. In addition to cost savings, organizing a collection of rulesets to your advantage allows you to improve your visibility and the security posture of your infrastructure. There is also some especially useful caching available to help cut down on the hammering of poor old AWS's API endpoints.

Before we go any further, here is a really important caveat: be exceptionally careful to test the policies that you create before running them over production services. You can cause total havoc and delete irreplaceable resources with tools like this. Make extensive use of the dryrun feature, which will save your skin on multiple occasions. You have been suitably warned!

Wrapper Installation

You can install Cloud Custodian via a useful Docker Go wrapper, known as custodian-cask, that will let you run it locally without having to satisfy the Python dependencies that might cause you installation headaches. It will allow you to use the contents of the provided Docker image via a cleaner CLI command. Both of the following container installation routes require Docker to be running beforehand.

If you want to use Docker directly, the following two commands show how you would run the containerized version once you have created a policy.yml file, which is referenced in the second command. However, note that we have not created it yet, and therefore, the following will not work if you run it now:

```
$ docker pull cloudcustodian/c7n
$ docker run -it \
  -v $(pwd)/output:/home/custodian/output \
  -v $(pwd)/policy.yml:/home/custodian/policy.yml \
  --env-file-file <(env | grep "^AWS\|^AZURE\|^GOOGLE") \
  cloudcustodian/c7n run -v \
  -s /home/custodian/output /home/custodian/policy.yml
```

To use the previous Docker command, first you would export your AWS credentials as environment variables, just as we did in Chapter 13, "Monitoring Cloud Operations," for Komiser.

If you prefer to use the Cask installation route, run the command that follows. It will dutifully download a binary into your user path and make it executable.

(Important: the long URL starting `https://` should be entered on one line, even though we cannot show that here. If you run into issues, try running the whole command as one line.)

```
$ sudo sh -c 'wget -q \
https://cloudcustodian.io/downloads/custodian-cask/
linux-latest/custodian-cask \
-O /usr/local/bin/custodian-cask \
&& chmod +x /usr/local/bin/custodian-cask'
```

Once the command completes, the executable `custodian-cask` file will reside in the `/usr/local/bin` directory, and you are all set. The previous command is the Cask installation method for Linux; Mac and Windows alternatives can be found on this page: `https://cloudcustodian.io/docs/tools/cask.html`.

Once you have run the downloaded binary file, pull the latest Cloud Custodian container image down to your container runtime, with the following command to trigger the image pull process:

```
$ custodian-cask --help
```

With some patience, you will see the container layers download; Listing 14.1 shows the slightly trimmed `--help` output.

Listing 14.1: The custodian-cask Help Output

```
usage: custodian [-h] {run,schema,report,logs,metrics,version,validate}
Cloud Custodian—Cloud fleet management
optional arguments:
  -h,--help             show this help message and exit
commands:
  {run,schema,report,logs,metrics,version,validate}
    run                 Execute the policies in a config file
    schema              Interactive cli docs for policy authors
    report              Tabular report on policy matched resources
    version             Display installed version of custodian
    validate            Validate config files against the json schema
```

Python Installation

It is definitely worth mentioning the Python installation route, too. On Debian derivatives you first install a package for Python to create a virtual environment as follows:

```
$ apt-get install python3-venv
```

Next, you need to activate a shell for Cloud Custodian to run within, using this command:

```
$ python3 -m venv custodian
$ source custodian/bin/activate
```

And, under that subshell, run the next command to install Cloud Custodian locally:

```
$ (custodian) $ pip install c7n
```

In Figure 14.1 we can see a successful installation (it appears that you can ignore some Python errors if it completes successfully), and again we can now run the `--help` command from within that subshell to get the same help output as we saw using the cask Go wrapper in Listing 14.1:

```
$ custodian --help
```

If you use this route, note that we are just using `custodian` and not `custodian-cask` as our executable's name.

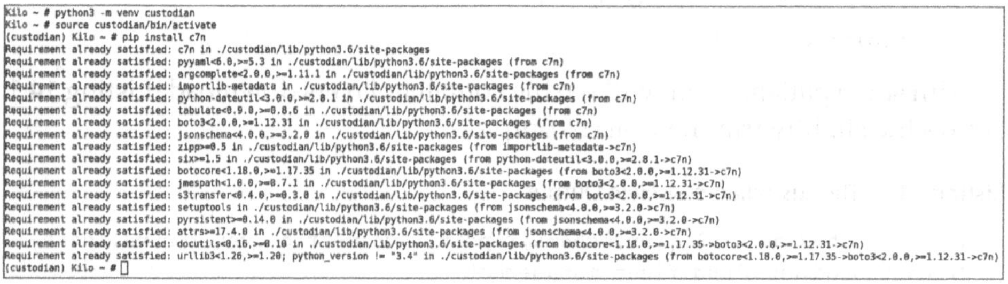
Kilo ~ # python3 -m venv custodian
Kilo ~ # source custodian/bin/activate
(custodian) Kilo ~ # pip install c7n
Requirement already satisfied: c7n in ./custodian/lib/python3.6/site-packages
Requirement already satisfied: pyyaml<6.0,>=5.3 in ./custodian/lib/python3.6/site-packages (from c7n)
Requirement already satisfied: argcomplete<2.0.0,>=1.11.1 in ./custodian/lib/python3.6/site-packages (from c7n)
Requirement already satisfied: importlib-metadata in ./custodian/lib/python3.6/site-packages (from c7n)
Requirement already satisfied: python-dateutil<3.0.0,>=2.8.1 in ./custodian/lib/python3.6/site-packages (from c7n)
Requirement already satisfied: tabulate<0.9.0,>=0.8.6 in ./custodian/lib/python3.6/site-packages (from c7n)
Requirement already satisfied: boto3<2.0.0,>=1.12.31 in ./custodian/lib/python3.6/site-packages (from c7n)
Requirement already satisfied: jsonschema<4.0.0,>=3.2.0 in ./custodian/lib/python3.6/site-packages (from c7n)
Requirement already satisfied: zipp>=0.5 in ./custodian/lib/python3.6/site-packages (from importlib-metadata->c7n)
Requirement already satisfied: six>=1.5 in ./custodian/lib/python3.6/site-packages (from python-dateutil<3.0.0,>=2.8.1->c7n)
Requirement already satisfied: botocore<1.18.0,>=1.17.35 in ./custodian/lib/python3.6/site-packages (from boto3<2.0.0,>=1.12.31->c7n)
Requirement already satisfied: jmespath<1.0.0,>=0.7.1 in ./custodian/lib/python3.6/site-packages (from boto3<2.0.0,>=1.12.31->c7n)
Requirement already satisfied: s3transfer<0.4.0,>=0.3.0 in ./custodian/lib/python3.6/site-packages (from boto3<2.0.0,>=1.12.31->c7n)
Requirement already satisfied: setuptools in ./custodian/lib/python3.6/site-packages (from jsonschema<4.0.0,>=3.2.0->c7n)
Requirement already satisfied: pyrsistent>=0.14.0 in ./custodian/lib/python3.6/site-packages (from jsonschema<4.0.0,>=3.2.0->c7n)
Requirement already satisfied: attrs>=17.4.0 in ./custodian/lib/python3.6/site-packages (from jsonschema<4.0.0,>=3.2.0->c7n)
Requirement already satisfied: docutils<0.16,>=0.10 in ./custodian/lib/python3.6/site-packages (from botocore<1.18.0,>=1.17.35->boto3<2.0.0,>=1.12.31->c7n)
Requirement already satisfied: urllib3<1.26,>=1.20; python_version != "3.4" in ./custodian/lib/python3.6/site-packages (from botocore<1.18.0,>=1.17.35->boto3<2.0.0,>=1.12.31->c7n)
(custodian) Kilo ~ #

Figure 14.1: Cloud Custodian courtesy of the Python installation route

EC2 Interaction

Now that you have installed the tool by any of the methods mentioned, to see it in action we will create a Cloud Custodian policy that attempts to stop an EC2 instance from running, based on a customized tag being added to that resource. The official AWS documentation for creating an instance over the AWS CLI can be found here (or do so using the AWS Console if you want): `https://docs.aws.amazon.com/cli/latest/userguide/cli-services-ec2.html`.

The first, simple policy that we will look at might be used for a number of purposes. It is extremely common to tag or label all of the resources that exist on enterprise cloud estates.

This can be so that ownership is immediately identifiable if there is an attack or some other issue with the resource, but most commonly organizations use tags to measure resource utilization for billing purposes.

EC2 instances are commonly tagged per environment (for example, development, staging, or production environments) for security monitoring, by cost center (which relates to the department that picks up the bill each month for any associated costs), and it is also not uncommon to have tags relating to an instance's operational hours.

By using tags, entire development environments can be torn down at 6 p.m. when developers go home for the day and then spun back up in time for 8 a.m. when they return. Imagine if that was fully automated and a company-wide policy for 200 developer teams, each with its own environment. This example hopefully helps illustrate how limiting the operational time for various resources can result in exceptional cost savings.

Let's see how Cloud Custodian uses tags now. We will begin by stopping a running instance. All we need to do is to add a tag to our EC2 instance named `Custodian`, as shown in Figure 14.2.

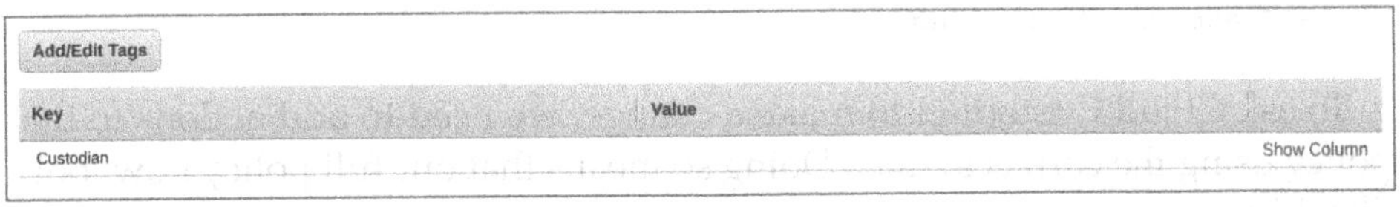

Figure 14.2: In the AWS Console or programmatically, add a tag to an EC2 instance.

Next, let's create a file called `custodian.yml` (this file would be the `policy.yaml` file in the vanilla Docker installation example shown earlier in the chapter) and enter the following contents:

```
policies:
   -name: stop-ec2-instance
    resource: aws.ec2
    filters:
     -tag:"Custodian": present
```

The logic within the policy is clear and straightforward, but make sure you follow it step-by-step for clarity. We are focusing on the `aws.ec2` resource and asking for the filters to check for tags on any of our EC2 instances. Filters might instead equally be used to check whether a storage volume is encrypted, for example, as follows:

```
filters:
  -Encrypted: false
```

Or instead, with reference to the previous mentions of ownership and billing, you might want to check that a resource has a tag with someone's username associated with it as so and prevent an EC2 instance from running if it is not present:

```
filters:
  -tag:CreatorName: absent
```

Filters are generally easy to read but can become more complex and include regular expressions. For example, if you have a number of filters for checking running EC2 instances that do not have the correct tags attached, think about combining them as one scenario. You might check for these conditions in a filter, for example, where we could stop active instances that did not comply to our tagging policy:

```
filters:
-or:
  -"tag:CostCenter": absent
  -"tag:OwnedBy": absent
  -"tag:DeployedEnv": absent
-not:
  -"State.Name": running
```

To ask Cloud Custodian to make a change, we need to add actions to that policy using the correct syntax. Doing so means that our full policy now looks like this:

```
policies:
-name: stop-ec2-instance
   resource: aws.ec2
   filters:
   -"tag:Custodian": present
   actions:
   -stop
```

Let's consider how we might improve the actions in our simple policy. What if we wanted to automatically tag EC2 instances that were noncompliant and not tagged correctly? We could incorporate simple changes by replacing the previous `actions` stanza with actions such as these:

```
actions:
-type: create-ownership-tag
   tag: OwnedBy
   principal_id_tag: CreatorId
```

In this example, we are ensuring that the user that created the instance is added to the value of the `OwnedBy` tag for that resource. You might also adopt a similar approach to preventing other users from shutting down EC2 instances that you own. (To learn more about the value of tagging, see the following interesting document from AWS, which should generate some food for thought: `https://aws.amazon.com/blogs/security/how-to-automatically-tag-amazon-ec2-resources-in-response-to-api-events`.)

Now that we have dissected a simple policy, let's assume we just want to stop any EC2 instances that are tagged "Custodian" so that we can see the sophisticated tool in action.

The next step is passing our AWS credentials to Cloud Custodian at execution time. For a sane security approach, we will use environment variables this way (note that we are using the `custodian` binary file in our example and not the `cask` binary):

```
$ AWS_ACCESS_KEY_ID="AKXXXXXXXXXXXXXXXXX"
$ AWS_SECRET_ACCESS_KEY="koNB7XXXXXXXXXXXXXX"
$ custodian run-output-dir=. custodian.yml
```

If you use the `aws configure` command to set up your `credentials` and `config` files in your `~/.aws` directory, you can omit the credentials set in environment variables on the command line.

Should you get complaints about a default AWS region not being set in your `config` file, you can simply pass the environment variable along the command line using these two commands or potentially as one command:

```
$ AWS_DEFAULT_REGION="eu-west-1"
$ custodian run-output-dir=. custodian.yml
```

The initial output from that command looks like this:

```
Custodian Cask 20190904.1 (cloudcustodian/c7n:latest)
Skipped image pull—Last checked 10 minutes ago.
```

This shows the beginning of processing output when the command is successful.

Note that if you have not allowed suitable permissions for your AWS IAM user or role to run the example `stop-ec2-instance` policy, then you might receive unceremonious `traceback` crash output. Because we know that we are running this command just for testing purposes and that we are dealing with only one AWS service, namely, EC2, we can offer our user or role the IAM policy as shown in Figure 14.3, noting again that you should definitely be testing this type of activity in a laboratory AWS account only.

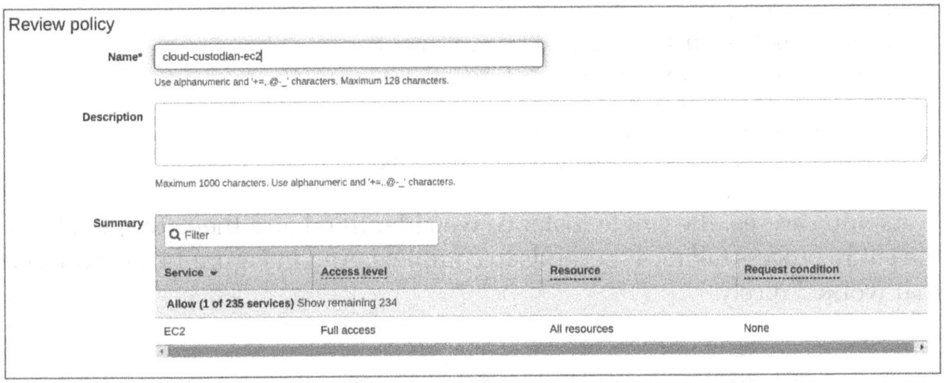

Figure 14.3: Highly permissive EC2 policy for our first test policy in Cloud Custodian

We can see that the IAM policy to stop our EC2 instance opens up everything for the EC2 service for our first Cloud Custodian policy to use. Listing 14.2 shows the far-from-ideal permissions in JSON format for that policy. It is a free-for-all with this policy when it comes to your EC2 service, so tune this policy if it is used in anything other than a laboratory account.

Listing 14.2: Laboratory-Only Permissions in JSON Format

```
{
  "Version": "2012-10-17",
  "Statement": [
    {
      "Effect": "Allow",
      "Action": ["ec2:*"],
      "Resource": ["*"]
    }
  ]
}
```

Another serious point to using tools like Cloud Custodian is that you absolutely must fine-tune your IAM permissions to suit your needs precisely as your policies evolve with Cloud Custodian. There is little point in improving your security posture with compliance-as-code automation if you leave gaping holes in your IAM configuration. You might only need to offer EC2 permissions such as `List`, `Read`, and `Stop` for our first policy.

Let's run our policy now, pointing at our local `custodian.yml` policy file with this command, in the subshell:

```
(custodian) Kilo ~ # custodian run—output-dir=. custodian.yml
```

We can see that our output directory is the current directory (denoted by the .), and we do not need many other switches because our configuration is in the policy file. What happens to our single EC2 instance that we tagged after we run that? That command's output is as follows:

```
2020-08-05 19:30:33,992:
custodian.policy:INFO policy:stop-ec2-instance
resource:aws.ec2 region:eu-west-1 count:1 time:0.40
2020-08-05 19:30:34,439:
custodian.policy:INFO policy:stop-ec2-instance
action:stop resources:1 execution_time:0.44
```

As you can see, the single instance was identified and then stopped, with the entire process taking 44 seconds to complete. And in Figure 14.4 we can see that worked nicely.

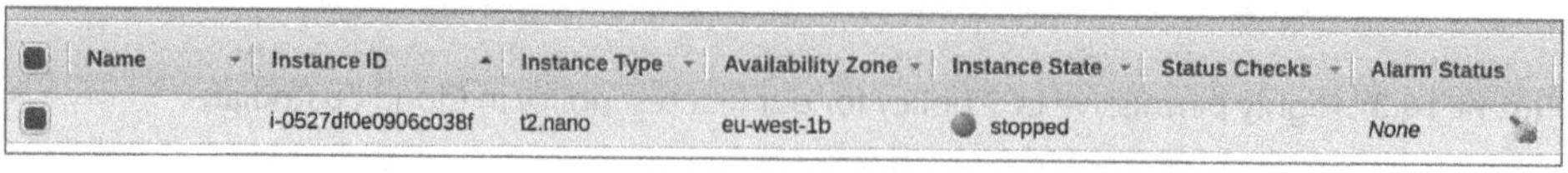
Name
Instance ID
Instance Type
Availability Zone
Instance State
Status Checks
Alarm Status
i-0527df0e0906c038f
t2.nano
eu-west-1b
stopped
None

Figure 14.4: We have stopped our instance successfully using a policy.

More Complex Policies

The documentation for Cloud Custodian is extremely thorough and well-presented. There are multiple ways to interact with the AWS, Azure, and GCP cloud platforms in a variety of useful ways.

In many cases, the scenarios covered by the official documentation can be readily adapted to your needs with only a little refactoring. The syntax is clear, and until you chain multiple conditions together (of which there are also many examples), the workflow is clear.

To avoid reinventing the wheel and repeating examples here, it is recommended that you decide what you are trying to achieve when it comes to compliance and look at some of the bundled examples, which you can find at `https://cloudcustodian.io/docs/aws/examples/index.html`.

The extensive compliance coverage of the examples is impressive. At a basic level, conditional tests can be made against logs for the source IP address of account logins, which can then be picked up by a Lambda function (`https://cloudcustodian.io/docs/aws/examples/accountinvalidiplogin.html`). The examples then move into Auto Scaling Groups (ASGs) being validated for sane configuration (`https://cloudcustodian.io/docs/aws/examples/asginvalidconfig.html`) and continue on to checking that the TLS ciphers and protocols are being used to run your Elastic Load Balancers (ELBs) (`https://cloudcustodian.io/docs/aws/examples/elbsslwhitelist.html`).

One policy that is highly recommended relates to the enabling of VPC flow logs in AWS (`https://cloudcustodian.io/docs/aws/examples/vpcflowlog.html`). Under this policy, any VPC in the current AWS region will be found that does not have flow logs enabled, and an email will be sent out asking the team to remediate them. VPC flow logs (`https://docs.aws.amazon.com/vpc/latest/userguide/flow-logs.html`) capture all traffic (or optionally, only accepted or denied traffic) that reach the network interfaces within a VPC and mean that low-level packet-sniffing traffic can be inspected for forensics and troubleshooting. You simply do not have the required visibility of the resources in your VPCs if you are not storing VPC flow logs in an S3 bucket or within CloudWatch logs. They are an essential bolt-on to any AWS VPC.

From an Azure perspective, the same level of effort has gone into the excellent examples, which can be found here: `https://cloudcustodian.io/docs/azure/gettingstarted.html`. Additionally, GCP has a wide range of examples to make adoption much smoother too, although they are marked as being in beta: `https://cloudcustodian.io/docs/gcp/gettingstarted.html`.

A reminder that every single remediation action that you attempt should be carefully tested in a laboratory before trying it on any valuable resources!

IAM Policies

Before leaving you to explore the exceptionally high-quality online examples, let's quickly look at an IAM example for some context about how Cloud Custodian interacts with other AWS resources. Within Listing 14.3 we can see how to detach a specific IAM policy if it is found to be attached to IAM roles. The obvious difference from our EC2 examples earlier is that we are using the `iam-role` resource type and not the `aws.ec2` resource. Also, note that we are explicitly listing the full Amazon Resource Name (ARN) including an AWS account number (123456789012 in this case) to make sure that we always deploy to the correct account and then detach the correct role.

Listing 14.3: Stop AWS Managed Policies Being Attached to Any Roles

```
policies:
- name: delete-an-insecure-iam-policy
  resource: iam-role
  filters:
  -type: has-specific-managed-policy
      value: specific-insecure-policy
  actions:
  -type: set-policy
      state: detached
      arn: arn:aws:iam::123456789012:policy/specific-insecure-policy
```

You might use a policy such as this one in Listing 14.3 because a legacy policy is being refactored or possibly because it is about to be deleted from multiple cloud accounts, and you do not want it used in the meantime, possibly for security reasons. You equally might be deprecating a service and want an automated cleanup of removing all access to it via IAM. Again, consider what suits you best and whether you want to execute such a policy within a Lambda function or via a `cron` job, for example.

A nice tip is that other than the `name:` entry (which names this Cloud Custodian policy), you could reverse the `actions` process simply. Think about it for a moment. To insist that this policy is attached to all IAM roles, you would simply change the `state:` entry to `attached` instead of `detached`. Again, test this carefully in case you lock yourself or other users out of your AWS accounts.

S3 Data at Rest

We will take a quick look at a storage policy next. The stalwart of AWS' storage services is S3, which offers highly available object storage for users and automation alike. When it comes to AWS' availability, a favorite marketing claim from AWS is this (`https://www.amazonaws.cn/en/s3/faqs`): "Amazon S3 is designed to provide 99.999999999% durability of objects over a given year.

This durability level corresponds to an average annual expected loss of 0.000000001% of objects. For example, if you store 10,000 objects with Amazon S3, you can on average expect to incur a loss of a single object once every 10,000,000 years." That is quite a claim, but AWS S3 has an excellent track record for data reliability. What we will see in Chapter 16, "AWS Cloud Storage," however, is that users struggle with protecting files stored on AWS S3 and need help to make sure that encryption is enabled.

You will not be surprised to discover that it is possible to enforce a setting so that all buckets are encrypted for data-at-rest security compliance using Cloud Custodian. In Listing 14.4 we are enforcing encryption but more specifically using the AES256 cipher, also known as Rijndael.

Listing 14.4: A Simple but Useful Policy for S3 Buckets

```
policies:
-name: s3-enforce-bucket-encryption
    resource: s3
    actions:
    -type: set-bucket-encryption
        crypto: AES256
        enabled: True
```

The policy is using the `s3` resource type this time and should need little explanation. You can also encrypt storage using AWS KMS keys (`https://docs.aws.amazon.com/AmazonS3/latest/userguide/UsingKMSEncryption.html`) so that only your custom-created secret will unencrypt the files.

NOTE **To enforce the policy shown in Listing 14.4, the custodian AWS user needs PutBucketEncryption as well as Read permission on S3 buckets.**

Generating Alerts

Although it is not particularly suited to Cloud Native tech, the example shown in Listing 14.5 shows how to trigger emails when policies spot something untoward. Developer teams usually prefer real-time messaging, so you would be better with ChatOps functionality (`https://www.atlassian.com/blog/software-teams/what-is-chatops-adoption-guide`), using Slack (`https://slack.com`) for example, for instant messages. This is quite also possible to set up with Cloud Custodian.

Listing 14.5: Fire Off Emails as an "Action" Should a Particular Policy Trigger a Match

```
actions:
  -type: notify
    template: default.html
    priority_header: 1
```

```
subject: "Root Login [custodian {{ account }} - {{ region }}]"
violation_desc: "AWS Console Root Login:"
action_desc: |
    "Please investigate if root access needs revoked."
to:
  -sysadmin@example.tld
transport:
  type: sqs
  queue: https://sqs.us-east-1.amazonaws.com/12345678900/cloud-custodian-mailer
  region: us-east-1
```

As Listing 14.5 demonstrates, it is possible to generate emails as "actions" and, by extension, also interact with ChatOps software. Cloud Custodian uses the `cloud-custodian-mailer` (`https://cloudcustodian.io/docs/tools/c7n-mailer.html`) to achieve this type of integration. The email templates can be a dynamic `jinja2` format, which allows for customization and creating a more useful message. These types of emergency notifications are critical to compliance monitoring and being informed when Cloud Custodian spots issues on a cloud estate.

On the `cloud-custodian-mailer` page there are also instructions on how to integrate with DataDog to fulfil real-time ChatOps requirements. When pushing messages out to Slack there is a simple-to-use example, as shown in Listing 14.6.

Listing 14.6: How to Integrate with Slack

```
-name: c7n-mailer-test
  resource: ebs
  filters:
 -Attachments: []
  actions:
  -type: notify
     slack_template: slack
     slack_msg_color: danger
     to:
       -slack://owners
       -slack://foo@bar.com
       -slack://#custodian-test
       -slack://webhook/#c7n-webhook-test
       -slack://tag/resource_tag
       -https://hooks.slack.com/services/T00000000/B00000000/XXXX
    transport:
      type: sqs
      queue: https://sqs.us-east-1.amazonaws.com/12345/mail-test
```

As you can see, the Slack example allows you to be able to set hashtags for labeling and set a custom color scheme to make sure that these types of alerts are noticed by all users who need to know that compliance has not been met for one reason or another. These notifications could also potentially be integrated with on-call engineer pagers in addition.

Cloud Custodian even makes light work of pushing data out to Splunk event collectors (`https://cloudcustodian.io/docs/tools/c7n-mailer.html#splunk-http-event-collector-hec`) so that you can ingest the data into a Security Information and Event Management (SIEM) system or make Security Operations Center (SOC) staff aware of the issues.

On the same page there are notes about how to deal with Microsoft Azure using Cloud Custodian and additionally how to create templates for your email so that the formatting is sane.

Summary

In this chapter, we looked at enforcing compliance as code across a number of different policies that the sophisticated Cloud Custodian can execute. The method of running scheduled tasks and their frequency is up to you; you might use a `cron` job or check for compliance via AWS Lambda functions, for example.

Thanks to the outstanding efforts made by Capital One developers in producing Cloud Custodian and its documentation, you should be able to get up and running relatively rapidly. That coupled with the logical policy language that the application uses makes for a formidable combination.

Do not forget either that the software is flexible enough to be applicable to multi-cloud environments, which means that transposing a consistent compliance posture across multiple cloud platforms should be easier to achieve.

As well as improving security, additionally you can keep your resources well organized, and a welcome side effect of doing so will be cutting down on your cloud estate's running costs.

CHAPTER 15

Cloud Auditing

Certain open source security tools focus specifically on one particular area, and others are more diverse. It is perfectly possible to audit multiple infrastructure components, whilst checking against a variety of detailed benchmarks, for no charge under the right licensing conditions.

As we saw in previous chapters, one set of criteria that is often used to audit systems and cloud platforms is from CIS Benchmarks (`https://www.cisecurity.org/cis-benchmarks`), where industry consensus offers a great deal of insight into how you might harden your infrastructure better.

In this chapter, we will look at three tools to assist with auditing: Lunar, Cloud Reports, and Prowler. Two of these tools focus on meeting rule definitions from CIS Benchmarks directly. We will begin with a sophisticated and diverse tool that is primed to cover multiple areas at once. These are some of the key areas that we have covered previously, so combining their coverage within one tool is a welcome proposition: container runtime security, hosts, and cloud platforms.

Runtime, Host, and Cloud Testing with Lunar

The first tool that we will look at is called Lunar (`https://github.com/lateralblast/lunar`). Although the tool is sophisticated enough to output Ansible code, to automatically assist with using its test results as Ansible playbooks, it has been created using shell scripts. The author unashamedly declares that coding is not necessarily his forte, and for compatibility with air-gapped systems, using shell scripts was the most logical approach. As we saw in Chapter 11, "Automated Host Security," Ansible has a relatively shallow learning curve and can provide sophisticated, automated configuration management.

You might be pleasantly surprised at how easy it is to get started with Lunar. There are just a couple of commands to run. Before we do that, though, let's look at some of its features.

Although we mentioned the CIS Benchmarks earlier, Lunar also pulls in its knowledge from other frameworks. However, when CIS Benchmarks is used, the author provides references within the codebase to help out as much as possible.

Unusually, it seems that Lunar can also make changes to a running system, but you are encouraged to avoid that unless you know exactly what is being changed. You have been warned! Instead, it is more sensible to use the auditing functionality and learn from the tool's findings. There is apparently a "backout" option for rewinding any changes that you make, but experienced admins will take heed from what the developer recommends for good reason. Downtime is never welcome, planned or otherwise. If you accidentally find yourself making changes, apparently pressing Ctrl+C will stop Lunar dead in its tracks. Reverting any changes already made might not be very easy, however.

With that caution in mind, we can look at the features that Lunar offers. Table 15.1 offers an insight into how diverse the tool is.

Table 15.1: The Many Areas of Coverage That Lunar Offers

PLATFORM/ SYSTEM/APPLICATION	AUDITING CAPABILITY
Docker	Detailed auditing across multiple criteria
AWS	In-depth multiservice auditing
Apache	Incomplete audits (work in progress)
Kubernetes	Incomplete audits (work in progress)
Operating systems	RHEL/CentOS 5, 6, 7; Scientific Linux; SLES 10, 11, 12; Debian; Ubuntu; Amazon Linux; Solaris 6, 7, 8, 9, 10, 11; macOS audits
Operating systems (work in progress)	FreeBSD, AIX, ESXi

As we can see, there is no doubt that Lunar boasts an exceptional range of coverage. Let's get it up and running.

Installing to a Bash Default Shell

We will use a Linux Mint laptop (based on Ubuntu 18.04) for the Lunar installation. As standard, Ubuntu has moved its default shell away from the venerable Bash to Dash to speed up boot times and lighten the load because Bash is brimming with features and a little more cumbersome. This means that when `/bin/sh` is called, `/bin/dash` is actually run instead of `/bin/bash`. It appears this does not play nicely with Lunar, so a simple fix is needed, as described in the following series of commands. Note that this may not apply to your system, so be careful, or potentially much of Lunar's functionality may not work on your machine if there is no default shell alteration. Reverse these changes after trying them if you do not want Bash as your default shell.

First, you can check that `/bin/sh` is just a symlink to Dash with this command:

```
$ ls -al /bin/sh
lrwxrwxrwx 1 root root 9 Aug  8 18:49 /bin/sh -> /bin/dash
```

As we can see, `/bin/sh` is just a symlink to `/bin/dash`.

We will temporarily delete the symlink from Dash to `/bin/sh` with this command:

```
$ rm /bin/sh
```

Next, we will re-create the symlink to point at Bash with this command:

```
$ ln -s /bin/bash /bin/sh
```

You could also globally change all references from `/bin/sh` to `/bin/bash` in the Lunar scripts if that seems less impactful.

Execution

We are all set to clone the Lunar GitHub repository and run Lunar next:

```
$ git clone https://github.com/lateralblast/lunar.git
```

Enter the `lunar` directory with the `cd` command, and in Listing 15.1 we can run the main shell script to generate the help output.

Listing 15.1: The Options That Lunar Can Support

```
$ cd lunar
$ ./lunar.sh -h

Usage: ./lunar.sh -[a|A|s|S|d|p|c|l|h|H|c|C|D|V|n] -[u] -[o] -[t]

-a: Run in audit mode (for Operating Systems- no changes made to system)
-A: Run in audit mode (for Operating Systems- no changes made to system)
    [includes filesystem checks which take some time]
```

```
-n: Output ansible code segments
-w: Run in audit mode (for AWS—no changes made to system)
-d: Run in audit mode (for Docker—no changes made to system)
-x: Run in recommendations mode (for AWS—no changes made to system)
-s: Run in selective mode (only run tests you want to)
-R: Print information for a specific test
-S: List all UNIX functions available to selective mode
-W: List all AWS functions available to selective mode
-D: List all Docker functions available to selective mode
-l: Run in lockdown mode (for Operating Systems- changes made to system)
-L: Run in lockdown mode (for Operating Systems- changes made to system)
    [includes filesystem checks which take some time]
-C: Show changes previously made to system
-c: Run docker-compose testing suite
    (runs lunar in audit mode without making changes)
-D: Run docker-compose testing suite
    (drops to shell in order to do more testing)
-o: Set docker OS or container name
-t: Set docker tag
-p: Show previously versions of file
-u: Undo lockdown (for Operating Systems—changes made to system)
-h: Display help
-H: Display usage
-V: Display version
-v: Verbose mode [used with -a and -A]
    [Provides more information about the audit taking place]
```

Here we can see `lockdown` options to make changes to systems; to preserve sanity, we will avoid those so that we do not make changes to the system. Instead, we will begin with a look at auditing operating systems, which is Linux in this case.

If we choose the lowercase `-a` switch for the script, it will not run all the exhaustive filesystem checks, whereas the `-A` switch would instead provide this functionality. Let's try that now with this command:

```
$ ./lunar.sh -a
```

The output of the command is extensive to say the least and completes with this summary:

```
Tests:      470
Passes:     191
Warnings:   279
```

Listing 15.2 shows a sample of the OS auditing output.

Listing 15.2: Operating System Audits, Heavily Abbreviated

```
Running:    In audit mode (no changes will be made to system)

Auditing:   OS
# SYSTEM INFORMATION:
Virtual:    LENOVO
Processor:  x86_64
Machine:    x86_64
Vendor:     LinuxMint
Name:       Linux
Version:    19
Update:     19
Checking:   Security Warning Message
Checking:   File permissions on /etc/issue
Secure:     File /etc/issue has correct permissions [1 Passes]
Checking:   Security message in /etc/issue
Warning:    No security message in /etc/issue [1 Warnings]
Checking:   File permissions on /etc/motd
Checking:   Notice:    File /etc/motd does not exist
Checking:   Security message in /etc/motd
Warning:    No security message in /etc/motd [2 Warnings]
Checking:   File permissions on /etc/issue.net
Secure:     File /etc/issue.net has correct permissions [2 Passes]
Checking:   Security message in /etc/issue.net
Warning:    No security message in /etc/issue.net [3 Warnings]
```

Here we see just the upper lines of the output generated. Other areas of the checks include PAM, squid, filesystem permission, NFS, apache2, SMB, tunable kernel parameters, syslog, system accounts, and password complexity policies, to name but a few. If you have worked with the CIS Benchmarks before, you will spot a number of familiar items that need to be hardened.

Let's look at the container runtime audits next. Running this type of audit is as simple as changing the command to use the following switch (Docker needs to be installed for this set of tests):

```
$ ./lunar.sh -d
```

Again, the output is impressive and completes without much of a wait. Some of the areas of coverage include the following:

- Checking for Linux kernel capabilities for running containers (including more privileged capabilities, such as `CAP_SYS_ADMIN`, `CAP_NET_ADMIN`, `CAP_SYS_MODULE`, and the like)
- Whether health checks configuration is present for containers
- Which logging level the Docker Engine is using
- Whether host-based networking is enabled

- Whether `auditd` is picking up the actions of the container runtime
- Whether the `root` filesystem is read-only

Again, CIS Benchmarks are put to good use here. If you search within the cloned repository directory locally by using the next command, you will see a number of references to CIS:

```
$ grep -R CIS *
```

This command produces lengthy output, including the following:

```
modules/audit_docker_security.sh:# Refer to Section(s) 5.4
Page(s) 132   CIS Docker Benchmark 1.13.0
modules/audit_docker_security.sh:# Refer to Section(s) 5.9
Page(s) 141   CIS Docker Benchmark 1.13.0
modules/audit_docker_security.sh:# Refer to Section(s) 5.12
Page(s) 146-7 CIS Docker Benchmark 1.13.0
modules/audit_docker_security.sh:# Refer to Section(s) 5.15
Page(s) 152-3  CIS Docker Benchmark 1.13.0
modules/audit_docker_security.sh:# Refer to Section(s) 5.16
Page(s) 154-5  CIS Docker Benchmark 1.13.0
```

This output is exceptionally useful because it translates into remediating issues much more easily. Visit the CIS website and download the benchmarks directly (`https://cisecurity.org/benchmark/docker`) to gain more insight into any discovered issues and find remediation tips there too. In Listing 15.3, we can see some sample output from running the excellent Lunar against our container runtime.

Listing 15.3: Container Runtime Auditing

```
Warning:  Traffic is allowed between containers [206 Warnings]
Checking: Docker daemon parameter iptables is unused and has value true
Secure:   Docker parameter iptables is unused [267 Passes]
Checking: Docker daemon parameter opt is used and has value encrypted
Warning:  Docker parameter opt is not used [207 Warnings]
Checking: Docker Logging
Checking: Docker daemon parameter log-level is unused and has value info
Secure:   Docker parameter log-level is unused [268 Passes]
Checking: Docker daemon parameter log-driver is used
Warning:  Docker parameter log-driver is not used [208 Warnings]
Checking: Docker daemon parameter log-opt is used
Warning:  Docker parameter log-opt is not used [209 Warnings]
```

The tool is comprehensive and does not fail to deliver from a runtime perspective either, with a significant number of checks summarized on the author's device as follows:

```
Tests:      1722
Passes:     1106
Warnings:   616
```

Cloud Auditing Against Benchmarks

To test against AWS, we need sufficient permissions attached to a role or user via a policy. Lunar offers some advice but does not provide a policy verbatim about exactly which permissions you will need to permit. You will need the AWS CLI tool installed locally. If you are not sure how to get this, the documentation can be found at `https://docs.aws.amazon.com/cli/latest/userguide/install-cliv2.html`. You may have had it installed to set up your credentials (with the `aws configure` command) previously.

Also, you need to fine-tune some rules, but Figure 15.1 shows a reasonable start.

Figure 15.1: Some of the permissions that your user/role will need in AWS, but not all

In Figure 15.1 we can see some read-only permissions. If you have not supplied the correct permissions, then certain checks will result in a permission-denied error of sorts.

There are two AWS modes to run Lunar in: recommendations mode and auditing mode. We will start with this "recommended" tests scan as follows:

```
$ ./lunar.sh -x
```

The output begins as follows:

```
Running:   In audit mode (no changes will be made to system)
Auditing:  AWS-Recommended Tests
# SYSTEM INFORMATION:
Virtual:   LENOVO
Processor: x86_64
Machine:   x86_64
Vendor:    LinuxMint
Name:      Linux
Version:   19
Update:    19
Checking:  EC2 Recommendations
```

We are then offered a number of useful suggestions such as tagging our security groups with recognizable names and pruning older EC2 snapshots. The checks include coverage of RDS, CloudWatch, RedShift, ElastiCache, Inspector, VPCs, security groups, DynamoDB, ELBs, and EC2. In Listing 15.4 we can see a sample of the output.

Listing 15.4: Redacted AWS Audits from Recommendations Mode

```
Warning:    AWS Security Group sg-0fXXXXXXX17 does not have a Name tag
            [7 Warnings]
Secure:     Number of Elastic IPs consumed is less than limit of 5
            [1 Passes]
Checking:   Elasticsearch Recommendations
Checking:   DynamoDB
Checking:   ELB Recommendations
Checking:   VPC Recommendations
Warning:    AWS VPC vpc-07c2XXXXXXb00 does not have a valid Name tag
            [8 Warnings]
```

Next, let's run "audit" mode over an AWS account and see the difference in output. We can do this using the following command:

```
$ ./lunar.sh -w
```

This time, the output is much more familiar and relates to CIS Benchmarks. Note that, at the time of writing, there seems to be a bug within the `lunar.sh` script with reference to the `-w` switch in the latest release. Once that bug is resolved, the sample output should again be as shown in Listing 15.5. There appears to be an issue with functions being disordered within the script.

Listing 15.5: Audit Mode Over an AWS Account

```
Secure:     Account XXXXXXXXXX has used AWS API credentials in the past
            90 days [11 Passes]
Secure:     Account XXXXXXXXX has rotated their AWS API credentials in
            the last 90 days [12 Passes]
Checking:   Password Policy
Secure:     The password policy has RequireUppercaseCharacters set to
            true [13 Passes]
Warning:    The password policy does not have RequireLowercaseCharacters
            set to true [7 Warnings]
Secure:     The password policy has RequireSymbols set to true
            [14 Passes]
Warning:    The password policy does not have RequireNumbers set to true
            [8 Warnings]
```

Because of the vast number of checks run in audit mode this time, the tool takes longer. If you want to select specific functions in AWS to check, use the `-W` switch to retrieve a list of available functions that you can choose from first. Once you've done so, you can then run Lunar using the `-s` switch to run in selective mode. Refer to Figure 15.1 to see the switches required for the other areas of coverage that the broad-reaching Lunar provides.

AWS Auditing with Cloud Reports

Now that we have looked at the uber-diverse Lunar, let's focus on a tool that deals only with AWS. Although this next tool is not focused on comparing its results with CIS Benchmarks, it is a valuable exercise to gain an understanding of the different output that varying tools provide.

There is a clever piece of software called Cloud Reports (`https://github.com/tensult/cloud-reports`) that will return shiny PDFs and HTML reports relating to your security posture. On its GitHub page there is a list of currently audited AWS services, according the AWS Well-Architected Framework best practices (`https://aws.amazon.com/architecture/well-architected`). Let's dive straight in and generate a report now.

You will need multiple Node packages available to you on the machine that will connect into AWS. Expect the packages shown in Listing 15.6; although there are many packages, they only use a little over 40MB of disk footprint. The command to use to install the packages on Debian derivatives is as follows:

```
$ apt install npm
```

Listing 15.6: Installing NodeJS on Debian Derivatives, Abbreviated

```
[. . .snip. . .] node-mime node-minimatch node-mkdirp node-mute-stream
node-node-uuid node-nopt node-normalize-package-data node-npmlog
node-once node-osenv node-path-is-absolute node-pseudomap node-qs
node-read node-read-package-json node-request node-retry node-rimraf
node-semver node-sha node-slide node-spdx-correct
node-spdx-expression-parse node-spdx-license-ids node-tar
node-tunnel-agent node-underscore node-validate-npm-package-license
node-which node-wrappy node-yallist nodejs nodejs-dev npm
```

The next task is to clone the repository from GitHub using this command:

```
$ git clone https://github.com/tensult/cloud-reports.git
```

Figure 15.2 shows the start of the build taking place, after we run the next command from within the `cloud-reports/` directory:

```
$ npm run build
```

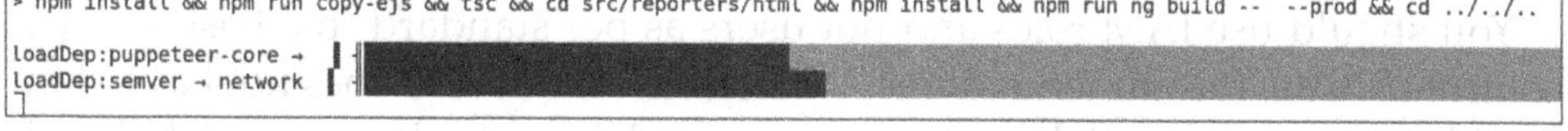

Kilo cloud-reports # npm run build
> cloud-reports@1.6.4 build /root/cloud-reports
> npm install && npm run copy-ejs && tsc && cd src/reporters/html && npm install && npm run ng build -- --prod && cd ../../..
loadDep:puppeteer-core →
loadDep:semver → network

Figure 15.2: The start of the Cloud Reports build process, courtesy of Node.js

You will need a modicum of patience to get through the build process, which includes downloading the Chromium Browser. If you become impatient, it is probably worth logging into AWS at this stage and getting ready to provide some credentials unless your machine is lightning fast. On a medium-spec laptop, it is probably going to take around 10 minutes to complete the build. The end of the process looks like the output in Figure 15.3.

```
> cloud-reports-final-report@0.1.0 ng /root/cloud-reports/src/reporters/html
> ng "build" "--prod"


Date: 2020-08-03T18:28:32.422Z
Hash: 935c40dfcb41e5395fae
Time: 80503ms
chunk {0} runtime.80ab492fe3d778817936.js (runtime) 1.41 kB [entry] [rendered]
chunk {1} main.2ff7df4a61ec467980c8.js (main) 718 kB [initial] [rendered]
chunk {2} polyfills.3581a49d7897af209067.js (polyfills) 61.7 kB [initial] [rendered]
chunk {3} styles.3b6045c8ab7f8185599d.css (styles) 55.8 kB [initial] [rendered]
Kilo cloud-reports # 
```

Figure 15.3: The end of the build process

For the purposes of this demonstration, we will create a new user called `cloud-reports` and attach an IAM policy directly to the user. For a nonproduction account, we can just brave the overly permissive ReadOnlyAccess to many of the AWS services that you will definitely want to fine-tune yourself in the future. Figure 15.4 shows List and Read permissions.

Allow (156 of 235 services) Show remaining 79		
Access Analyzer	**Full**: List, Read	All resources
Alexa for Business	**Full**: List **Limited**: Read	All resources
Amplify	**Limited**: List, Read	All resources
API Gateway	**Full**: Read	All resources
App Mesh	**Full**: List **Limited**: Read	All resources
Application Auto Scaling	**Full**: Read	All resources
Application Discovery	**Full**: List, Read	All resources

Figure 15.4: The IAM policy is very permissive, even as read-only, so be sure to tune it to your security needs.

To scrutinize the existing policy and create a customized policy afterward, you can visit the IAM page directly here:

```
https://console.aws.amazon.com/iam/home?region=us-east-
   1#/policies/arn:aws:iam::aws:policy/ReadOnlyAccess$jsonEditor
```

You should use IAM roles and not users as per standard role-based access control (RBAC) recommendations. AWS states that "a role does not have standard long-term credentials such as a password or access keys associated with it. Instead, when you assume a role, it provides you with temporary security credentials for your role session." Further information can be found at `https://docs.aws.amazon.com/IAM/latest/UserGuide/id_roles.html`.

Finally, we will run the CLI command from the `awscli` command to add our credentials. This step depends on how many AWS accounts you are using at the same time; for our needs we will just use `default` as the profile name as per this redacted command output:

```
$ cat ~/.aws/credentials
[default]
aws_access_key_id = AKIAYSXXXXXXXXRSPK
aws_secret_access_key = XXXXXXXXXXXXXXXXXXXXXX
```

Generating Reports

We are all set to run the tool and generate reports. That was an easy process, even if the build took a little while. To get started, enter the `default` profile name and use the following command, which creates a PDF named `scan_report.pdf`:

```
$ npm run scan -- --profile default
```

Make sure that you execute that file within the `cloud-reports/` directory and wait patiently for the AWS API to respond to an abundance of requests. Do not be too alarmed if, during the process, you see some errors related to `createPDF`; they appear to be innocuous, but if your scan fails, use the instructions that follow to output to HTML instead. Should you be unsure if the process is working, check the Last Used section in the Security Credentials tab to see which service the tool last accessed. It will show an AWS service name and an accessed time and date associated with it (under the Last Used column), as shown in Figure 15.5.

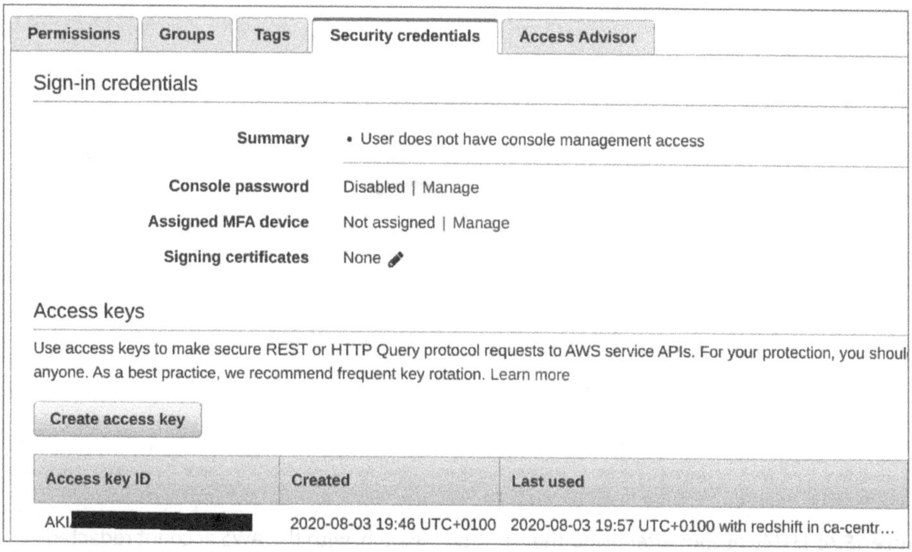

Figure 15.5: Check your progress via the Last Used column in IAM for your user or role.

Cloud Reports recommends running on an EC2 instance directly and, to speed things up, making sure that you have at least 2GB of RAM available. If, however, you do not want to scan everything and scan remotely, for example, then you can name specific AWS services with a command this way:

```
$ npm run scan -- -m s3,acm
```

You can also limit your regions, as follows:

```
$ npm run scan -- -m s3,acm -r us-east-1,eu-west-2
```

If you add `-f html` to your command, you will output to HTML format instead of to PDF. The same is true if you choose `csv` for a CSV file format. Adding `-o` will change the generated report name to something more familiar. If you have opted for HTML to avoid `createPDF` errors, just hit Ctrl+C when you are presented with some error output and look for the `scan_report.html` file. The command that generated the HTML report in Figure 15.5 was as follows:

```
$ npm run scan -- --profile default -m s3 -r eu-west-1 -d -u -f html
```

Note the `-d` and `-u` flags. The first is for debugging output to assist with troubleshooting, and the second is to reuse some of the data from previous scans in order to speed up the processing and then reduce the time it takes to produce a report. If you are frustrated with processing time because you are on a slow machine, start with as few services as possible.

The output from the tool is clean and easy to fathom. We can see in Figure 15.6 that we have only scanned AWS S3, and 21 buckets have been discovered. There are explanations in text about what Failed, Warning, Passed, and Info results mean, and there are a couple of things to note from this report.

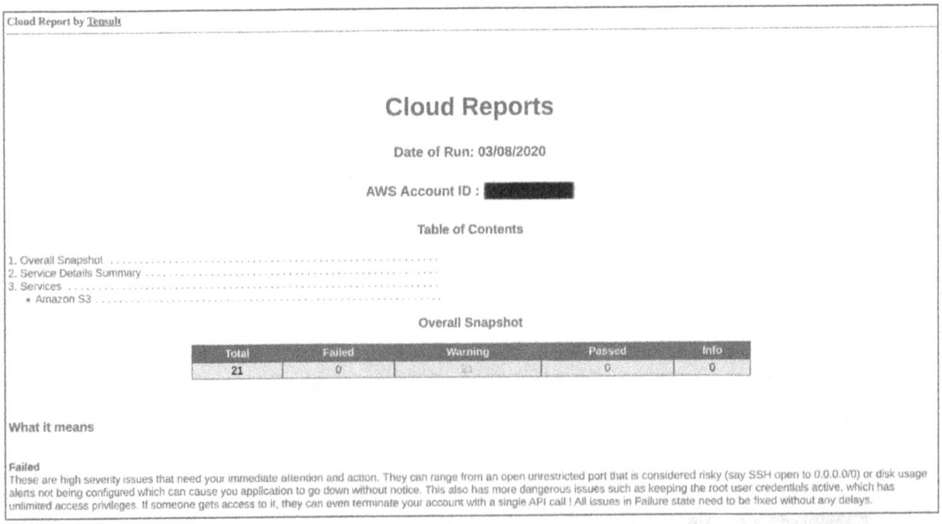
Cloud Report by Tensult
Cloud Reports
Date of Run: 03/08/2020
AWS Account ID : [redacted]
Table of Contents
1. Overall Snapshot
2. Service Details Summary
3. Services
• Amazon S3
Overall Snapshot
Total Failed Warning Passed Info
21 0 21 0 0
What it means
Failed
These are high severity issues that need your immediate attention and action. They can range from an open unrestricted port that is considered risky (say SSH open to 0.0.0.0/0) or disk usage alerts not being configured which can cause you application to go down without notice. This also has more dangerous issues such as keeping the root user credentials active, which has unlimited access privileges. If someone gets access to it, they can even terminate your account with a single API call ! All issues in Failure state need to be fixed without any delays.

Figure 15.6: HTML output after using the `-f html` switch, with the AWS account redacted

First, out of the 21 buckets, one has been identified as having public access permissions, which is usually not a good thing at all for data loss prevention (DLP). In this case, however, it is a bucket plugged into the AWS CloudFront CDN service with public assets such as website images, so it is safe. The other warnings are that the buckets do not have cost optimization enabled with "Bucket Life cycle rules are not configured," and we are dutifully told to "Configure life cycle rules" as a result.

EC2 Auditing

The report for EC2 on this particular AWS account is not quite as complimentary. The command used was as follows:

```
$ npm run scan -- --profile default -m s3 -r eu-west-1 -d -u -f html
```

For example, two keypairs were unused and in two different security groups: "SSH Port is open to entire world." What did pass with flying colors, however, were the MySQL, RDS, Oracle, and Postgres ports, which were all closed within the security groups.

The welcome detail from Cloud Reports is that the auditing is still very comprehensive, even though in that region there were not any running EC2 instances. In Figure 15.7 we can see just how thorough it is.

Overall Snapshot

Total	Failed	Warning	Passed	Info
16	2	2	12	0

Figure 15.7: A relatively empty region in the AWS account still produced 16 findings.

You can apparently also run Cloud Reports against Microsoft Azure, too. When it is processing the associated API data, it first sorts them into collectors, which look something like the JSON shown in Listing 15.7.

Listing 15.7: A Sample from the `Collector_Report.Json` File, Captured During the API Queries

```
{
  "aws.account": {
    "id": "XXXXXXXXXX"
  },
  "aws.ec2": {
    "reserved_instances": {
      "eu-west-1": [
        {
          "AvailabilityZone": "eu-west-1a",
          "Duration": 94608000,
          "End": "2013-03-31T23:59:59.000Z",
```

```
            "FixedPrice": 1032,
            "InstanceCount": 1,
            "InstanceType": "m1.large",
            "ProductDescription": "Linux/UNIX"
```

The next part of the process involves what are called *analyzers*. As you may have guessed, these rules, of sorts, check against known best practices on the cloud platform of choice and are then run past the data found by the collectors. Listing 15.8 shows the analyzer output for reference.

Listing 15.8: How an Analyzer File Is Constructed and Then Saved to the `Analyzer_Report.Json` File

```
"untagged_instances": {
      "type": "OperationalExcellence",
      "what": "Are there EC2 any instances without tags?",
      "why": "Tags help to follow security practices easily",
      "recommendation": "Recommended to add tags to all instances",
      "regions": {
        "eu-west-1": []
      }
    },
```

Finally, the reporters generate the file type from the analysis as you would expect.

The excellent Cloud Reports is well worth a look. The attention to detail is invaluable to assist in periodically auditing the security posture of your AWS accounts.

CIS Benchmarks and AWS Auditing with Prowler

Another outstanding tool designed to compare findings against CIS Benchmarks is called Prowler (`https://github.com/toniblyx/prowler`). It produces colorful output and can be used in a CI/CD pipeline for testing.

If you have the Python package installer available on your system (named `pip`), then you are all set to install Prowler by using this single command:

```
$ pip install awscli detect-secrets
```

On modern Debian derivatives, you should be able to install `pip` with this command:

```
$ apt install python3-pip
```

You will also need the `jq` package available for formatting JSON output more cleanly:

```
$ apt install jq
```

Next, clone the GitHub repository and enter the directory, as follows:

```
$ git clone https://github.com/toniblyx/prowler
Cloning into 'prowler'..
remote: Enumerating objects: 6, done.
remote: Counting objects: 100% (6/6), done.
remote: Compressing objects: 100% (6/6), done.
remote: Total 5012 (delta 0), reused 2 (delta 0), pack-reused 5006
Receiving objects: 100% (5012/5012), 1.58 MiB | 70.00 KiB/s, done.
Resolving deltas: 100% (3377/3377), done.

$ cd prowler
```

We will assume that our AWS credentials are present in the file `~/.aws/credentials.`

Or the preferred route is to export your AWS details with Environment Variables as so:

```
$ export AWS_ACCESS_KEY_ID="AXXXXXXXXXXX"
$ export AWS_SECRET_ACCESS_KEY="XXXXXXXXXXXXXXX"
$ export AWS_SESSION_TOKEN="XXXXXXXXXXXX"
```

For IAM permissions, we will need our user or role to have the following permissions attached from a policy or multiple policies. In this case, we will just attach the SecurityAudit and ViewOnlyAccess AWS Managed Policies. In Figure 15.8, we can see the UI version of listing these policies.

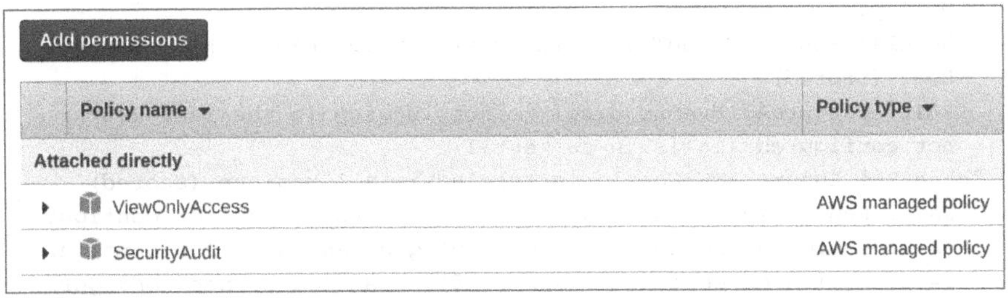

Figure 15.8: Prowler needs two IAM policies attached to an IAM user or role.

Run this command to execute Prowler:

```
$ ./prowler
```

The results are extremely comprehensive, just as the CIS Benchmarks are. We can see the start of the redacted output in Figure 15.9.

The auditing is not particularly speedy, because of the large number of checks made. As already mentioned, you will be offered insight into what each finding means, but it is important to cross-check with the CIS Benchmarks themselves to gain more information to assist with remediating issues.

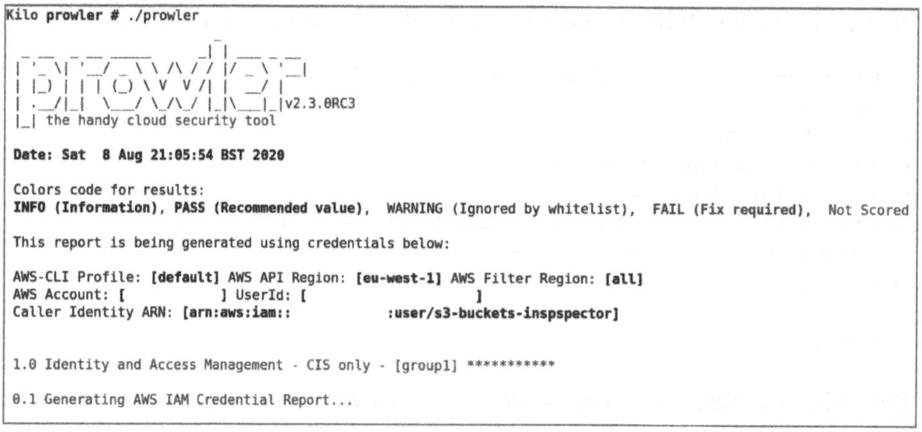
Kilo prowler # ./prowler
v2.3.0RC3
the handy cloud security tool
Date: Sat 8 Aug 21:05:54 BST 2020
Colors code for results:
INFO (Information), PASS (Recommended value), WARNING (Ignored by whitelist), FAIL (Fix required), Not Scored
This report is being generated using credentials below:
AWS-CLI Profile: [default] AWS API Region: [eu-west-1] AWS Filter Region: [all]
AWS Account: [ ] UserId: [ ]
Caller Identity ARN: [arn:aws:iam:: :user/s3-buckets-inspspector]
1.0 Identity and Access Management - CIS only - [group1] ***********
0.1 Generating AWS IAM Credential Report...

Figure 15.9: Prowler is firing up and ready to scan a (redacted) AWS account.

In Listing 15.9 we can see a sample of the output with the CIS item reference listed next to the findings.

Listing 15.9: A Sample of the Prowler Output

```
 2.2  [check22] Ensure CloudTrail log file validation is enabled (Scored)
        PASS! CaptureAllEvents trail in eu-west-1 has log file validation
        enabled
  2.3 [check23] Ensure the S3 bucket CloudTrail logs to is not publicly
        accessible (Scored)
        FAIL! check your acc-cloudtrail-events CloudTrail bucket ACL and
        Policy!
  2.4 [check24] Ensure CloudTrail trails are integrated with CloudWatch
        Logs (Scored)
        FAIL! CaptureAllEvents trail is not logging in the last 24h or
        not configured (it is in eu-west-1)
  2.5 [check25] Ensure AWS Config is enabled in all regions (Scored)
        FAIL! Region eu-north-1 has AWS Config disabled or not configured
        FAIL! Region ap-south-1 has AWS Config disabled or not configured
        FAIL! Region eu-west-3 has AWS Config disabled or not configured
```

The output for FAIL entries is always in red text for clarity, and PASS entries are in green text. The AWS account that the audit has run against is producing multiple FAIL warnings. The account is a laboratory account and not used in production, but the sheer volume of issues Prowler is capturing demonstrates nicely how many default settings you should change in order to harden your AWS accounts. In Listing 15.10 we can see more sample output.

Listing 15.10: More Auditing Output Information from Prowler

```
3.7  [check37] Ensure a log metric filter and alarm exist for
       disabling or scheduled deletion of customer created CMKs
       (Scored)
       FAIL! No CloudWatch group found for CloudTrail events
3.8  [check38] Ensure a log metric filter and alarm exist for S3
       bucket policy changes (Scored)
        FAIL! No CloudWatch group found for CloudTrail events
3.9  [check39] Ensure a log metric filter and alarm exist for
       AWS Config configuration changes (Scored)
       FAIL! No CloudWatch group found for CloudTrail events
```

Summary

In this chapter, we looked at three invaluable tools to help you secure your cloud estate. The first tool, Lunar, was incredibly diverse and gave instant feedback on Linux hosts, the container runtime, and AWS. Being written in shell scripts means it is more versatile than some other tools. Its output is thorough and provides useful information across all facets that it audits. Additionally, if you dare, it can also make changes to running systems in order to improve their security posture automatically.

The second tool we looked at, Cloud Reports, offers a useful perspective on multiple AWS services and presents findings in useful human-readable reports.

The third tool, the highly popular Prowler, also looked at AWS and focuses heavily on the recommendations found in CIS Benchmarks. The output, whether run once or periodically, is a real eye-opener on the level of work that you need to undertake to ensure that your AWS accounts are in good standing from a security perspective.

It would be prudent to run a combination of these tools against your hosts, container runtime, and AWS accounts to gain as much information as possible about the potential security flaws present. Creating a historical audit trail, in which periodic reports are archived, can be an excellent way of tracking changes to your infrastructure in addition.

CHAPTER 16

AWS Cloud Storage

Attackers target cloud systems around the clock and often focus on cloud storage. They tend to take advantage of misconfigurations thanks to the fact that there are nuanced configuration settings that are not immediately obvious. Although this chapter focuses on AWS specifically, such issues are far from just being an AWS problem, and Azure and GCP, for example, require similar levels of prudence and attention paid to misconfigurations and overly permissive access settings.

On AWS, the dominant cloud platform, storage repositories are called *buckets* in relation to the AWS S3 service. Buckets have what you might call parent permissions relating to the entire bucket, and it is possible to set varying levels of access to that upper level of each bucket.

However, it is also possible to get caught out, more so until recent improvements made by AWS were made available, because some of the child assets within buckets, called *objects* in S3 terms, can inherit different permissions.

In this chapter, we will look at ways of auditing where misconfiguration problems might exist within AWS S3 buckets to help with your cloud storage's security posture.

Buckets

We will begin by looking at software called S3 Inspector (`https://github.com/clario-tech/s3-inspector`). It has a relatively simple raison d'etre: to programmatically list your AWS S3 buckets, note whether they are publicly accessible, and then display any URLs that are pointing at them. Consider that simple statement from the perspective of an attacker. It is possible to promptly enumerate storage resources and their weaknesses with ease.

To install S3 Inspector, start by creating a suitable IAM role or user, with a policy, namely, `AmazonS3ReadOnly`. Figure 16.1 shows what that looks like with Programmatic Access chosen for a new user in the AWS Console.

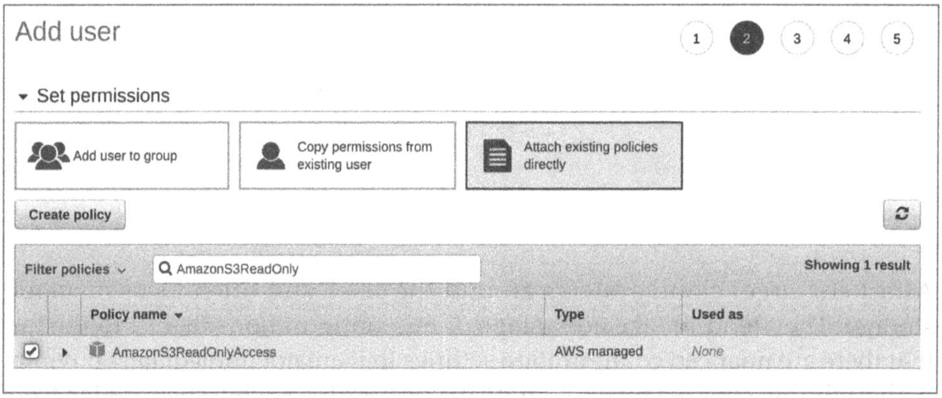

Figure 16.1: You should only give S3 Read access to S3 Inspector for obvious reasons because it is all it requires.

Following the principle of least privilege, we have chosen the minimum permissions for S3 Inspector and attached the relevant policy to a user or role to suit our needs. Using the managed AWS policy (AmazonS3ReadOnly), you might want to start with a test against a nonproduction account first, but as it only contains read-only permissions, you should be comforted by their innocuous nature.

Next, clone the S3 Inspector GitHub repository with this command:

```
$ git clone https://github.com/clario-tech/s3-inspector.git
Cloning into 's3-inspector'.
remote: Enumerating objects: 145, done.
remote: Total 145 (delta 0), reused 0 (delta 0), pack-reused 145
Receiving objects: 100% (145/145), 157.12 KiB | 160.00 KiB/s, done.
Resolving deltas: 100% (67/67), done.
```

We can now enter that directory and run the tool against our AWS S3 buckets using these commands:

```
$ cd s3-inspector/
$ python s3inspector.py
```

TIP **If you are struggling with getting Python running correctly, some online searching should help. For Debian derivatives, try the Hitchhiker's Guide to Python (`https://docs.python-guide.org/starting/install3/linux`).**

After running the command: `python s3inspector.py` we see the output in Listing 16.1.

Listing 16.1: You Can Choose Profiles to Run S3 Inspector Against

```
/usr/share/python-wheels/requests-2.18.4-py2.py3-none-any.whl/
requests/__init__.py:80: RequestsDependencyWarning:
urllib3 (1.23) or chardet (3.0.4) doesn't
match a supported version!
Collecting termcolor
  Downloading https://files.pythonhosted.org/packages/8a/48/
  a76be51647[. . .snip. . .]/termcolor-1.1.0.tar.gz
Building wheels for collected packages: termcolor
  Running setup.py bdist_wheel for termcolor . done
  Stored in directory: /root/.cache/pip/wheels/7c/06/
  54/[. . .snip. . .]aee85f68b4b0c5ab2c6
Successfully built termcolor
Installing collected packages: termcolor
Successfully installed termcolor-1.1.0
Enter your AWS profile name [default]:
```

As we can see in Listing 16.1, you are able to change your AWS profile name in the `~/.aws/credentials` file to choose multiple AWS login profiles. In our case, we just choose Default by pressing Enter.

In Listing 16.2, we can see the redacted output of what the simple, but invaluable, S3 Inspector has discovered.

Listing 16.2: The Results from Scanning an AWS Account

```
Found credentials in shared credentials file: ~/.aws/credentials
____________________
Bucket XXXXXXXXX: Not public
Location: None(probably Northern Virginia)
____________________
Bucket XXXXXXXXX: Not public
Location: None(probably Northern Virginia)
____________________
```

```
Bucket XXXXXXXXX: Not public
Location: EU
--------------------------------
Bucket XXXXXXXXX: Not public
Location: EU
--------------------------------
Bucket XXXXXXXXX: Not public
Location: EU
--------------------------------
Bucket XXXXXXXXX: Not public
Location: None(probably Northern Virginia)
--------------------------------
Bucket XXXXXXXXX: PUBLIC!
Location: EU
Permission: readable & permissions readable by Everyone
URLs:
https://XXXXXXXXX.s3.amazonaws.com
http://XXXXXXXXX.s3.amazonaws.com
https://XXXXXXXXX.amazonaws.com/XXXXXXXXX
http://XXXXXXXXX.amazonaws.com/XXXXXXXXX
--------------------------------
Bucket XXXXXXXXX: Not public
Location: eu-west-1
--------------------------------
Bucket XXXXXXXXX: Not public
Location: None(probably Northern Virginia)
--------------------------------
Bucket terraform-state-XXXXXXXXX: Not public
Location: eu-west-1
```

With a little scrutiny, the output is easy to fathom, as shown in Figure 16.2, where we are just focusing on the public findings.

```
----------------------------------------
Bucket      : PUBLIC!
Location: EU
Permission: readable & permissions readable by Everyone
URLs:
https://     .s3.amazonaws.com
http://    .s3.amazonaws.com
https://s3.amazonaws.com/
http://s3.amazonaws.com/
----------------------------------------
```

Figure 16.2: Redacted output from the same results as Listing 16.1, focusing on the main issue

Although the content is redacted, you can see how useful the output of a simple tool like this can be when run on a periodic schedule or in some kind of per-build CI/CD pipeline process to check for public buckets.

Native Security Settings

As mentioned, in recent years AWS has made a number of key improvements in the security of its S3 service. In the left column in Figure 16.3, you can see a warning that objects within S3 buckets can be public and that permissions are independent of the security settings of the bucket itself.

Objects can be public	EU (Ireland)	Sep 15, 2010 10:15:52 AM GMT+0100
Objects can be public	EU (Ireland)	Sep 15, 2010 10:21:44 AM GMT+0100
Objects can be public	EU (Ireland)	Feb 2, 2011 9:59:18 AM GMT+0000

Figure 16.3: The top-level listing in the AWS Console of S3 buckets reminds you that objects can be public.

Additionally, on the same screen is an orange Public icon next to buckets that allow public access to draw your attention to them further. At the top of the list of buckets there is now an Edit Public Access Settings option to click. Clearly, with these extra warnings and tools AWS has made the effort to improve the perception of the S3 service's security and also to educate users of the service's inherent configuration dangers. The AWS site states that "Public access is granted to buckets and objects through access control lists (ACLs), bucket policies, access point policies, or all."

Over time this is one element that has led to confusion and misconfiguration of AWS buckets, which has resulted in successful attacks. After clicking Edit Public Access Settings in the S3 section of the AWS Console, we are greeted with the dialog box shown in Figure 16.4. These settings are unique to an individual AWS account; so if you have multiple accounts, within an AWS Organization, for example, you must check each account for these options. AWS encourages you to start with a "default deny" approach to all S3 resources and then carefully open up individual buckets or objects that must be public to operate correctly.

For clarity, as shown in Figure 16.4, you are offered the ability to make a single sweeping change to ensure that all public access options are blocked, or as listed in Table 16.1, you can fine-tune each of the settings.

As Table 16.1 demonstrates, the powerful access controls that AWS offers add a level of complexity to securing your files. When in doubt, blocking all access and working your way through the objects that you intend to make publicly accessible is really the only sensible, pragmatic approach to be absolutely certain you have achieved what is required.

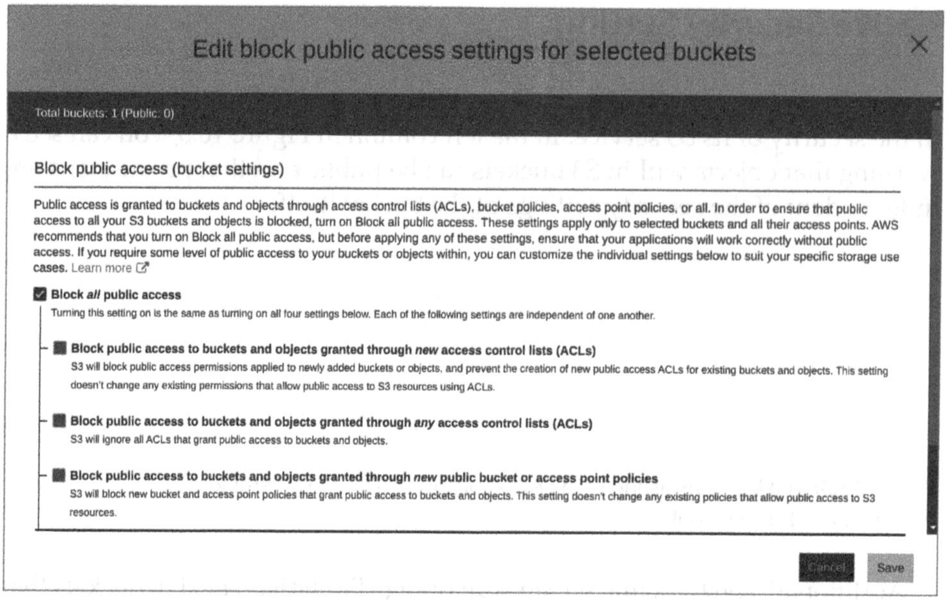

Figure 16.4: There are relatively new Edit Public Access Settings options now in AWS S3.

Table 16.1: Public Access Settings for S3 Buckets and Objects

SECURITY OPTION	PURPOSE
Block All Public Access	Effectively chooses all the options below with a single change. Useful for commercial data so you are certain that none of the settings has been missed.
Block Public Access To Buckets And Objects Granted Through New Access Control Lists (Acls)	Ensures that access is denied for newly added buckets and objects. Existing resources will not be changed. This maintains compatibility with apps relying on public access but can enable private use of some data.
Block Public Access To Buckets And Objects Granted Through Any Access Control Lists (Acls)	Blocks access that is permitted by ACLs. Handy to avoid mistakes if you are certain that you want settings to be private.
Block Public Access To Buckets And Objects Granted Through New Public Bucket Or Access Point Policies	New buckets and access point policies won't be allowed to be public.
Block Public And Cross-Account Access To Buckets And Objects Through Any Public Bucket Or Access Point Policies	Ignore public access for any bucket or access point policies. Useful to fine-tune cross-account access.

To assist users further, AWS has detailed documentation that, among other topics, helps with our understanding of the definition of concepts like *public*, for example. The docs (`https://docs.aws.amazon.com/AmazonS3/latest/dev/access-control-block-public-access.html#access-control-block-public-access-policy-status`) are worth a read to help you be certain that you are clear about what you are trying to achieve by loosening rules for access.

There are also detailed API docs (`https://docs.aws.amazon.com/cli/latest/reference/s3api/put-public-access-block.html`) available that help clear up any misconceptions that users might have. For example, one such warning is as follows: "If the PublicAccessBlock configurations are different between the bucket and the account, Amazon S3 uses the most restrictive combination of the bucket-level and account-level settings." You are encouraged to tread carefully before making changes and potentially opening up unwelcome access to nefarious visitors.

Automated S3 Attacks

With the potentially devastating brand damage that can be inflicted when data loss prevention (DLP) controls fail a business, not forgetting the commercial value of some of the information held within S3 buckets, it is no wonder that attackers pay close attention to them. The incentives for attackers to extort funds from commercial victims and individuals alike, or sell information on to interested parties, are obvious. The attraction of targeting individuals is often for the purposes of identity theft. Sadly, there are simply too many examples to list all the high-profile data breaches in recent years, but there are so many that the list is extensive.

Let's look at another simple tool, one that goes a step further. This tool will attempt to retrieve objects it finds in S3 buckets that are publicly accessible.

The clever, lightweight tool in question is called S3Scanner (`https://github.com/sa7mon/S3Scanner`). You can clone it as follows:

```
$ git clone https://github.com/sa7mon/S3Scanner.git
Cloning into 'S3Scanner'.
remote: Enumerating objects: 9, done.
remote: Counting objects: 100% (9/9), done.
remote: Compressing objects: 100% (7/7), done.
remote: Total 1088 (delta 3), reused 4 (delta 2), pack-reused 1079
Receiving objects: 100% (1088/1088), 225.58 KiB | 33.00 KiB/s, done.
Resolving deltas: 100% (634/634), done.

$ cd S3Scanner/
```

The tool is written in Python and easily installed. After cloning the repository and entering the directory, enter the following command:

```
$ pip install -r requirements.txt
```

After some packages are installed as per those shown in the `requirements.txt` file, listed here, we are all set:

```
awscli
pytest-xdist
coloredlogs
boto3
requests
```

Next, we need to add some S3 bucket names to a file for the scanner to check. You can list the buckets using the various formats shown in Table 16.2.

Table 16.2: Ways to List S3 Buckets in S3Scanner

FORMAT	EXAMPLE
Bucket name	*bucketname*
Domain name	*something*.tld or *subdomain.something*.tld
Fully qualified S3 bucket name	*bucketname*.s3-us-west-1.amazonaws.com
Bucket:AWS region	*bucketname:region*

For simplicity we can just use the *bucketname:region* approach, as shown here (real bucket names are redacted because you should keep them secret unless they are public for a reason):

```
bucket:s3-eu-west-1
anotherbucket:s3-eu-west-1
```

Having added a bucket to the file `names.txt`, we can run through it for processing and then expect to see the results in a file called `results.txt`.

The command to run S3Scanner is as follows. Ensure that you have your AWS credentials in place before you begin (if not, run the `aws configure` command first):

```
$ python s3scanner.py --out-file results.txt names.txt
```

The results file now has two bucket names present and this redacted entry, which looks like there is a hit for public access on the top line:

```
[found]: bucket | 27169172 bytes | ACLs: {'authUsers': [], 'allUsers':
['READ', 'READ_ACP']}
[found]: anotherbucket | 852221073 bytes | ACLs: {'authUsers': [],
'allUsers': []}
```

As the developer of S3Scanner says in the docs, the tool will take care of the findings, but it is up to you to interpret them into useful information. The second line in the previous output is a private bucket, and the top entry is what to expect when a public bucket is found. The tool will look for `list` and `write` settings for objects and for ACL access. You are warned that even if a bucket returns an access denied error, thanks to ACL settings, it does not necessarily mean that the bucket cannot be read from (and possibly written to). In some cases, however, there is a chance that you can list ACLs but not be allowed to read or write to a bucket. You can see why users make mistakes when setting up AWS S3 configuration; it can be a minefield for novice users. The intricacies of ACLs can be found here if you want to learn more: `https://docs.aws.amazon.com/AmazonS3/latest/userguide/acl-overview.html`.

Let's add a simple switch to the excellent S3Scanner to get a directory listing of the public bucket that we have just found:

```
$ python s3scanner.py --list --out-file results.txt names.txt
```

If we go into the `list-buckets/` directory, you might be somewhat surprised to see a `.txt` file prepended with the name of the S3 bucket. Listing 16.3 shows a sample of the findings.

Listing 16.3: Without Breaking a Sweat, S3Scanner Has Directory-Listed All the Contents of a Public S3 Bucket

```
2011-06-30 10:17:27 423 blog10.png
2011-06-30 10:29:38 245 blog11.png
2011-06-30 08:10:30 423 blog9.png
2011-06-28 15:27:24 473 bofh.png
2011-06-30 10:17:28 473 bofh2.png
2011-06-30 10:29:38 284 bofh3.png
2011-06-05 15:12:48 709 bold.png
```

The directory listing feature is impressive. Let's run the tool next with the intention of downloading all the contents of the bucket locally as if you were an attacker stealing data:

```
$ python s3scanner.py --dump --out-file results.txt names.txt
```

The output while the tool is running is as follows:

```
[found]: s3cdn | 27169172 bytes | ACLs: {'authUsers': [], 'allUsers':
['READ', 'READ_ACP']}
2020-08-08 12:23:25        [found]: bucket—Attempting to dump.
this may take a while.
```

If we look inside the `buckets/` directory, there is now a subdirectory named after the public bucket name. And, low and behold, there are the files from the public S3 bucket stored on the local machine.

For a different deployment approach, if you want to use the Dockerfile to build a container to run S3Scanner, you can find it in the repository; it is listed in Listing 16.4.

Listing 16.4: The Dockerfile for S3Scanner If You Want to Go Down the Container Route

```
FROM python:3-alpine
COPY . /app
WORKDIR /app
RUN pip install -r requirements.txt
ENTRYPOINT ["python", "s3scanner.py"]
```

Just build the image in the same way as usual but from the S3Scanner remote repository URL:

```
$ docker build -t s3scanner https://github.com/sa7mon/S3Scanner.git
```

To run the container, you need to pass the AWS credentials as environment variables. Note as well that we are mounting a volume to the current working directory:

```
$ docker run -e AWS_ACCESS_KEY_ID="AKIAYXXXXXXWE" \
-e AWS_SECRET_ACCESS_KEY="wi30XXXXXXXnjYOLr8yQAL" \
-v $(pwd):/data s3scanner–out-file /data/results.txt /data/names.txt
```

The output is just as expected and the same as the Python approach:

```
[found]: bucket | 27169172 bytes | ACLs: {'allUsers':
['READ', 'READ_ACP'], 'authUsers': []}
```

Storage Hunting

Another approach that piques many people's interest is using a bone fide website to hunt for exposed storage. A website called GrayhatWarfare (`https://buckets.grayhatwarfare.com`), which was set up to search the internet for interesting files, is worth looking at in detail.

As mentioned earlier, the list of high-profile victims of sensitive files being exposed via misconfigurations of storage permissions is too lengthy to list. However, that said, to help educate developers, and indeed users of all kinds, there is a repository (`https://github.com/nagwww/s3-leaks`) that lists some S3 bucket leaks, and GrayhatWarfare references that repository as one of the reasons why its website was created.

In that repository, you can see some horror stories. Scanned passports, sensitive tax information, Social Security numbers, credit reports, driver licenses, and many other types of information have been leaked in the past. It also includes commercially sensitive data.

Before we take a quick look at the GrayhatWarfare website, note that the developer hopes, time permitting, to add exposed internet-connected cameras and internet of things (IoT) to the search functionality in the future.

In Figure 16.5, we can see the GrayhatWarfare splash page, visible when you first visit.

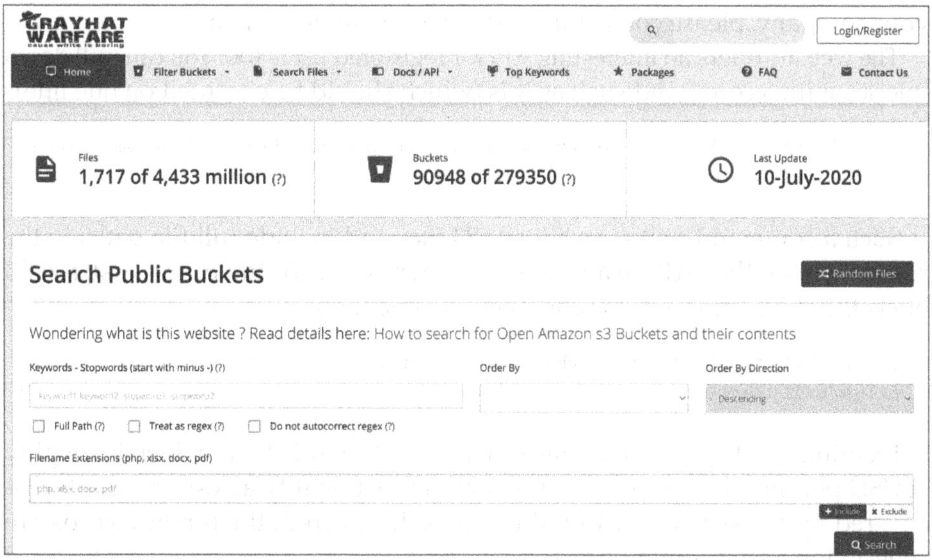

Figure 16.5: GrayhatWarfare is an excellent resource for learning about storage issues.

As we can see in Figure 16.5, apparently 1,717 files of 4,433 million have been tagged as being of interest. If you navigate up to the top menu, pull down Filter Buckets, and select Random Buckets, you can grab a list of random S3 buckets.

This produces a list of S3 buckets that you can visit; this list contains, at the time of the last update (the top right of Figure 16.5 in this case), publicly exposed files. In Figure 16.6 we can see the random list of buckets.

Figure 16.6: Public files discovered in S3 buckets

The site asks you to sign up to become a registered user to see the directory listings. Of course, the tools earlier in the chapter would offer insight too. There is a code of ethics when it might involve sensitive files, and the site states, "We exclude of course, sensitive buckets that some person or organization asked us to remove." The site also says, "The purpose of this website is to raise awareness on the open buckets issue. If you see any files or buckets that harm you or your company, please contact us so that we can remove them."

The website offers an interesting API for registered users too. You can pull down queries with a command such as this (which should be executed on one line):

```
$ curl https://buckets.grayhatwarfare.com/api/v1/files/mp3?access_token=
{apiKey}&full-path=1
```

Such a command will search for MP3 files and include full file paths in the response. Another API example is to generate a CSV file of the first 100 S3 buckets held (again, run this command on one line):

```
$ curl https://buckets.grayhatwarfare.com/api/v1/bucket/5/
files/0/100?access_token={apiKey}&keywords=csv
```

Premium packages, at the time of writing, start at 25EUR, which is roughly 30USD per month, and provide full search functionality across any assets discovered by the service. Within those files discovered, the top keywords are collected in a list for reference, too.

It is well worth taking a few minutes to check whether any of your important data has been leaked from S3 buckets via the site. And, for your organization, you could do worse than automate checks through API calls to periodically ensure that your data is secure.

Summary

In this chapter, we extolled the virtues of securing your cloud storage. There is simply no room for complacency when it comes to securing important files that are stored in the cloud.

We looked at two Open Source tools initially. The first, S3 Inspector, showed how to enumerate AWS S3 buckets that were marked as "public" quickly, and we saw that such a simple process could be integrated into CI/CD pipeline tests potentially with relative ease.

The second tool, S3Scanner, went a little further. Not only did the tool enumerate any buckets marked as public, but it offered a directory listing of any buckets that were discovered. Additionally, the tool also offered functionality to then download any discovered assets as would be the case when data was stolen.

Finally, we looked at a paid-for service that collates a list of publicly available files that users might query. And, without a fee, the service can help you search for the names of public S3 buckets, which could be inspected further using tools mentioned earlier in the chapter for testing purposes.

The straightforward, unequivocal message about cloud storage that has been conveyed in this chapter should be crystal clear. If you do not want your precious files to end up on the dark web or appearing in Google search indexes, you must make sure that you fully understand the ramifications of adjusting the potentially confusing and nuanced access permissions on your cloud storage. Take some time to get the permissions correct in order to protect your valuable data assets.

Part

IV

Advanced Kubernetes and Runtime Security

As Kubernetes is now such a pervasive feature of most Cloud Native deployments, it makes sense to delve into its security more deeply. While we've already covered some tools you might use to assess the security of a cluster, over the next four chapters we're going to take a deeper look at this topic.

We'll start by focusing on how an attacker might look at a cluster from an external perspective and the key configuration items to look for. Then we'll look at some of the major topics in ensuring that your clusters are operating securely and that attackers will have a hard time in exploiting them.

In This Part

CHAPTER 17

Kubernetes External Attacks

When assessing the security of any system, one of the first points to be considered is the "threat model" you'll be thinking about. Different groups of attackers have different capabilities and motivations, so when you're thinking about what controls are needed, it's important to think about what they have access to.

One of the most basic common threat models is that of the external attacker. Attackers in this category are typically looking at remotely available starting points, such as listening network services, and have no existing access to the system that they're attempting to compromise.

So when we're thinking about securing Kubernetes systems, it makes sense to first look at the attack surface available to these external attackers, before moving on to consider more advanced threat models. Kubernetes clusters can have a number of listening network ports, and several of these are susceptible to attack, if incorrectly configured.

This chapter will look at each of the main ports used by Kubernetes clusters in turn from an attacker's perspective, showing what kinds of attacks are possible via that service. Understanding the attacker's approach is an important element of security, as the techniques can be used by defenders to test the systems they've built and also to improve security detection and response techniques.

The Kubernetes Network Footprint

To assess the network attack surface of a Kubernetes cluster, we can use a port scanner like `nmap`. The results for scanning a Kubernetes cluster are likely to be quite variable, depending on the distribution in use. For the purposes of demonstration we'll use a `kubeadm` (`kubernetes.io/docs/reference/setup-tools/kubeadm/`) cluster as it presents a fairly standard configuration without too many additional features. For a `kubeadm` 1.18 cluster, the open ports could look like this:

```
Not shown: 65527 closed ports
PORT      STATE SERVICE
22/tcp    open  ssh
179/tcp   open  bgp
2379/tcp  open  etcd-client
2380/tcp  open  etcd-server
5473/tcp  open  apsolab-tags
6443/tcp  open  sun-sr-https
10250/tcp open  unknown
10256/tcp open  unknown
```

From this output we can see ports belonging to some of the key Kubernetes services. The most important are these:

6443/TCP: The API Server Port This is the core of any Kubernetes cluster. It presents a REST API and manages communications between the other components of the cluster and also handles requests from users.

The API server listening port can vary depending on the distribution used; common choices are `443/TCP`, `6443/TCP`, and `8443/TCP`. Because the API server is a standard HTTP API, it can be assessed and attacked using any tooling that works with web services.

2379/TCP & 2380/TCP: The etcd Ports Etcd (`https://etcd.io`) is the main key-value datastore for most Kubernetes clusters. Earlier versions presented a standard HTTP API; however, more recent versions have moved to gRPC for communications. The two ports showing externally in the port scan are for client-server and server-server communications, respectively.

10250/TCP: The kubelet Port This is the kubelet that manages the container runtime (such as Docker) used to launch containers on the host. The kubelet won't always run on master cluster nodes, but it will always be running on cluster worker nodes.

As we'll see from the rest of this chapter, an attacker who is able to exploit vulnerabilities in any of these ports is likely to gain privileged access to cluster nodes, or the entire cluster. Mitigating the risks of misconfiguration is generally a matter of ensuring that each component is correctly configured when the cluster is established and confirming that this secure starting point does not change over time.

Attacking the API Server

From an attacker's perspective, the API server is the main target, as control of this service would allow for full control of the cluster. By default, Kubernetes allows only a limited level of access without authentication; however, it is possible for the API server to be misconfigured to allow attackers additional access.

NOTE **Examples of misconfigured API servers can be seen on services like Shodan** (`unit42.paloaltonetworks.com/misconfigured-and-exposed-container-services/`) **and Binary Edge** (`blog.binaryedge.io/2019/06/06/new-module-and-type-kubernetes/`)**. The latter, in particular, makes it possible to find Kubernetes clusters that allow unauthenticated access to the API server by using a search term of** `kubernetes.auth_required:false`**.**

API Server Information Discovery

Once an open port that appears to be running a Kubernetes API server has been located, the first step in most attackers' methodologies is to fingerprint it (`owasp.org/www-project-web-security-testing-guide/latest/4-Web_Application_Security_Testing/01-Information_Gathering/02-Fingerprint_Web_Server`) to positively identify the service running.

Attackers do this to allow them to choose specific exploits that are known to affect the running software, and from a defensive perspective, it's generally a good idea to avoid disclosing this kind of information, to make the attacker's job harder.

Most Kubernetes clusters make the process of identification fairly simple as they have identifying information in their TLS certificates and also make known paths available to unauthenticated users. Using `nmap` it's possible to retrieve the certificate information from the API server:

```
nmap -v -n -sTC -p 6443 --script +ssl-cert [IP]
```

The output from this command will include the CN and SAN fields, which can be used to confirm that a Kubernetes API server is running on this port, as shown in Listing 17.1.

Listing 17.1: Port Scan of Kubernetes API Server

```
PORT     STATE SERVICE
6443/tcp open  sun-sr-https
| ssl-cert: Subject: commonName=kube-apiserver
| Subject Alternative Name: DNS:k8smaster, DNS:kubernetes,
 DNS:kubernetes.default, DNS:kubernetes.default.svc,
 DNS:kubernetes.default.svc.cluster.local,
IP Address:10.96.0.1, IP Address:192.168.41.100
| Issuer: commonName=kubernetes
| Public Key type: rsa
| Public Key bits: 2048
| Signature Algorithm: sha256WithRSAEncryption
| Not valid before: 2020-08-24T16:25:17
| Not valid after:  2021-08-24T16:25:17
| MD5:   6798 802d ee67 d020 1b94 54de 9e97 4f01
| SHA-1: 518d f120 ecf7 fd88 b687 42e4 3eb0 1d6a cf97 42f2
```

In addition to the information available from the TLS certificate, there are also some paths that are typically available that are unauthenticated.

The most useful of these is the `/version` endpoint, which provides information about the Kubernetes version in use and the platform architecture, as shown in Listing 17.2.

Listing 17.2: Retrieving Version Information from the Kubernetes API Server

```
curl -k https://192.168.41.100:6443/version
{
  "major": "1",
  "minor": "18",
  "gitVersion": "v1.18.8",
  "gitCommit": "9f2892aab98fe339f3bd70e3c470144299398ace",
  "gitTreeState": "clean",
  "buildDate": "2020-08-13T16:04:18Z",
  "goVersion": "go1.13.15",
  "compiler": "gc",
  "platform": "linux/amd64"
}
```

Avoiding API Server Information Disclosure

The best way to reduce the risk of attackers fingerprinting clusters via the API server is to restrict access to the port at a network level. Avoid putting Kubernetes clusters directly onto the internet, and for internal deployments consider, restricting access to the API server to specific sets of whitelisted source

IP addresses. The set of systems whitelisted for access will depend on how the cluster is managed. Where deployments are handled using a CI/CD system (such as Jenkins), it may be possible to limit API server access to those hosts and jump host(s) used by systems administrators for administering the cluster.

It is also possible to remove unauthenticated access to API server endpoints by setting the `--anonymous-auth` flag to false in the API server static manifest file (`/etc/kubernetes/manifests/kube-apiserver.yaml`); however, this can have the effect of blocking some monitoring tools that make use of unauthenticated access to operate.

Exploiting Misconfigured API Servers

Where an API server has been misconfigured to allow anonymous access to sensitive paths, exploiting this should be relatively simple. The `kubectl` tool can be configured to access a specific API server from the command line.

For this to work, there are a couple of options that need to be specified:

```
--insecure-skip-tls-verify
```

This allows the user to trust unverified certificates. Alternatively, to install the files for the private certificate authority used, there's information at `kubernetes.io/docs/concepts/security/controlling-access/`.

```
--username=system:unauthenticated
```

The API server needs a username to be provided for access, in this case the generic group for unauthenticated users.

```
-s
```

Use this switch to specify the host and port to connect to.

The whole command looks like this:

```
kubectl --insecure-skip-tls-verify --username=system:unauthenticated
 -shttps://[IP]:6443 get po -n kube-system
```

NOTE **In addition to the standard API server, Kubernetes also supports an option for an "insecure" API server. If configured, this service provides complete access to the cluster with no authentication or authorization. Although it is not commonly configured, the default for Kubernetes (as of 1.18) is to have this listen on localhost on the API server.**

Once you have established that you have access to the API server without authentication, it's just a question of establishing what rights you have and how that can be leveraged. That's usually done by role-based access control (RBAC); you can find more details on how to do this in Chapter 18, "Kubernetes Authorization with RBAC."

Preventing Unauthenticated Access to the API Server

In addition to restricting network-level access to the service, the main way to avoid issues with unauthenticated API server access is to ensure that no excessive rights are provided to the `system:anonymous` user or the `system:unauthenticated` group (if RBAC is used) and to ensure that the authorization modes configured on the API server do not include `AlwaysAllow`. The API server parameter can be checked by reviewing the startup flags passed to it; you can find more details on checking the permissions assigned to these special accounts in Chapter 18.

Attacking etcd

The `etcd` datastore is another valuable target for an attacker, as it stores all the state information about the cluster it is part of. In addition to general configuration information, this includes Kubernetes secrets that can be used by an attacker to gain additional access to a cluster.

etcd Information Discovery

Unlike the API server, a standard configuration of `etcd` (as used by `kubeadm`) will not provide any unauthenticated endpoints remotely. There is a metrics endpoint, but the current default setting for this is to be available only on localhost.

If an `etcd` server has been configured to allow unauthenticated access, then a first step in fingerprinting it is to request the `/version` endpoint:

```
curl -k https://[IP]:2379/version
```

This will return a JSON array looking something like this:

```
{"etcdserver":"3.3.15","etcdcluster":"3.3.0"}
```

Exploiting Misconfigured etcd Servers

`etcd`'s authentication and authorization configurations, when used with Kubernetes, are fairly simplistic. Once a client has access to the service, it will provide access to any data stored by `etcd`, so if unauthenticated access is available, it should be possible to dump all the information stored by `etcd`.

The easiest way to do this is to use the `etcdctl` utility. Before using this on any client system, an important first step is to ensure that the environment variable is set like so: `ETCDCTL_API=3`. This tells `etcdctl` that it's addressing a version 3 server; without it you're likely to see errors from your commands.

Once that's set, you can start extracting information from the target `etcd` service. The first step is to see what information is stored in the database, with a command like this:

```
etcdctl --insecure-skip-tls-verify --insecure-transport=false
--endpoints=https://[IP]:2379 get / --prefix --keys-only
```

This will list all of the available keys in the database. From an attacker's perspective, likely the most interesting information will be the Kubernetes secrets. Each of the service accounts that Kubernetes uses has a corresponding secret in the `etcd` database, so with access to that, we can dump it out and use it. For example, to get the secret for the `daemonset-controller` service account, we can use something like the following:

```
etcdctl --insecure-skip-tls-verify --insecure-transport=false
--endpoints=https://[IP]:2379 get
/registry/secrets/kube-system/daemon-set-controller-token-[RAND]
```

The area in the previous line that says `[RAND]` will be a set of five alphanumeric characters that vary per installation. This will return the service account token information. There are some nonprintable characters in the output that are a result of how the data is stored in `etcd`, but it is possible to extract the important value, which will start `ey....` This is a JWT token that can then be used when communicating using `kubectl`, for example:

```
kubectl --token="[TOKEN]" -s https://[IP]:6443 --insecure-skip-tls-verify
 get po -n kube-system
```

Preventing Unauthorized etcd Access

`etcd` can be configured to restrict access to clients that present a certificate signed by a specific certificate authority. The `--trusted-ca-file` and `--client-cert-auth` flags should always be configured on `etcd` to ensure that this restriction is in place.

In a standard Kubeadm cluster, the options would look like this:

```
--client-cert-auth=true
--trusted-ca-file=/etc/kubernetes/pki/etcd/ca.crt
```

Additionally, it is important to note that `etcd` will trust any certificate signed by the specified CA, so it is important to ensure that this CA is only used for `etcd` authentication and not for other purposes. With Kubernetes, this means that multiple CAs are needed to separate the main Kubernetes CA from the CA used for the connection from the API server to `etcd`.

Attacking the Kubelet

Because the kubelet controls the container runtime used on every node in the cluster that runs containers, it is an important potential avenue for attackers to explore. There are two ports that can be listening on a cluster node related to the kubelet.

Kubelet Information Discovery

In addition to port 10250/TCP, which was mentioned earlier, it is possible to see the kubelet listening on 10255/TCP, although this is less common in newer clusters. This port provides a read-only view of the kubelet API and, if configured, is always available without authentication or authorization.

The API can be queried via `curl`. Requests to the root path will just return a 404; however, requesting the `/pods/` endpoint should return a list of all the containers running on the host:

```
curl http://[IP]:10255/pods/ | jq
```

NOTE **The JSON query tool `jq` (`stedolan.github.io/jq/`) is useful when dealing with large amounts of JSON output on the command line. In addition to making the output more readable, it can be used to query JSON documents for specific elements.**

From the output that this returns, likely the most useful information for an attacker will be the command-line flags passed to the pods. Kubernetes system components like the API server and `etcd` generally specify their arguments as command-line flags, and this information is included in the output of the kubelet's pods endpoint, shown in Listing 17.3.

Listing 17.3: Information Disclosure from Kubelet API

```
"name": "kube-apiserver",
"image": "k8s.gcr.io/kube-apiserver:v1.18.2",
"command": [
  "kube-apiserver",
  "--advertise-address=172.18.0.3",
  "--allow-privileged=true",
  "--authorization-mode=Node,RBAC",
  "--client-ca-file=/etc/kubernetes/pki/ca.crt",
  "--enable-admission-plugins=NodeRestriction",
  "--enable-bootstrap-token-auth=true",
```

```
"--etcd-cafile=/etc/kubernetes/pki/etcd/ca.crt",
"--etcd-certfile=/etc/kubernetes/pki/apiserver-etcd-client.crt",
"--etcd-keyfile=/etc/kubernetes/pki/apiserver-etcd-client.key",
"--etcd-servers=https://127.0.0.1:2379",
"--insecure-port=0",
```

The previous excerpt shows parameters passed to the API server pod on the vulnerable host. Information like the location of TLS keys can be useful to attackers in targeting other issues that may be present in the cluster.

Exploiting Misconfigured Kubelets

While the read-only kubelet can provide useful information for attackers, the read-write kubelet that runs on 10250/TCP provides the opportunity for command execution.

If you find a kubelet port that accepts unauthenticated requests, then it's just a question of working out the exact syntax of the API request to execute commands inside any of the pods on the affected cluster node. The format for this was first detailed in the kubelet-exploit from kayrus (`github.com/kayrus/kubelet-exploit`), which was useful as the kubelet API itself doesn't have user-facing documentation.

The following is the general form for executing commands via the kubelet:

```
curl https://[IP]:10250/run/[namespace]/[pod name]/[container name] -k
-XPOST -d "cmd=[command]"
```

This will execute the command as the user running the pod; it's the equivalent of using `kubectl exec` to execute a command in a running container.

To make use of commands similar to the previous, the following information can be filled in to requests to the API:

`[namespace]`	The Kubernetes namespace of the pod
`[pod name]`	The name of the pod the container belongs to
`[container name]`	The name of the container to execute the command in
`[command]`	The name of the command to be run

The kubelet has other available endpoints that can be used, if they have been made available unauthenticated or an attacker has been able to get valid credentials for the kubelet. As an alternative to manual exploitation, Cyberark released a tool called `kubeletctl` (`github.com/cyberark/kubeletctl`) that can automate the process of using the kubelet API.

Preventing Unauthenticated Kubelet Access

The read-only kubelet can be disabled by setting the read-only-port flag to 0. Access to the read-write kubelet should be restricted to authenticated users, anonymous authentication should be disabled, and the authorization-mode flag should be set to `Webhook` and not `AlwaysAllow`.

The stanzas in a kubelet configuration file on a kubeadm cluster (held in /`var/lib/kubelet/config.yaml` by default) would look like Listing 17.4.

Listing 17.4: kubelet Authentication and Authorization Configuration

```
authentication:
  anonymous:
    enabled: false
  webhook:
    cacheTTL: 0s
    enabled: true
  x509:
    clientCAFile: /etc/kubernetes/pki/ca.crt
authorization:
  mode: Webhook
  webhook:
    cacheAuthorizedTTL: 0s
    cacheUnauthorizedTTL: 0s
```

Summary

All Kubernetes clusters have a set of APIs that could be vulnerable to attack, if misconfigured. It's important to ensure that access to these APIs is restricted appropriately, both at a network level and by ensuring that the APIs are correctly configured to require authentication and authorization for all requests to them.

Ideally, most modern Kubernetes distributions assume a "secure by default" posture; however, it is always possible for cluster configurations to be modified during their operation, and often a solution to one issue can open a cluster up to attack.

CHAPTER

18

Kubernetes Authorization with RBAC

Once users have authenticated to a Kubernetes cluster, a key security control is limiting what access they have to create and manage objects within the Kubernetes API. Allowing overly broad permissions to users or applications running in your cluster can easily allow attackers who gain access to those credentials to escalate their privileges in the cluster and get access to all the workloads running on it.

Kubernetes provides several mechanisms for authenticating users to control the rights they have; this chapter explores the most commonly used method, role-based access control (RBAC), including possible pitfalls and tools for auditing RBAC.

Kubernetes Authorization Mechanisms

Kubernetes provides multiple authorization mechanisms, which can be used to control what rights a user has. An important initial point to note is that where multiple authorization mechanisms are configured in a cluster, the rights provided to users will be the sum of all rights provided from each mechanism, so it is generally safer to configure a single authorization mechanism for each cluster.

These are the main modes that can be used for user authorization:

ABAC
Attribute-based access control (ABAC) is generally a legacy mechanism that uses JSON files held on the control plane nodes of the cluster to detail user permissions.

Webhook
With this authorization mechanism, the cluster defers the decision to an external service.

AlwaysAllow
This allows any authenticated user to make any request to the API server.

AlwaysDeny
This rejects all requests.

RBAC
This uses Kubernetes role-based access control (RBAC) objects for authorization decisions.

Of the available options, RBAC is the most commonly deployed and generally provides the best compatibility with third-party software used in the cluster. For that reason, it is the focus of this chapter.

RBAC Overview

Kubernetes RBAC makes use of rights provided to principals (which can be groups, users, or service accounts) at either a cluster or namespace level. There are four object types used as part of this process:

Role
An object whose rights are defined to be provided in a single specified namespace

RoleBinding
An object that links a role or cluster role to a set of principals

ClusterRole
A set of rights defined to be provided either cluster-wide or to a specific namespace

ClusterRoleBinding
An object that links a cluster role to a set of principals

These objects can be combined in these three ways:

Role ➪ RoleBinding
This method provides rights in a single namespace.

ClusterRole ➪ ClusterRoleBinding
This method provides rights at a cluster level.

ClusterRole ➪ RoleBinding
Perhaps unintuitively, this method provides rights in a single namespace. Typically it is used to create a template set of rights that can be applied to individual namespaces, without needing one role per namespace.

RBAC Gotchas

When assigning rights to Kubernetes principals, to reduce the risk of unintended privilege escalations, there are a number of things to be aware of.

Avoid the *cluster-admin* Role

Kubernetes provides a number of default cluster roles that can be used when providing rights to users; one of these is `cluster-admin`, which provides totally unlimited access to the cluster. You can see the rights provided by reviewing the contents of the cluster role with `kubectl`, as shown in Listing 18.1.

Listing 18.1: `cluster-admin` **ClusterRole Rights**

```
kubectl get clusterrole cluster-admin -o yaml

apiVersion: rbac.authorization.k8s.io/v1
kind: ClusterRole
metadata:
 annotations:
   rbac.authorization.kubernetes.io/autoupdate: "true"
 labels:
   kubernetes.io/bootstrapping: rbac-defaults
 name: cluster-admin
 selfLink: /apis/rbac.authorization.k8s.io/v1/clusterroles/cluster-admin
rules:
- apiGroups:
  - '*'
  resources:
  - '*'
  verbs:
  - '*'
- nonResourceURLs:
  - '*'
  verbs:
  - '*'
```

The rules applied here are all wildcards, which means that not only does this role provide full rights to all objects in the cluster that are available now but that it will automatically provide rights to any objects created in the cluster in the future. This level of access is unlikely to be necessary and should be avoided wherever possible.

It's also worth noting the annotation on this cluster role:

```
rbac.authorization.kubernetes.io/autoupdate
```

This indicates that the API server should re-create and reset permissions on this role when the API server is restarted, so if it's removed or modified, it will just be re-created.

There is also a special group in Kubernetes, called `system:masters`, whose members will always have `cluster-admin` rights, even if there are no `clusterrolebindings` mentioning it. Any user-assigned membership of this group will always have full access to the cluster if they can present valid credentials, so generally it should never be used. This is particularly dangerous when combined with client certificate authentication as it can result in an irrevocable `cluster-admin` credential being available.

Built-In Users and Groups Can Be Dangerous

Kubernetes provides two built-in groups and a built-in user that are used for RBAC decisions in specific circumstances. It's important to be careful when assigning rights to these principals as they can provide access to unauthorized parties who can connect to the Kubernetes API server.

The `system:anonymous` user is the default user account used for RBAC decisions when no username is supplied with requests to the API server. Similarly, rights assigned to the `system:unauthenticated` group will also be provided to unauthenticated requests.

The `system:authenticated` group is also available, and rights provided to it are given to any user who presents valid authentication credentials to the cluster.

Read-Only Can Be Dangerous

It's important to note that unlike many systems, the Kubernetes API allows read-only access that can enable users to gain additional access to the cluster and potentially get cluster administrator access. It behaves this way because Kubernetes stores secrets in the API and will return them to any user who has read (or even list) access to that object type.

It's possible to demonstrate this using a relatively simple test cluster. First create a namespace called `secretlist`:

```
kubectl create ns secretlist
```

Then create a cluster role that provides only list access to secrets:

```
kubectl create clusterrole "secretlist" --verb=list --resource=secrets
```

and bind that cluster role to the default service account in the `secretlist` namespace.

```
kubectl create clusterrolebinding secretlist --clusterrole=secretlist
--serviceaccount=secretlist:default
```

This command also illustrates an important point about service account rights in Kubernetes, which is that any rights applied to the default service account in a namespace will be given to every pod in that namespace, unless a pod explicitly uses a different service account.

Once you have these commands set up, you can run a pod in that namespace to demonstrate the issue:

```
kubectl -n secretlist run -it testpod
--image=raesene/alpine-containertools /bin/bash
```

This will drop you into a Bash shell with the rights from the previous cluster role. Although you can't actually retrieve the details on individual secrets, Kubernetes has an option to direct output to YAML; using it on our pod shows that the list right will let you see all the secrets in, for example, the `kube-system` namespace. This will include all the service account tokens for system components, some of which have considerable levels of access to the API:

```
kubectl -n kube-system get secrets -o yaml
```

As shown in Listing 18.2, the tokens and namespaces are base64 encoded, but once decoded, the secrets can be used to authenticate to the cluster.

Listing 18.2: `attachdetach-controller` **Service Account Token**


```
namespace: a3ViZS1zeXN0ZW0=
    token: ZXlKaGJHY2lPaUpTVXpJMU5pSXNJbXRwWkNJNkltS1BWMkY2VXpsdVVFZFBRV
zVtVWpCRWJFaEZOMDVETVhJMVRHdzRZalppYUdoYWVVcHpXSG95VFVVaWZRLmV5SnBjM01p
T21KcmRXSmxjbTVsZEdWekwzTmxjblpwWTJWaFkyTnZkVzUwSWl3aWEzVmlaWEp1WlhSbGN5
NXBieTl6WlhKMmFXTmxZV05qYjNWdWRDOXVZVzFsYzNCaFkyVWlPaUpyZFdKbExYTjVjM1J
sYlNJc0ltdDFZbVZ5Ym1WMFpYTXVhVzh2YzJWeWRtbGpaV0ZqWTI5MWJuUXZjM1ZqY21WME
xtNWhiV1VpT2lKaGRIUmhZMmhrWlhSaFkyZ3RZMjl1ZEhKdmJHeGxjaTEwYjJ0bGJpMWpkR
3g2T0NJc0ltdDFZbVZ5Ym1WMFpYTXVhVzh2YzJWeWRtbGpaV0ZqWTI5MWJuUXZjM1Z5ZG1s
alpTMWhZMk52ZFc1MExtNWhiV1VpT2lKaGRIUmhZMmhrWlhSaFkyZ3RZMjl1ZEhKdmJHeGx
jaUlzSW10MVltVnlibVYwWlhNdWFXOHZjM1Z5ZG1salpXTmpZMjkxYm5RdmMyVnlkbWxqWl
MxaFkyTnZkVzUwTG5WcFpDSTZJbUZsWlRJM05HHTXdMV1ZqTW1JdE5EWXhNUzFpWkdJMExUQ
XhNakU0TmpRM1pqWXdOU01lzSW5OMVlpSTZJbk41YzNSbGJUcHpaWEoyYVdObFlXTmpiM1Z1
ZERwcmRXSmxMWE41YzNSbGJUcGhkSFJoWTJoa1pYUmhZMmd0WTI5dWRISnZiR3hsY21lKOS5
QTkZ1eG1IRVp1bUlrR0o1SWphRHNGWWF3NmJOOVU0TWNPRGx2WFZDaUk1RF9nX2tvRW80aX
BuUzRCYTVkME01djNmOUY1MHhxaVZrWm5hMXI5aVZqLTJaVy1Wa2haY1lhZjFHdTFxaF9mT
mxQNndLNXhBS2R3eWwxMWNYRUpPaGtfMmQtUVA5NXducHpHWnlEQ3pEamhQQWd1Q09OdHhj
bWpBYmpfMWN4NFZxMzhfeDk5TkY5dVpyZTRoYlF5ZUpRdWVtNmdXUVplZDR1UVhxVTk4b3d
yaGVVUVdFa2xneDBBY185S0dEekJSQVZmeTFKeVpIWUotZTB5Z1I0TnR4bUdVTXlKRU9YSX
hJaEVqV0Fydk1rdENFLTJybzF5MEF5VWktZFlHcHdfcFV3ckVWSEZ4V1hfc2tjSnByTXN4M
jUtMXNUX0xkaFRqWl9sVGEtVGNJV2c=
```

```
kind: Secret
metadata:
  annotations:
    kubernetes.io/service-account.name: attachdetach-controller
    kubernetes.io/service-account.uid:
aee274c0-ec2b-4611-bdb4-01218647f605
```

In addition to service account tokens, any other secrets stored in the cluster (for example, API tokens or database credentials) would be accessible.

As a result of this potential exposure, it's important to ensure that get and list rights to secret objects are strictly controlled. This is also another reason to avoid using wildcard rights' grants as they can include things such as secret objects.

Create Pod Is Dangerous

In addition to challenges in providing read-only access to cluster resources, it's important to note that, without additional controls, providing the ability for a user to create pods presents risks of privilege escalation. This can present a tricky problem, as allowing developers or application owners in a multitenant cluster to create and manage their own resources is a fairly common Kubernetes use case.

Although we'll cover some of the options for mitigating this risk in Chapter 19, "Network Hardening," it's worth looking at how various rights around pod creation and management could lead to privilege escalation.

The simplest of these occurs where a user is able to create pods and also execute commands inside them (using `kubectl exec`). In this case, getting root access to the underlying node is a relatively trivial task. To see for yourself, first create a pod manifest, as shown in Listing 18.3.

Listing 18.3: `NodeRoot` **Pod Manifest**

```
apiVersion: v1
kind: Pod
metadata:
  name: noderootpod
  labels:
spec:
  hostNetwork: true
  hostPID: true
  hostIPC: true
  containers:
-name: noderootpod
    image: busybox
    securityContext:
      privileged: true
    volumeMounts:
```

```
  -mountPath: /host
       name: noderoot
     command: [ "/bin/sh", "-c", "—" ]
     args: [ "while true; do sleep 30; done;" ]
   volumes:
 —name: noderoot
     hostPath:
       path: /
```

This will create a pod based on the busybox image from Docker Hub. It then sets a number of parameters to true; these remove parts of the isolation provided by standard Linux container runtimes, set the infamous (from a security perspective) privileged flag to true, and create a volume mount to the underlying node root filesystem.

With this manifest saved as `noderoot.yml`, it takes only two commands to get root on the underlying host, with the only rights needed being `create` on pod resources and `pod/exec` subresources. First run this command:

```
kubectl create -f noderoot.yml
```

This will create the pod. Then run the following:

```
kubectl exec -it noderootpod chroot /host
```

You should get a root shell on the underlying node. This technique is based on the article "The Most Pointless Docker Command Ever" from Ian Miell:

`zwischenzugs.com/2015/06/24/the-most-pointless-docker-command-ever/`

It is a useful demonstration that without additional hardening, it's relatively easy to remove the isolation provided by Linux containers and run commands on the underlying host.

It's also worth noting that, even without the pod/exec rights needed for this attack, it's possible to use techniques such as reverse shells to get access to a host with just create pod rights.

Kubernetes Rights Can Be Transient

An interesting feature of how Kubernetes creates resources is that, in many cases, the principal creating a pod resource won't actually be the user who issued the command, but instead a controller running as part of the cluster.

There are many resource types that, if rights to them are provided to a user, will effectively allow for the user to create pods.

Deployment objects are a simple example. When a deployment is created by a user, the deployment controller creates a Replica Set object, and then the Replica Set object creates the pods. As such, a user who can create deployment objects effectively has create pod rights, without actually explicitly having that right granted.

This is important given the possibility of privilege escalation resulting from allowing users unrestricted create pod rights.

Other Dangerous Objects

In addition to pods and secrets, there are other objects that require careful attention when allowing users to manage them. As flagged in the 2019 Security audit report (`github.com/kubernetes/kubernetes/issues/81110`), a user with the ability to create PersistentVolume objects can effectively gain privileged access to the underlying host filesystem. It's important to note that this object type is not governed by PodSecurityPolicies, so access needs to be restricted in RBAC to ensure that only trusted Kubernetes users can create or manage these objects.

Auditing RBAC

When running clusters it's important to ensure that the rights that users and service accounts have are kept to a minimum, so periodically reviewing RBAC assignments is a good way to ensure that this is the case. There are a number of ways to approach this task.

Using *kubectl*

kubectl has some facilities to assess the rights that an account has. The `kubectl auth can-i` command will provide yes/no answers about whether the authenticated user can carry out specific operations:

```
kubectl auth can-i get pods
yes
```

Importantly, it's possible to provide flags to this command to execute it as another user (or service account), allowing you to check the permissions of another user (note that to use this feature your account needs to have impersonation rights for the target account). For example, the following command confirms that the `certificate-controller` service account in the `kube-system` namespace is not able to get pods:

```
kubectl auth can-i get pods
--as=system:serviceaccount:kube-system:certificate-controller
no
```

Additionally, the `-list` flag can be used to see all the permissions available to a user in a given namespace. For example, the following command will show the rights available to the default service account in the default namespace:

```
kubectl auth can-i --as=system:serviceaccount:default:default --list
```

Note that it can be difficult to tell if you have misspelled the name of the user account you're requesting information as. That's because Kubernetes does not have a user database, so it can't tell you whether a user is nonexistent or just doesn't have any specifically provided rights.

In a similar vein, if you request information about an object type that doesn't exist, even though Kubernetes will warn you it doesn't know about that object type it will still provide yes/no responses to the command. Here's an example:

```
kubectl auth can-i get pies
Warning: the server doesn't have a resource type 'pies'
Yes
```

One last area where using `kubectl auth can-i` may be challenging is in looking at the rights provided to the special user `system:anonymous` and the special group `system:unauthenticated`. By default these two principals do not have enough rights to review their own permissions, so the method described earlier of using the `-as` parameter will not be effective.

To review rights assigned to these principals, one option would be to dump all `clusterrolebindings` from the cluster in JSON format and then use a text editor or grep to look for mentions of them.

Additional Tooling

In addition to using `kubectl` for auditing RBAC permissions, there are a number of useful external tools that can be used. These tools provide alternate ways of looking at the same information and are invaluable in analyzing the information from Kubernetes RBAC, which can get quite complex in larger clusters.

Rakkess

`Rakkess` (`github.com/corneliusweig/rakkess`) is a useful tool for getting a listing of rights available to either your current user or to another user/service account that you specify when running it.

Like many Golang tools, `rakkess` comes as a single binary that can be run directly without requiring dependencies to be installed.

If run without any parameters, it will analyze the rights of the current user. In Figure 18.1, the user has `cluster-admin` rights, so all objects and operations are ticked.

```
rorym@dsob:~$ rakkess
NAME                                              LIST  CREATE  UPDATE  DELETE
apiservices.apiregistration.k8s.io                ✔     ✔       ✔       ✔
bgpconfigurations.crd.projectcalico.org           ✔     ✔       ✔       ✔
bgppeers.crd.projectcalico.org                    ✔     ✔       ✔       ✔
bindings                                                ✔
blockaffinities.crd.projectcalico.org             ✔     ✔       ✔       ✔
certificatesigningrequests.certificates.k8s.io    ✔     ✔       ✔       ✔
clusterinformations.crd.projectcalico.org         ✔     ✔       ✔       ✔
clusterrolebindings.rbac.authorization.k8s.io     ✔     ✔       ✔       ✔
clusterroles.rbac.authorization.k8s.io            ✔     ✔       ✔       ✔
componentstatuses                                 ✔
configmaps                                        ✔     ✔       ✔       ✔
controllerrevisions.apps                          ✔     ✔       ✔       ✔
cronjobs.batch                                    ✔     ✔       ✔       ✔
csidrivers.storage.k8s.io                         ✔     ✔       ✔       ✔
csinodes.storage.k8s.io                           ✔     ✔       ✔       ✔
customresourcedefinitions.apiextensions.k8s.io    ✔     ✔       ✔       ✔
daemonsets.apps                                   ✔     ✔       ✔       ✔
deployments.apps                                  ✔     ✔       ✔       ✔
endpoints                                         ✔     ✔       ✔       ✔
endpointslices.discovery.k8s.io                   ✔     ✔       ✔       ✔
events                                            ✔     ✔       ✔       ✔
events.events.k8s.io                              ✔     ✔       ✔       ✔
felixconfigurations.crd.projectcalico.org         ✔     ✔       ✔       ✔
globalnetworkpolicies.crd.projectcalico.org       ✔     ✔       ✔       ✔
globalnetworksets.crd.projectcalico.org           ✔     ✔       ✔       ✔
```

Figure 18.1: `Rakkess` output

To run `rakkess` against another principal (user or service account), just specify that as a parameter. For example, to review the rights provided to the `certificate-controller` account in the `kube-system` namespace, you would run this:

```
rakkess --sa kube-system:certificate-controller
```

Figure 18.2 shows the result.

```
rorym@dsob:~$ rakkess --sa kube-system:certificate-controller
NAME                                              LIST  CREATE  UPDATE  DELE
apiservices.apiregistration.k8s.io                ✖     ✖       ✖       ✖
bgpconfigurations.crd.projectcalico.org           ✖     ✖       ✖       ✖
bgppeers.crd.projectcalico.org                    ✖     ✖       ✖       ✖
bindings                                                ✖
blockaffinities.crd.projectcalico.org             ✖     ✖       ✖       ✖
certificatesigningrequests.certificates.k8s.io    ✔     ✖       ✖       ✔
clusterinformations.crd.projectcalico.org         ✖     ✖       ✖       ✖
clusterrolebindings.rbac.authorization.k8s.io     ✖     ✖       ✖       ✖
clusterroles.rbac.authorization.k8s.io            ✖     ✖       ✖       ✖
componentstatuses                                 ✖
configmaps                                        ✖     ✖       ✖       ✖
controllerrevisions.apps                          ✖     ✖       ✖       ✖
cronjobs.batch                                    ✖     ✖       ✖       ✖
csidrivers.storage.k8s.io                         ✖     ✖       ✖       ✖
csinodes.storage.k8s.io                           ✖     ✖       ✖       ✖
customresourcedefinitions.apiextensions.k8s.io    ✖     ✖       ✖       ✖
daemonsets.apps                                   ✖     ✖       ✖       ✖
deployments.apps                                  ✖     ✖       ✖       ✖
endpoints                                         ✖     ✖       ✖       ✖
endpointslices.discovery.k8s.io                   ✖     ✖       ✖       ✖
events                                            ✖     ✔       ✔       ✖
events.events.k8s.io                              ✖     ✔       ✔       ✖
felixconfigurations.crd.projectcalico.org         ✖     ✖       ✖       ✖
```

Figure 18.2: `Rakkess` output for the `certificate-controller` account

In short, `rakkess` is useful for visualizing the rights provided to various service accounts and users and getting an idea of whether they have any incorrect or excessive permissions.

kubectl-who-can

This tool, from Aqua Security (`github.com/aquasecurity/kubectl-who-can`), takes a different approach to showing information from a Kubernetes RBAC system, one that can be useful when reviewing permissions in a cluster. You can use it to find out which principals have specific rights. It works similarly to `rakkess` in that it is available as a static Golang binary that can be downloaded and executed, and it makes use of the running user's `kubeconfig` file to determine which cluster to run against. When auditing the permissions of a cluster, it's a good idea to first check for likely dangerous permissions (for example, get secrets):

```
kubectl-who-can get secrets
```

Figure 18.3 shows the results.

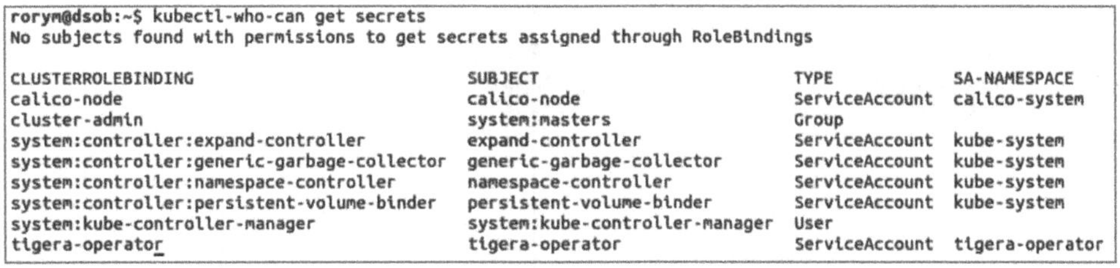

```
rorym@dsob:~$ kubectl-who-can get secrets
No subjects found with permissions to get secrets assigned through RoleBindings

CLUSTERROLEBINDING                           SUBJECT                           TYPE            SA-NAMESPACE
calico-node                                  calico-node                       ServiceAccount  calico-system
cluster-admin                                system:masters                    Group
system:controller:expand-controller          expand-controller                 ServiceAccount  kube-system
system:controller:generic-garbage-collector  generic-garbage-collector         ServiceAccount  kube-system
system:controller:namespace-controller       namespace-controller              ServiceAccount  kube-system
system:controller:persistent-volume-binder   persistent-volume-binder          ServiceAccount  kube-system
system:kube-controller-manager               system:kube-controller-manager    User
tigera-operator                              tigera-operator                   ServiceAccount  tigera-operator
```

Figure 18.3: `kubectl-who-can get secrets`

The output shows a list of principals that can access that resource both at a namespace level where applicable (via `rolebindings`) and at a cluster level. Figure 18.3 shows the output for a default `kubeadm` 1.18 cluster set up to use Calico networking (`www.tigera.io/tigera-products/calico/`) and shows a potentially interested result, which is that the `tigera-operator` used to manage networking has the ability to get secrets at a cluster level.

A good first approach to auditing RBAC on a cluster is to look at some of the dangerous rights listed earlier in the chapter and confirm that the principals listed as having those rights are what you'd expect.

Rback

Rback (`github.com/team-soteria/rback`) is a useful visualization tool for RBAC rights. What it does is parse the cluster's RBAC objects and create a graphical representation of them, which can be reviewed for unexpected entries. Rback uses Graphviz to create the image file, so a standard run of the tool looks like this:

```
kubectl get sa,roles,rolebindings,clusterroles,clusterrolebindings
--all-namespaces -o json | rback | dot -Tpng
> /tmp/rback.png && open /tmp/rback.png
```

From that an image is generated, which will likely require quite a lot of horizontal scrolling to view; however, the format is useful in understanding what rights have been applied. Figure 18.4 shows a `podreader` role and `rolebinding`, which look reasonable, but then also a `podwriter` role that appears to be misnamed as it provides access to a range of resources including secrets.

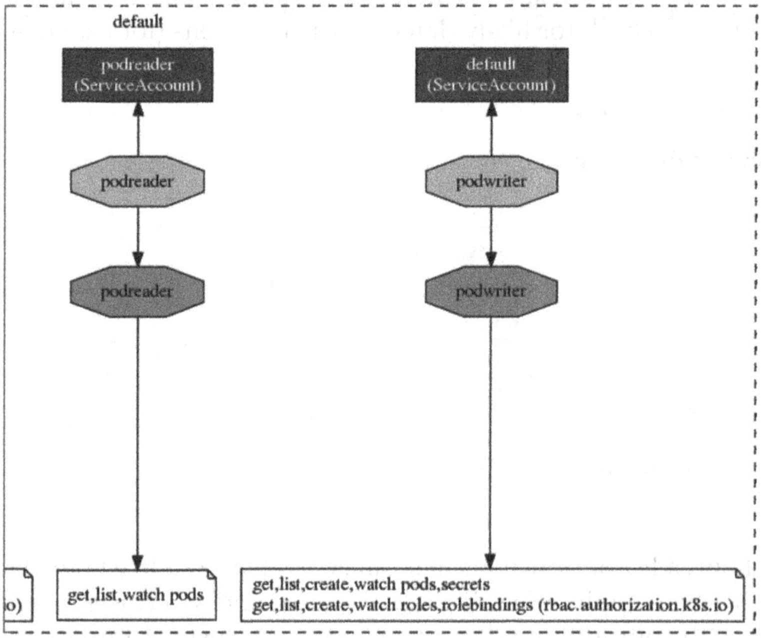

Figure 18.4: Example of `rback` output

This kind of visualization is a useful technique in locating inappropriate rights assignments in clusters.

Summary

Kubernetes RBAC is a key control for the security of the cluster, and it's important to ensure that rights provided using it are given out on a least-privilege basis. In addition to more obvious dangerous permissions, such as the use of `cluster-admin` rights, there are a number of other areas like the rights to create pods and read-only access to the API, which can be dangerous and should be carefully controlled.

In addition to the built-in tooling available with `kubectl`, we looked at a number of third-party open source tools that can be used to help review RBAC rules that have been implemented in a cluster.

CHAPTER

19

Network Hardening

One of the key capabilities provided by Kubernetes is the container network, which allows workloads to contact each other easily when the containers are running on different nodes or even in different networks.

Kubernetes' default approach to container networks is to provide a flat unrestricted environment where every container can contact every other container. From a security standpoint, this obviously presents some challenges, in that it's generally advisable to reduce the attack surface of your environment by restricting which applications can contact each other, at a network level. Exactly how restrictive you want to be will depend, as with most things in security, on the threat model of your cluster.

Kubernetes provides a default API, called Network Policy, which can be used by cluster operators and users to restrict access between workloads. This API provides a Kubernetes and container-aware interface to networking controls like firewall rules, which restrict the traffic flowing over the container network.

Container Network Overview

Before we delve directly into how Network Policy is configured, it's worth reviewing how container networks are deployed, as there are some complexities there that can trip you up if you're coming from a more traditional VM-based infrastructure.

There are multiple discrete sets of IP addresses you're likely to see in a Kubernetes cluster, each of which has a different role in handling cluster traffic.

Node IP Addresses

These are the addresses assigned to nodes in the cluster, typically virtual machines or physical servers. They'll be either handed out by DHCP servers on the LAN that the cluster node sits on or statically assigned there. You can see the IP addresses of your nodes by using the `-o wide` option on `kubectl get nodes` or by using a custom column to just get that information, as shown in Listing 19.1.

Listing 19.1: Getting Node Addresses and Node Name

```
kubectl get nodes -o custom-columns=Address:status.addresses[*].address

Address
192.168.41.100,k8smaster
192.168.41.101,k8sworker1
192.168.41.102,k8sworker2
```

Pod IP Addresses

These addresses are handed out to individual pods when they're started. The network they are part of will usually (but not always) be entirely different from the network containing the node IP addresses. Assignment of the IP addresses to pods is governed by the Container Network Interface (CNI) plugin that's used by the cluster (such as Calico or Cilium).

It's worth noting that, usually when connecting to an application running in a Kubernetes cluster, you would not connect directly to a pod IP address, as those addresses are as ephemeral as the pods themselves. You would instead connect to the service addresses, as discussed in the next section. However, pod addresses can be useful when troubleshooting connectivity issues.

You can see a pod's IP address by looking at the IP column in the output of Listing 19.2.

Listing 19.2: Getting Pod IP Addresses

```
kubectl -n kube-system get po -o custom-columns=IP:.status.podIP

IP
10.1.8.31
10.1.16.131
192.168.41.100
192.168.41.100
192.168.41.102
192.168.41.100
192.168.41.101
192.168.41.100
```

This listing shows an example of a case where a pod's IP address might not be on a separate network. We've listed the IP addresses of the pods in the `kube-system` namespace, and some of the IP addresses returned are the same as the node IP addresses we saw in the previous section.

This occurs where a pod makes use of *host networking*, which means that instead of being given a separate address, a pod is given the address of the node to which it is assigned.

Service IP Addresses

The third set of IP addresses you'll typically see in a cluster consists of service IP addresses. Services provide a consistent IP address for an application running in a Kubernetes cluster and are necessary because pods, by their very nature, are ephemeral and may move from node to node, causing their IP addresses to change. The SVC-IP column of output in Listing 19.3 shows some service IP addresses.

Listing 19.3: Getting Service IP Addresses

```
kubectl get svc -o custom-columns=SVC-IP:.spec.clusterIP

SVC-IP
10.96.0.1
```

One important element of service IP addresses to know about is that, unlike pod IP addresses and node IP addresses, there's no network interface associated with a service IP address. In reality it's associated with a set of `iptables` rules. This is relevant when you're testing connectivity (or the implementation of network policies) in a cluster as you can't expect to ping a service IP address. Typically, they'll respond only on the port number(s) that the service exposes.

Restricting Traffic in Kubernetes Clusters

With this background in the basics of Kubernetes networking, we can look at how to restrict access using the Network Policy API provided by Kubernetes. An important prerequisite for using this API is to ensure that the Container Network Interface (CNI) plugin that you're using supports it. That's the case with most common CNI plugins; however, there are still some (`flannel` is an example) that don't include that support as part of their base functionality.

Network policies operate at a namespace level, and once there are any policies that apply to a given namespace in a given direction (inbound or outbound), all traffic is blocked unless it is specifically allowed. This approach is often called the *white list* model.

Because some of the concepts surrounding network policies can be a little abstract, we'll use a hands-on example to illustrate how it works.

Setting Up a Cluster with Network Policies

To demonstrate and test network policies, we'll need to make sure that our cluster supports them. Some of the common development cluster options (including KinD and minikube) default to CNI providers that don't handle the Network Policy API.

There are instructions to enable cilium on minikube on the Kubernetes documentation site (`kubernetes.io/docs/tasks/administer-cluster/network-policy-provider/cilium-network-policy/`). To set up a network policy capable CNI with KinD, use the `disableDefaultCNI` option (`kind.sigs.k8s.io/docs/user/configuration/#disable-default-cni`) and then just use the installation instructions for a CNI, like Calico or Cilium (both discussed later in the chapter).

Getting Started

With access to a (nonproduction) Kubernetes cluster, first we can create a couple of namespaces to represent a two-tier application (web application and database):

```
kubectl create namespace webapp
kubectl create namespace database
```

Next start an instance of the `nginx` web server in the webapp namespace and expose port 80 using a service:

```
kubectl -n webapp run testwebapp --image=nginx --expose=true --port=80
```

We'll also start an instance of `postgres` in the database namespace:

```
kubectl -n database run testdb --image=postgres
--env="POSTGRES_PASSWORD=database" --expose=true --port=5432
```

WARNING **In a real cluster, of course, you should never set your database password using an environment variable!**

We can demonstrate that, at this point, the web application will be available from another namespace in the cluster. First run a shell in a container in the default namespace:

```
kubectl run -it client --image=raesene/alpine-containertools /bin/bash
```

and then we can access the webapp using `curl`:

```
curl http://testwebapp.webapp
```

Note that we can use the hostname shown here thanks to the way Kubernetes uses DNS for service discovery. This is generally a useful feature for being able to communicate between services in a predictable fashion.

If all is working well, you should get a response from the web application:

```
<!DOCTYPE html>
<html>
<head>
<title>Welcome to nginx!</title>
```

We can also confirm that the database service is accessible using `nmap`:

```
nmap -Pn -v -n -sTV -p5432 testdb.database
```

This command should return output similar to Listing 19.4.

Listing 19.4: `nmap` Scan of the Database Service

```
nmap -Pn -sTV -p5432 testdb.database
Starting Nmap 7.70 ( https://nmap.org ) at 2020-10-10 12:57 UTC
Nmap scan report for testdb.database (10.111.98.83)
Host is up (0.000082s latency).
rDNS record for 10.111.98.83: testdb.database.svc.cluster.local

PORT     STATE SERVICE    VERSION
5432/tcp open  postgresql PostgreSQL DB 9.6.0 or later
```

The way this initial environment is configured will be similar to most base Kubernetes clusters, and traffic will be able to move freely, as shown in Figure 19.1.

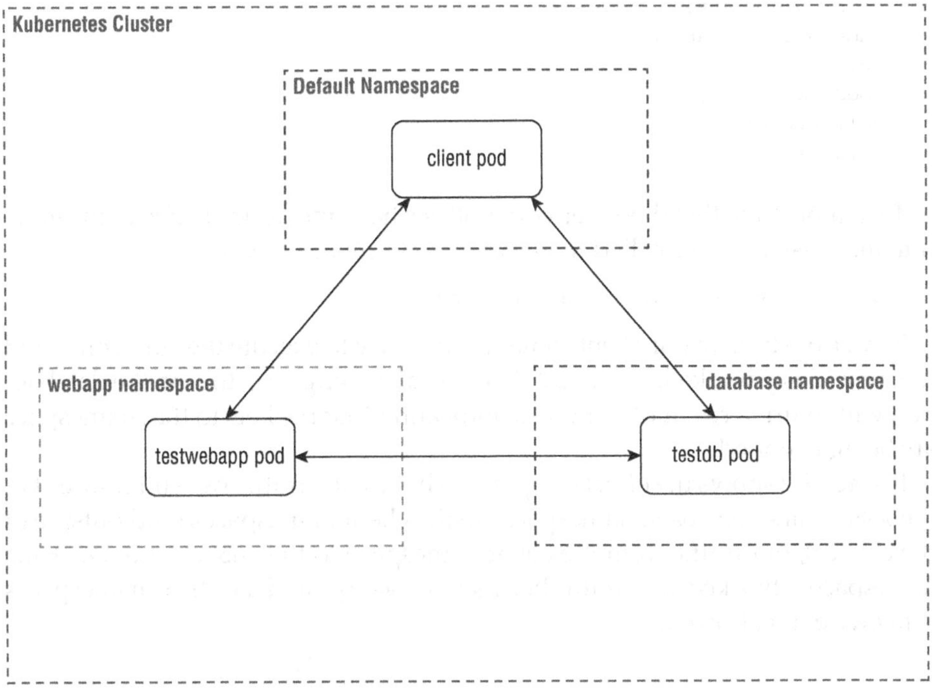

Figure 19.1: Traffic flow in the base Kubernetes cluster

Now that we have the basic environment set up, we can demonstrate the operation of network policies. With network firewalling, it's always best to take a policy of denying by default, so let's start by denying all ingress traffic to the `webapp` namespace:

```
apiVersion: networking.k8s.io/v1
kind: NetworkPolicy
metadata:
  name: deny-ingress-webapp
  namespace: webapp
spec:
  podSelector: {}
  policyTypes:
  - Ingress
```

This basic policy has the usual required elements for a Kubernetes manifest, namely, the `apiVerison`, `kind`, `metadata`, and `spec`. Within the `spec`, we have a `podSelector` field that is empty, which means it will apply to all pods in the namespace, and a `policyTypes` field stating that this applies to ingress traffic to the namespace.

We will also apply a similar policy to the database namespace:

```
apiVersion: networking.k8s.io/v1
kind: NetworkPolicy
metadata:
  name: deny-ingress-database
  namespace: database
spec:
  podSelector: {}
  policyTypes:
  - Ingress
```

To demonstrate that these network policies have the desired effect, first apply it to the cluster (we've called it `default-deny-inbound.yaml`):

```
kubectl create -f default-deny-inbound.yaml
```

Now, from back in our client container, if we try to execute the `curl` command that previously worked, it will just time out, and using `nmap` to scan the database pod will return a result of `filtered`, indicating that packets to that namespace are being dropped.

Figure 19.2 shows the effect our policies have had. Traffic can still flow out of the `webapp` and `database` namespaces to the client namespaces (and outside of the cluster), but traffic from the client namespace to the `webapp` and `database` namespace is blocked, and traffic between the `webapp` and `database` namespaces is likewise not allowed.

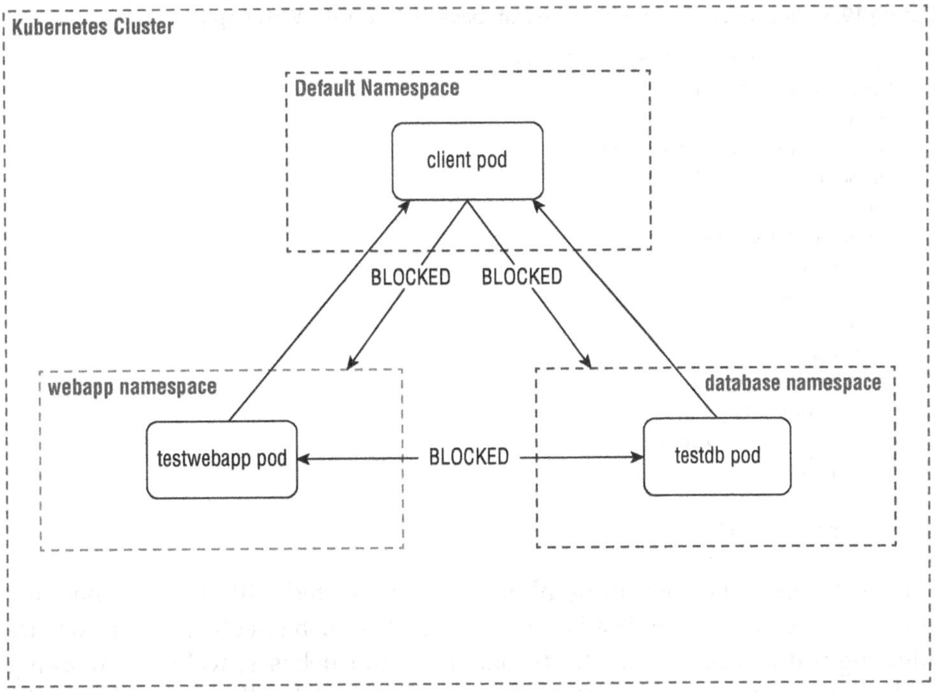

Figure 19.2: Network traffic after default deny policies applied

Allowing Access

Of course, an application that doesn't allow any access is somewhat useless, so we need to provide the ability for necessary traffic to pass. A good example of this is that the web application pod will likely need to communicate with the database pod, so we can allow access into the database namespace from the `webapp` namespace on the port we're using (5432/TCP).

To do this we're going to first need to apply a label to our namespace. As of version 1.20 of Kubernetes, it's not possible to address a namespace directly by name (`kubernetes.io/docs/concepts/services-networking/network-policies/#what-you-can-t-do-with-network-policies-at-least-not-yet`), but we can apply a label to a namespace and use that:

```
kubectl label namespace/webapp tier=webapp
```

Labels are arbitrary name-value pairs, so in this case we're giving our namespace a label `tier` with a value of `webapp`.

Once we've applied that label, we can create our policy, shown in Listing 19.5.

Listing 19.5: Network Policy to Allow the Database to Access the Web Application

```
apiVersion: networking.k8s.io/v1
kind: NetworkPolicy
metadata:
  name: allow-webapp-access
  namespace: database
spec:
  podSelector: {}
  policyTypes:
  - Ingress
  ingress:
  - from:
    - namespaceSelector:
        matchLabels:
          tier: webapp
    ports:
    - protocol: TCP
      port: 5432
```

In addition to the basic deny-all policies we started with, this one has two additional sections. The first is a `from` section, which specifies where we are allowing traffic from. Unlike traditional firewall rulebases, we're not working with CIDR ranges for this; instead, we're using the label that we added to the `webapp` namespace as a means of declaring where traffic should be allowed from.

The other new section is `ports`, which specifies the protocol (TCP or UDP) and port numbers to be allowed. It's important to be as specific as possible when specifying firewall rules to avoid inadvertently allowing excess access. Wherever possible, specifying individual ports here is helpful.

To apply this rule, we can just use `kubectl` as before:

```
kubectl create -f allow-webapp-access.yaml
```

Figure 19.3 shows the effect of this rule. The access is as before, except that we can now go from the `webapp` namespace to the database port in the database namespace.

Now that we've applied this rule, we can test first that access is still not allowed from our client pod in the default namespace using `nmap`. Execute another shell inside the pod:

```
kubectl exec -it client /bin/bash
```

and then run the same `nmap` command as before. This will return another filtered result. Now to test that our access is now allowed from the `webapp` namespace as expected, we'll run a pod in that namespace:

```
kubectl run -n webapp -it webappclient --image=raesene/alpine-containertools
/bin/bash
```

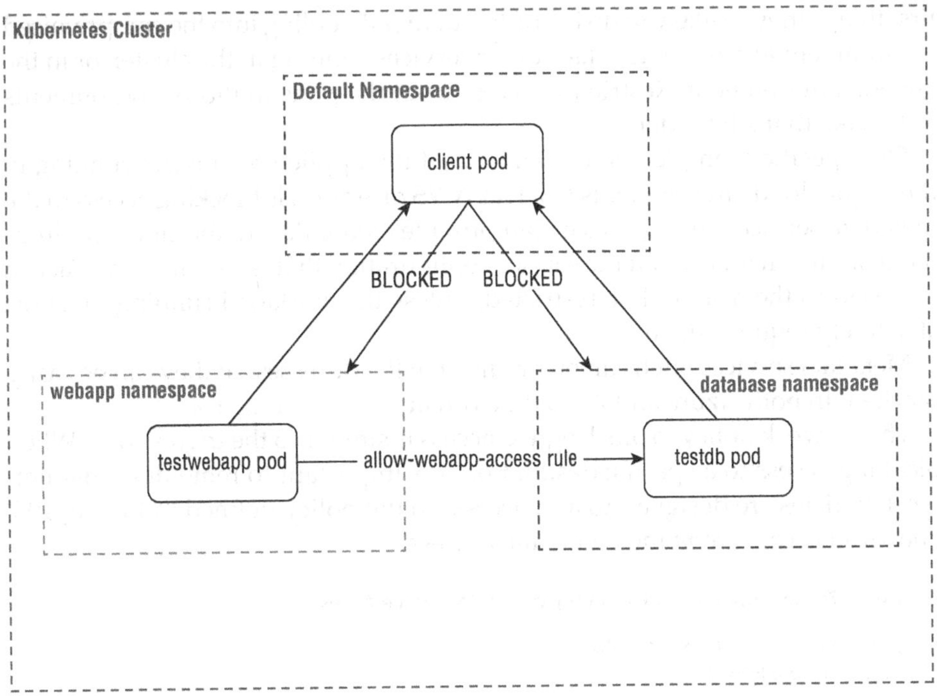

Figure 19.3: Network traffic after `allow-webapp-access` policy added

Now run the same `nmap` command we used before:

```
nmap -Pn -sTV -p5432 testdb.database
```

You'll get back an open response, as shown in Listing 19.6.

Listing 19.6: Open Port Scan of the Database Service

```
Starting Nmap 7.80 ( https://nmap.org ) at 2021-02-27 10:53 UTC
Nmap scan report for testdb.database (10.111.98.83)
Host is up (0.00026s latency).
rDNS record for 10.111.98.83: testdb.database.svc.cluster.local

PORT     STATE SERVICE    VERSION
5432/tcp open  postgresql PostgreSQL DB 9.6.0 or later
```

Egress Restrictions

In addition to restricting access inbound to a namespace, network policies can be used to restrict outbound access. Egress restrictions can be useful in making attackers lives harder and preventing inadvertent privilege escalation. If an attacker is able to compromise a pod running in a Kubernetes cluster, one of the first things they're likely to do is to attempt to pull tooling into the compromised environment to attempt to attack other services running in the cluster, or in the general environment. Restricting access from the pods to those environments will make that job harder.

One specific example, which can be usefully applied to clusters running in the major cloud environments (such as AWS or Azure) is blocking access to the metadata service. These services can provide credentials to the cloud environment or information about the service configuration that is useful to an attacker, so access to them should be restricted, unless the workload running in a port absolutely requires them.

Metadata services often run on predictable IP addresses, so they can be easily blocked. In both Azure and AWS they run at `169.254.169.254`.

The network policy to block egress access is similar to the ingress one. When blocking access to a specific destination, it's important to remember that network policies are designed to add access, so the policy defined in Listing 19.7 allows all access *except* the metadata address.

Listing 19.7: Network Policy Restricting Metadata Service Access

```
apiVersion: networking.k8s.io/v1
kind: NetworkPolicy
metadata:
  name: block-metadata
  namespace: webapp
spec:
  policyTypes:
  - Egress
  podSelector:
    matchLabels: {}
  egress:
  - to:
    - ipBlock:
        cidr: 0.0.0.0/0
        except:
          - 169.254.169.254/32
```

This policy blocks access from the `webapp` namespace to the metadata service address and can be applied to our cluster with the following command:

```
kubectl create -f block-metadata.yaml
```

Network Policy Restrictions

When using network policies as a security control, it's important to note restrictions on how they're applied. Specifically, standard Kubernetes network policies are implemented by the CNI plugin and apply only where a workload's networking is managed by that plugin. If a workload connects directly to the underlying host network (using the directive `hostNetwork: true` in the pod specification), then standard network policies will not apply to it.

CNI Network Policy Extensions

In addition to the base functionality provided by the Kubernetes Network Policy API, there are also additional capabilities provided by some CNI providers. These extensions often make scaling network policies and making consistent network policies across larger clusters easier. The trade-off with using them is that the objects used to manage them will be tied to the CNI provider choice, and if you want to have flexibility to use other CNI providers, you'll need to look at re-implementing the restrictions on each CNI provider you implement. Two of these providers are Cilium and Calico.

Cilium

Cilium is a popular CNI provider that makes use of eBPF to provide enhanced performance for Kubernetes networking. It also implements some additional network policy capabilities, with the `CiliumNetworkPolicy` and `CiliumClusterWideNetworkPolicy` objects.

Among its useful capabilities, `CiliumNetworkPolicy` can address nodes directly in policy and apply policies to DNS names, which are not currently available in base Kubernetes network policies.

For example, in the policy shown in Listing 19.8, access will be allowed from a namespace called `webapp` to Google domain sites on ports 80 and 443. Note that to use DNS-based policies, access from the affected workloads to DNS services is necessary.

Listing 19.8: Cilium Network Policy DNS Example

```
apiVersion: cilium.io/v2
kind: CiliumNetworkPolicy
metadata:
  name: cilium-google-allow
  namespace: webapp
spec:
  endpointSelector: {}
  egress:
    - toEndpoints:
        - matchLabels:
            io.kubernetes.pod.namespace: kube-system
            k8s-app: kube-dns
      toPorts:
        - ports:
```

```
            - port: "53"
              protocol: UDP
          rules:
            dns:
              - matchPattern: "*"
    - toFQDNs:
        - matchPattern: "*.google.com"
      toPorts:
        - ports:
            - port: "443"
        - ports:
            - port: "80"
```

Applying the policy can be done with only `kubectl`:

```
kubectl create -f cilium-google-allow.yaml
```

`CiliumClusterWideNetworkPolicy` objects allow you to define policies that are not namespaced and apply to the whole cluster. This is useful for establishing baseline security policies where there are a large number of namespaces in a cluster.

Looking at the example shown in Listing 19.9, we can see that it is possible to establish a default deny on traffic entering the cluster from any entity outside the cluster. This policy makes use of a Cilium-specific concept of the `world` entity, which matches anything outside the managed cluster.

Listing 19.9: Cilium Cluster-Wide Lockdown Policy

```
apiVersion: cilium.io/v2
kind: CiliumClusterwideNetworkPolicy
metadata:
  name: cilium-external-lockdown
spec:
  endpointSelector: {}
  ingressDeny:
  - fromEntities:
    - "world"
  ingress:
  - fromEntities:
    - "all"
```

You can find more information on the available entities that can be used in Cilium policies in its documentation (`docs.cilium.io/en/stable/policy/language/#entities-based`).

Calico

Another popular CNI provider is Calico, which also provides extensions to the base Kubernetes Network Policy API. Calico's approach is to have an object type called `NetworkPolicy` (the same as the Kubernetes object name) but to have that in a separate API namespace (`projectcalico.org/v3`), so care should be taken when writing manifests to choose the correct value for the `apiVersion` field.

When using Calico-specific policies, it's currently necessary to use their `calicoctl` tool to apply the policies, although there is an intention to allow `kubectl` to be used it the future (`github.com/projectcalico/calico/issues/2923`). This tool can be installed using the documentation on their site (`docs.projectcalico.org/getting-started/clis/calicoctl/install`).

`Calicoctl` will use the same `kubeconfig` file as `kubectl`, by default, although it is possible to configure it to connect to a specific cluster independently (`docs.projectcalico.org/getting-started/clis/calicoctl/configure/`).

Calico's network policy provides useful features missing from base Kubernetes, including the ability to log where network policies block traffic in the cluster. This kind of feature is handy, both for troubleshooting and also for security monitoring.

As an example, the policy shown in Listing 19.10 could be used to allow access to web applications running in the `webapp` namespace on port 80/TCP, while logging the allowed access. Logs generated by Calico network policies will be placed in the node's `iptables` log location (typically the kernel logs).

Listing 19.10: Calico Policy to Allow and Log Access

```
apiVersion: projectcalico.org/v3
kind: NetworkPolicy
metadata:
  name: calico-allow-and-log-webapp
  namespace: webapp
spec:
  ingress:
  - action: Log
    protocol: TCP
    destination:
      ports:
        - 80
  - action: Allow
    protocol: TCP
    destination:
      ports:
        - 80
```

Applying this is done using `calicoctl`:

```
curl -O -L
https://github.com/projectcalico/calicoctl/releases/download/v3.18.1/
calicoctl
chmod +x calicoctl
calicoctl create -f calico-allow-and-log-webapp.yaml
```

Calico also has a `GlobalNetworkPolicy` object that, similarly to the facility provided by Cilium, allows network policies to be defined that work across whole clusters.

The example in Listing 19.11 provides a default deny base policy that would apply across the whole cluster apart from `kube-system`, which should be protected from generalized policies because of its sensitive nature as it is the heart of the cluster.

Listing 19.11: Calico Default Deny Global Policy

```
apiVersion: projectcalico.org/v3
kind: GlobalNetworkPolicy
metadata:
  name: calico-default-deny
spec:
  selector: projectcalico.org/namespace != "kube-system"
  types:
  - Ingress
  - Egress
```

Again, this policy would be applied using `calicoctl`:

```
calicoctl create -f calico-default-deny.yaml
```

Summary

An important part of securing Kubernetes clusters is understanding how cluster networking works. Features like Kubernetes services can be somewhat unintuitive when you first encounter them but are important in working out how communication between parts of the cluster occurs.

Effective use of the network policy features provided by base Kubernetes and the CNI provider(s) used in your clusters is also important for a well secured cluster. By applying a sensible set of network policies to applications when they're deployed, it's possible to make attackers' lives significantly harder when they're trying to expand an attack from initial compromise to wider cluster access.

CHAPTER

20

Workload Hardening

One of the key properties of Linux containerization is the flexibility of the security model, which allows for individual security layers to be modified as required. Although the default settings created by common container runtimes like Docker are fairly good, an important part of improving cluster security is ensuring that these defaults are strengthened as much as possible.

In addition to workloads voluntarily improving their security by setting security contexts, cluster operators can use Kubernetes features like PodSecurityPolicy (`https://kubernetes.io/docs/concepts/policy/pod-security-policy/`) and other admission controllers such as OPA or Kyverno to ensure that workloads that do not meet their security requirements are not run on the cluster.

It's worth noting that although Kubernetes clusters can include Windows nodes running Windows containers, most of the hardening options available are specific to Linux containers.

Using Security Context in Manifests

Kubernetes provides a number of features that can be used, when applications are being deployed to the cluster, to improve their security. Some of these are likely to be easily deployed with limited impacts, but others will require more preparation to effectively deploy. The mechanisms exposed as part of a security context are largely mirrors of similar features available at the container runtime level.

Setting security contexts in manifests is an important hardening step, particularly when developing applications that will be deployed in arbitrary clusters (for example, when developing open source applications). Having a good idea of the rights required for your application and ensuring that the security context matches those requirements as closely as possible will help users in improving the security of their clusters.

General Approach

Security contexts can either be set at the level of a container or apply to all containers in a pod. If both are defined, the container-level settings will override pod settings. In most cases, it is advisable to set these items at one level only to avoid potential unexpected results.

Within a container, the security context is defined at the same level as the container name and image, as shown in Listing 20.1.

Listing 20.1: Setting a Container Security Context

```
containers:
    -name: db
        image: mongo
        ports:
      -name: mongo
          containerPort: 27017
        securityContext:
          capabilities:
            drop:
            -all
            add:
            -CHOWN
            -SETGID
            -SETUID
          readOnlyRootFilesystem: true
```

allowPrivilegeEscalation

This is one of the available hardening options that should almost always be set, as it has limited risk of causing issues with running workloads. When set to `false`, this flag instructs the container runtime (and thereby the Linux kernel) to prevent any requests from the contained process to acquire additional privileges.

To illustrate this effect, imagine we have a container that is set to run as a non-root user. If there was a setUID root instance of a Bash shell inside the container image, it would be possible for an attacker who had gained access to the container to escalate their privileges to root.

However, if `allowPrivilegeEscalation` is set to false, when the shell is run, it won't escalate privileges to root.

To demonstrate this, we can use Docker commands on a standard image and an image on Docker Hub that has a setUID shell present. The Docker Hub image `raesene/setuidexample` has a setUID shell located at `/bin/setuidbash`.

After launching a container based on this image:

```
docker run -it raesene/setuidexample /bin/bash
```

you can run `whoami`, which should show your user as `newuser`:

```
newuser@83ddb9714a5e:/$ whoami
newuser
```

Then, after running the setUID shell, we can confirm the user has changed:

```
newuser@83ddb9714a5e:/$ /bin/setuidbash -p
setuidbash-4.4# whoami
root
```

To demonstrate `no-new-privileges` in effect, we can pass that option to `docker run`, which has the same effect as using a security context in a Kubernetes workload.

```
docker run -it --security-opt=no-new-privileges raesene/setuidexample /bin/bash
```

Now trying to use the setUID shell, we can see it has no effect:

```
/bin/setuidbash -p
newuser@15e5a64014a4:/$ whoami
newuser
```

Capabilities

By default, when a Linux container runs, it will be assigned a set of capabilities (Linux capabilities were discussed in Chapter 1, "What Is A Container?"), which are portions of the rights provided traditionally to the `root` user in a Linux system. The default set of capabilities will depend on the container runtime in use (for example, Docker may provide a different set than CRI-O). As a result, for applications, specifying the capabilities they require helps the application to run smoothly on unknown clusters as they're not depending on the default set of capabilities assigned by the CRI being correct.

Dropping capabilities can be an effective method of hardening a container and reducing the risk that an attacker can break out to attack other applications running in a Kubernetes cluster.

It's possible to see the capabilities assigned by default to a container by running `amicontained` (`https://github.com/genuinetools/amicontained`) from inside a container.

We can use the Docker Hub image `raesene/alpine-containertools` to demonstrate this by running the following:

```
kubectl run -it amicontained --image=raesene/alpine-containertools
/bin/bash
```

and then running `amicontained`. If your cluster is using Docker as a runtime, you should see output similar to that shown in Listing 20.2.

Listing 20.2: Capabilities Under a Docker Runtime

```
Container Runtime: kube
Has Namespaces:
        pid: true
        user: false
AppArmor Profile: docker-default (enforce)
Capabilities:
        BOUNDING -> chown dac_override fowner fsetid kill setgid setUID
 setpcap net_bind_service net_raw sys_chroot mknod audit_write setfcap
Seccomp: disabled
Blocked Syscalls (22):
        MSGRCV SYSLOG SETSID VHANGUP PIVOT_ROOT ACCT SETTIMEOFDAY
UMOUNT2 SWAPON SWAPOFF REBOOT SETHOSTNAME SETDOMAINNAME
INIT_MODULE DELETE_MODULE LOOKUP_DCOOKIE KEXEC_LOAD
PERF_EVENT_OPEN FANOTIFY_INIT OPEN_BY_HANDLE_AT FINIT_MODULE
KEXEC_FILE_LOAD
Looking for Docker.sock
```

For our purposes, the important section is under `Capabilities`. This shows the default set of capabilities assigned to the container.

There are two approaches that can be taken to hardening this container. The first option is easier to implement: drop capabilities that you don't require from the default set. A prime example of a capability that should be dropped from most container workloads is `net_raw`. From an attacker's perspective, this capability can be used to attempt ARP spoofing attacks, which can be a useful mechanism for them to attempt to increase their access to a cluster. On the flip side from the perspective of an application running in a container, this capability is required only if there is a requirement to send raw network packages (for example, ICMP ping), which is often not required.

If you wanted to drop that capability from a manifest, it would be specified in the security context this way:

```
securityContext:
  capabilities:
    drop:
    —NET_RAW
```

The other approach to handling capabilities in a container is to drop all of them and then add back those that are explicitly required. This requires some more work as the application should be analyzed to see which, if any, capabilities are required. Remember, though, that capabilities are facets of root's privileges; so if you are porting applications that previously ran as nonprivileged users, it's quite likely that they don't need any capabilities at all.

In the example shown earlier in this chapter, we can see that after all capabilities were dropped, three were added back, `CHOWN`, `SETGID`, and `SETUID`. In this case, it would allow the process running in the container to modify the ownership and permissions of files it can access.

privileged

This should always be set to false. Setting `privileged` to true will cause the container to run with the security isolation provided by the container sandbox effectively disabled. Given the flexibility and number of other, less drastic options you can set to provide a container with additional rights, it should almost never be necessary to set this flag to true.

readOnlyRootFilesystem

This setting prevents files from being written to the root filesystem of the container and can often be applied to improve container security. Because containers are meant to be ephemeral, they should generally avoid holding any state within the container, so setting the root filesystem to be read only should not impact their operation.

From an attacker's perspective, this kind of control can make exploiting issues in the application more difficult, as a common step in many attacks is placing a tool onto the compromised system.

Where the contained application does need to write to disk (such as log or temporary files) a good pattern to use is to mount something like an `emptyDir` volume (for more information, see `https://kubernetes.io/docs/concepts/storage/volumes/#emptydir`), and if something like a database server will run in the container, you can use persistent volumes to provide the storage and still make the main root filesystem of the container read-only.

seccompProfile

Another layer of isolation that comes with Linux container runtimes like Docker is the ability to specify a `seccomp` profile (`https://docs.docker.com/engine/security/seccomp/`) for a container. `Seccomp` profiles provide the most granular approach to Linux container isolation as they allow specific sets of Linux kernel syscalls to be blocked or allowed. By default, Docker has a seccomp profile that is enabled for every container and blocks a number of potentially dangerous syscalls, but it is important to note that Kubernetes will disable this filter unless explicitly told to enable it.

To illustrate this difference, we can use amicontained first on a container run directly via Docker (that is, without using Kubernetes):

```
docker run -it raesene/alpine-containertools /bin/bash -c amicontained
```

The output includes a list of blocked syscalls:

```
Blocked Syscalls (63):
        MSGRCV SYSLOG SETSID USELIB USTAT SYSFS VHANGUP
PIVOT_ROOT _SYSCTL ACCT SETTIMEOFDAY MOUNT UMOUNT2 SWAPON
SWAPOFF REBOOT SETHOSTNAME SETDOMAINNAME IOPL IOPERM
CREATE_MODULE INIT_MODULE DELETE_MODULE GET_KERNEL_SYMS
QUERY_MODULE QUOTACTL NFSSERVCTL GETPMSG PUTPMSG AFS_SYSCALL
 TUXCALL SECURITY LOOKUP_DCOOKIE CLOCK_SETTIME VSERVER MBIND
 SET_MEMPOLICY GET_MEMPOLICY KEXEC_LOAD ADD_KEY REQUEST_KEY
 KEYCTL MIGRATE_PAGES UNSHARE MOVE_PAGES PERF_EVENT_OPEN
 FANOTIFY_INIT NAME_TO_HANDLE_AT OPEN_BY_HANDLE_AT
CLOCK_ADJTIME SETNS PROCESS_VM_READV PROCESS_VM_WRITEV
 KCMP FINIT_MODULE KEXEC_FILE_LOAD BPF USERFAULTFD
MEMBARRIER PKEY_MPROTECT PKEY_ALLOC PKEY_FREE RSEQ
```

Running the same container image in a Kubernetes 1.18 cluster that uses Docker as the CRI produces a smaller set of block syscalls, as the items from Docker's seccomp filter are not included:

```
Blocked Syscalls (22):
        MSGRCV SYSLOG SETSID VHANGUP PIVOT_ROOT ACCT SETTIMEOFDAY
 UMOUNT2 SWAPON SWAPOFF REBOOT SETHOSTNAME SETDOMAINNAME
INIT_MODULE DELETE_MODULE LOOKUP_DCOOKIE KEXEC_LOAD
PERF_EVENT_OPEN FANOTIFY_INIT OPEN_BY_HANDLE_AT FINIT_MODULE
 KEXEC_FILE_LOAD
```

In versions of Kubernetes up to version 1.18, enabling seccomp profiles for your containers requires adding an annotation to the pod manifest in the metadata section. For example, to set the runtime default profile for containers running in a pod, you would add the following annotation to your definition:

```
annotations:
    seccomp.security.alpha.kubernetes.io/pod: runtime/default
```

Since version 1.19, it is possible to set the seccomp profile using security contexts, although it is worth noting that this can be set only on new pods defined in the cluster; you can't edit the specification of an existing workload to add it.

```
securityContext:
  seccompProfile:
    type: RuntimeDefault
```

Mandatory Workload Security

In addition to the voluntary controls that we can place into the security context section of workload manifests, cluster operators will likely want to add mandatory controls on what deployed workloads can do in their clusters.

Kubernetes handling for this mandatory workload security is currently evolving (see `https://kubernetes.io/blog/2021/04/06/podsecuritypolicy-deprecation-past-present-and-future/` for more information and updates). Traditionally, Pod Security Policies (PSPs) are the built-in mechanism for this; however, as a feature, they never hit full release and were stuck as a beta feature for a large number of releases. As a result, the Kubernetes project decided to deprecate them in version 1.21 and plan to remove them in version 1.25 (although this is subject to change). Fortunately, there are a number of options we can consider when looking to achieve this goal.

Pod Security Standards

In preparation for the deprecation of PSPs, the Kubernetes project has defined a set of generic recommendations for security settings to be applied to cluster workloads, known as Pod Security Standards (`https://kubernetes.io/docs/concepts/security/pod-security-standards/`). The concept is that this could form a reference point for practical implementations of workload restriction tools.

These standards define three levels of restriction that could be placed onto cluster workloads: Privileged, Baseline, and Restricted.

The Privileged level is entirely unrestricted. Allowing a user to create workloads that can use this policy would allow them to gain access to the underlying node, should they want to do so. It's mainly required for trusted cluster components, which need to interoperate with the node operating system, like the kube-proxy process.

The baseline level provides a minimal level of restrictions that should block known privilege escalation points. It restricts specific things like the `privileged` flag discussed earlier in this chapter, but still allows things like the `NET_RAW` capability that can cause security issues. Using tools that implement this policy should allow most common containers to run without modification.

The restricted level takes a far stricter approach, providing what the Kubernetes project says is a best-practice level of restrictions. In addition to mandating the removal of known privilege escalation paths, things like volume types allowed and the user running the container are restricted. Implementing this policy is likely to be a challenge in many clusters, as it will require workload manifests to be modified in many cases; however, it serves as a good target operating model.

PodSecurityPolicy

Although Pod Security Policies are scheduled for deprecation, it is likely that many existing clusters will have them deployed for some time, so it is worth discussing how they operate and some of the challenges of using them.

Setting Up PSPs

Before enabling PSPs it's important to understand a bit about how they operate. Once PSPs are enabled, when a workload is launched on the cluster, the PSP controller will be called to confirm that the user or service account launching the workload has access to a PSP that matches the security contexts requests made by the workload. If no matching PSP can be found, the workload will be rejected.

As such, if you enable the PSP admission controller in your cluster before creating any policies, it won't be possible to create any new workloads, until you create some policies! So it's important to have some basic policies worked out before trying to enable PSPs in a production cluster.

One option is to create a default "allow all" policy before enabling PSPs and then work to restrict access to that high-privileged policy as you add new ones. This is the approach taken by some managed Kubernetes distributions, such as Amazon EKS (`https://docs.aws.amazon.com/eks/latest/userguide/pod-security-policy.html`), and it enables you to enable PSPs without risking the operation of the cluster.

Another approach is to set up a couple of basic policies before enabling PSPs; one would be a "high-privileged" policy for system components that need that level of access, and the other a "low-privileged" policy for standard workloads. This has the advantage that you aren't allowing all access by default, so the PSP enforcement will be having some effect from the point it's enabled. If you're aligning your policies with the generic Pod Security Standards, these levels would likely correlate to using their "privileged" and "baseline" policies.

Which approach you take for the initial PSP setup will likely depend on whether you're trying to retrofit PSPs to an existing cluster or developing the cluster workloads as you create PSPs.

To illustrate the two-policy approach, let's look at a couple of example PSPs. Listing 20.3 shows the first one, which we'll call `highpriv` as it allows most security options that a workload might need.

Listing 20.3: High-Privileged PodSecurityPolicy

```
apiVersion: policy/v1beta1
kind: PodSecurityPolicy
metadata:
  name: highpriv
spec:
  privileged: true
  allowPrivilegeEscalation: true
  allowedCapabilities:
  - '*'
  volumes:
  - '*'
  hostNetwork: true
  hostPorts:
  - min: 0
    max: 65535
  hostIPC: true
  hostPID: true
  runAsUser:
    rule: 'RunAsAny'
  seLinux:
    rule: 'RunAsAny'
  supplementalGroups:
    rule: 'RunAsAny'
  fsGroup:
    rule: 'RunAsAny'
```

A key point is that this PSP allows for privileged containers. As mentioned earlier, a user who can create privileged containers will be able to gain access to the underlying node, likely as the `root` user, so care must be taken when enabling this policy.

Next, in Listing 20.4, we have a more restrictive policy we'll call `lowpriv`.

Listing 20.4: Low-Privileged PodSecurityPolicy

```
apiVersion: policy/v1beta1
kind: PodSecurityPolicy
metadata:
  name: lowpriv
spec:
  privileged: false
  allowPrivilegeEscalation: false
  requiredDropCapabilities:
    - ALL
  volumes:
    - 'configMap'
    - 'emptyDir'
    - 'secret'
```

```
hostNetwork: false
hostPID: false
runAsUser:
  rule: 'MustRunAsNonRoot'
seLinux:
  rule: 'RunAsAny'
supplementalGroups:
  rule: 'MustRunAs'
  ranges:
    - min: 1
      max: 65535
fsGroup:
  rule: 'MustRunAs'
  ranges:
    - min: 1
      max: 65535
readOnlyRootFilesystem: false
```

This policy prevents users who use it from adding a number of potentially dangerous options, like privileged containers, or using the underlying node's network interfaces. Note that it also restricts the volume types that workloads can use as part of their specification; it does this because there are risks in allowing pods to mount files from the underlying node. Specifically, they could mount directories with sensitive information (for example, the TLS private key that the kubelet uses to communicate with the Kubernetes API server).

Setting Up PSPs

Once you have the PSPs you want to use in the cluster, the next step is to create them. This can be done by just applying the YAML files via `kubectl`:

```
kubectl create -f lowpriv.yaml
kubectl create -f highpriv.yaml
```

We can then view the created PSPs, as shown in Figure 20.1, with the command `kubectl get psp`.

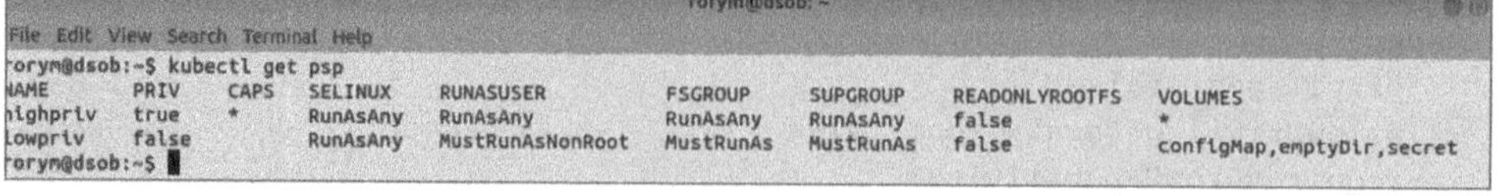

Figure 20.1: PodSecurityPolicies

At this point, however, these PSPs will have no effect on cluster behavior, because the PSP admission controller isn't active yet.

To enable that, we need to edit the API server startup flags that specify the admission controllers to enable. For a `kubeadm`-based cluster, we do this by editing the API server static pod manifest here:

```
sudo nano /etc/kubernetes/manifests/kube-apiserver.yaml
```

Add the string `PodSecurityPolicy` to the end of the `--enable-admission-plugins` parameter. In a standard cluster, it should now look like this:

```
--enable-admission-plugins=NodeRestriction,PodSecurityPolicy
```

Once the API sever manifest is modified and saved, it should, in a `kubeadm` cluster, automatically be reloaded while the kubelet watches the directory it's in for any changes.

PSPs and RBAC

With policies created, the next step to consider when making use of PSPs is ensuring that your RBAC settings are correctly configured to support them. The way this works is that users and service accounts need the "USE" right on a given PSP to be able to make use of it, and if a user has access to multiple PSPs, then any of them can be used by a workload they're creating.

When you have both a high-privileged and low-privileged policy, as in our earlier example, a generally suitable approach is to give access to the low-privileged policy to the `system:authenticated` group. This is a special group that is provided to any authenticated users and means that any cluster user can create workloads that comply with the requirements of the `lowpriv` PSP.

To do this, create a cluster role, as shown in Listing 20.5.

Listing 20.5: LowPriv Cluster Role

```
kind: ClusterRole
apiVersion: rbac.authorization.k8s.io/v1
metadata:
  name: psp-lowpriv
rules:
- apiGroups:
  - extensions
  resources:
  - podsecuritypolicies
  resourceNames:
  - lowpriv
  verbs:
  - use
```

Then create a cluster role binding that ties this cluster role to the `system:authenticated` group, as shown in Listing 20.6.

Listing 20.6: LowPriv Cluster Role Binding

```
kind: ClusterRoleBinding
apiVersion: rbac.authorization.k8s.io/v1
metadata:
  name: psp-default
subjects:
  - kind: Group
  name: system:authenticated
roleRef:
  kind: ClusterRole
  name: psp-lowpriv
  apiGroup: rbac.authorization.k8s.io
```

Applying these two objects to the cluster API will leave us in a position where any user can create basic pods for the cluster.

The next step is to consider what rights to provide for the high-privileged role that was created earlier. This provides extensive rights for pods and should be used with care. Users with cluster-admin rights will already have access to this policy, so there's no need to explicitly create role bindings for them; however, if a cluster admin user tries to create a deployment, replicaset, or similar object, it will be denied. Explaining this requires a bit of background into how Kubernetes creates objects in the cluster.

When a user creates a pod, the permissions used are those of the user, but when a user creates a higher-level object like a deployment, it is actually one of Kubernetes controllers that carries out the pod creation process; and therefore it is the controller service accounts that require access to PSPs as part of the setup process.

For example, with a deployment, the user creates a deployment object, the deployment controller uses its permissions to create a replicaset object, and then the replicaset object creates the pods using its permissions.

This means that to allow privileged containers to be deployed, the controller service accounts will need to have access to that PSP. Typically, the way this is done, without giving access to every user who can create deployments, is to restrict it by namespace.

For example, we would usually want privileged containers to be deployed in the `kube-system` namespace, as some of the components there are likely to need elevated rights.

To make that possible, you can create a role, as shown in Listing 20.7.

Listing 20.7: HighPriv PSP Cluster Role

```
kind: ClusterRole
apiVersion: rbac.authorization.k8s.io/v1
metadata:
  name: psp-highpriv
rules:
```

```
- apiGroups:
  - extensions
  resources:
  - podsecuritypolicies
  resourceNames:
  - highpriv
  verbs:
  - use
```

Then, in the `kube-system` namespace, define role binding, as shown in Listing 20.8.

Listing 20.8: HighPriv PSP Role Binding

```
apiVersion: rbac.authorization.k8s.io/v1
kind: RoleBinding
metadata:
  name: psp-permissive
  namespace: kube-system
roleRef:
  apiGroup: rbac.authorization.k8s.io
  kind: ClusterRole
  name: psp-highpriv
subjects:
- kind: ServiceAccount
  name: daemon-set-controller
  namespace: kube-system
- kind: ServiceAccount
  name: replicaset-controller
  namespace: kube-system
- kind: ServiceAccount
  name: deployment-controller
  namespace: kube-system
```

This will provide the rights the controller service accounts need, but only where they are deploying workloads to the `kube-system` namespace.

Using this approach, any user who is able to create daemonsets, replicasets, or deployments in the kube-system namespace will be able to make use of this PSP. So, to prevent it being misused by users of the cluster, it's important to ensure that only trusted users have rights to create workloads in the `kube-system` namespace.

PSP Alternatives

Now that PSPs are scheduled for deprecation, it is worth considering alternatives that can be used to implement similar controls. While there will be an in-tree option for this, it is expected to be limited in scope, so for more complex requirements an external admission controller is likely to be the best option.

There are a number of projects that can be configured to perform similar checks to those carried out by PSPs on workloads being launched on the cluster. As an added bonus, these solutions are generally more flexible and can be used for other policy management duties.

Here we will examine two of the more popular options for this:

- Open Policy Agent (`https://www.openpolicyagent.org/`)
- Kyverno (`https://kyverno.io/`)

These two programs take quite different approaches to the problem of enforcing policies on Kubernetes workloads, so it's worth considering both when working out which will be the most applicable to your environment.

Open Policy Agent

Open Policy Agent (OPA) is a general policy control system for Cloud Native environments and is part of the CNCF. It allows users to define policies to ensure that a wide variety of systems meet specific requirements.

With the context of Kubernetes, there is a specific program that OPA provides called Gatekeeper (`https://github.com/open-policy-agent/gatekeeper`), which can be installed into a cluster to enforce policies. The gatekeeper component runs as a controller inside the cluster and hooks into the API server using a validating admission webhook (`https://kubernetes.io/docs/reference/access-authn-authz/extensible-admission-controllers/`). This mechanism essentially allows Gatekeeper to define a range of events that will be sent to it for review. Once the Gatekeeper component sees an event, it can apply the policies that it has to decide whether to admit or reject it.

Installation

Installing Gatekeeper into a cluster is a relatively straightforward process, and the documentation is clear and easy to follow (`https://open-policy-agent.github.io/gatekeeper/website/docs/install/`). In common with a lot of Cloud Native software, it can be installed either by directly applying a manifest or by using the helm package manager.

Once we've applied the Gatekeeper manifest, it's possible to see some of the changes that have been made to the cluster. As shown in Listing 20.9, Gatekeeper will install itself into its own namespace.

Listing 20.9: Gatekeeper Installed

```
kubectl get ns
NAME                 STATUS   AGE
default              Active   6m58s
gatekeeper-system    Active   6m45s
```

```
kube-node-lease       Active   7m
kube-public           Active   7m
kube-system           Active   7m
local-path-storage    Active   6m55s
```

In Listing 20.10, we can see the webhook that Gatekeeper uses to gain access to API server events.

Listing 20.10: Gatekeeper Webhook

```
kubectl get validatingwebhookconfigurations
NAME                                          WEBHOOKS   AGE
gatekeeper-validating-webhook-configuration   2          12mOperation
```

Once Gatekeeper is installed, it will need policies to apply. OPA provides a policy library covering common use cases and has a specific set of policies covering the same ground as Pod Security Policy, which can be found at `https://github.com/open-policy-agent/gatekeeper-library/tree/master/library/pod-security-policy`.

To apply a policy to a cluster, two objects need to be created. The first is a *constraint template*. This object describes the constraint to be applied and provides the rego code used to implement it. Rego (`https://www.openpolicyagent.org/docs/latest/policy-language/`) is a query language designed by OPA. Having its own programming language does provide a lot of flexibility; however, it does place a bit of a learning curve on designing your own constraints.

Looking at the sample constraint template provided for restricting privileged containers (`https://github.com/open-policy-agent/gatekeeper-library/blob/master/library/pod-security-policy/privileged-containers/template.yaml`), we can see the main elements in Listing 20.11.

Listing 20.11: OPA Constraint Template for Privileged Containers

```
apiVersion: templates.gatekeeper.sh/v1beta1
kind: ConstraintTemplate
metadata:
  name: k8spspprivilegedcontainer
  annotations:
    description: Controls running of privileged containers.
spec:
  crd:
    spec:
      names:
        kind: K8sPSPPrivilegedContainer
  targets:
    - target: admission.k8s.gatekeeper.sh
      rego: |
```

```
        package k8spspprivileged

        violation[{"msg": msg, "details": {}}] {
            c:= input_containers[_]
            c.securityContext.privileged
            msg:= sprintf("Privileged container is not allowed: %v,
securityContext: %v", [c.name, c.securityContext])
        }

        input_containers[c] {
            c:= input.review.object.spec.containers[_]
        }

        input_containers[c] {
            c:= input.review.object.spec.initContainers[_]
        }
```

The Constraint template essentially creates a custom resource definition that will then be available in the cluster to be applied using constraint objects. Inside the object spec, we can see the layout of the custom resource definition (CRD) element. (See `https://kubernetes.io/docs/concepts/extend-kubernetes/api-extension/custom-resources/#customresourcedefinitions` for more information about CRDs.) The name to be used is set with `kind: K8sPSPPrivilegedContainer`, which will then be available as an object type.

After that, the detail of the constraint template is the `rego` section, which lays out the policy to be applied. Within that block we can see that there is code to review the containers and `initContainers` sections of any manifest and to see if the `securityContext.privileged` setting is present and deny admission if it is.

Because this object is just a template, on its own it won't have any effect, so an additional object is needed to apply the template to the cluster. This is done using a constraint object. Let's look at the sample for privileged containers, as shown in Listing 20.12.

Listing 20.12: Privileged Containers Constraint

```
apiVersion: constraints.gatekeeper.sh/v1beta1
kind: K8sPSPPrivilegedContainer
metadata:
  name: psp-privileged-container
spec:
  match:
    kinds:
      - apiGroups: [""]
        kinds: ["Pod"]
    excludedNamespaces: ["kube-system"]
```

We can see how the constraint ties the template to the cluster. The constraint template to be used is specified using the `kind` of this object. In this case, we see `kind: K8sPSPPrivilegedContainer`, which is the same as we saw in our constraint template.

After that, the constraint lays out which type of objects should have the template applied to them (in this case pod objects) and then any excluded namespaces. This is an important element of the constraint to avoid disrupting the cluster.

As mentioned in the PSP section of this chapter, namespaces like kube-system will often need privileged pods to be deployed into them, so we need to exclude that namespace from this kind of policy.

Enforcement Actions

Another useful feature that OPA has over PSP is that it is possible to set constraints to only log occasions where they would usually deny access (`https://open-policy-agent.github.io/gatekeeper/website/docs/violations`).

This is done via the `enforcementAction` parameter in the constraint specification. To see how it works, consider our previous example of denying privileged containers. If you are deploying this constraint to a new cluster and want to see whether any workloads would fail, without actually blocking things, you can add the constraint as shown in Listing 20.13.

Listing 20.13: Dry Run Privileged Containers Constraint

```
apiVersion: constraints.gatekeeper.sh/v1beta1
kind: K8sPSPPrivilegedContainer
metadata:
  name: psp-privileged-container
spec:
  enforcementAction: dryrun
  match:
    kinds:
      - apiGroups: [""]
        kinds: ["Pod"]
    excludedNamespaces: ["kube-system"]
```

Once this constraint has been set, you can see whether there are any violations for newly created resources, by looking at the `totalViolations` field in the object specification. To get just that value the following `jsonpath` statement can be used for this constraint:

```
kubectl get k8spspprivilegedcontainer -o
jsonpath='{.items[*].status.totalViolations}'
```

Kyverno

Kyverno (`https://kyverno.io/`) is a policy engine designed for Kubernetes. Like OPA, it is a CNCF project. Unlike OPA, Kyverno uses standard YAML files to define policies, and the scope of the project is purely as a policy engine for Kubernetes clusters.

Installation

Kyverno can be installed either by running a manifest directly from their GitHub repository or by using the helm package manager (`https://kyverno.io/docs/introduction/#quick-start`). Once the manifest has been applied to the cluster, we can see that, similarly to OPA, there's a new namespace for Kyverno, as shown in Listing 20.14.

Listing 20.14: Namespaces with Kyverno Installed

```
kubectl get ns
NAME                 STATUS   AGE
default              Active   79s
kube-node-lease      Active   80s
kube-public          Active   80s
kube-system          Active   80s
kyverno              Active   65s
local-path-storage   Active   75s
```

Kyverno also installs validating admission webhooks that will be used to check workloads as they are deployed to the cluster, as we can see in Listing 20.15.

Listing 20.15: Validating Admission Webhooks for Kyverno

```
kubectl get validatingwebhookconfigurations
NAME                                        WEBHOOKS   AGE
kyverno-policy-validating-webhook-cfg       1          118s
kyverno-resource-validating-webhook-cfg     1          118s
```

Operation

With Kyverno installed, we need to define policies for it to apply. There is a library of policies that replicate the requirements of PSP on Kyverno's GitHub account (`https://github.com/kyverno/policies/tree/main/pod-security`). Kyverno allows for two types of policies: `ClusterPolicy` objects will apply restrictions across the whole cluster, while `Policy` objects are used for individual namespaces. Unlike OPA, Kyverno provides no separation between templates and constraints.

A sample policy for blocking privileged containers, as shown in Listing 20.16, demonstrates the structure of a Kyverno policy.

Listing 20.16: Kyverno ClusterPolicy for Blocking Privileged Containers

```
apiVersion: kyverno.io/v1
kind: ClusterPolicy
metadata:
  name: disallow-privileged-containers
```

```
  annotations:
    policies.kyverno.io/category: Pod Security Standards (Default)
    policies.kyverno.io/description: >-
      Privileged mode disables most security mechanisms and must not be
allowed.
spec:
  validationFailureAction: enforce
  background: true
  rules:
  - name: privileged-containers
    match:
      resources:
        kinds:
        - Pod
    exclude:
      resources:
        namespaces:
        - kube-system
    validate:
      message: >-
        Privileged mode is disallowed. The fields
spec.containers[*].securityContext.privileged
        and spec.initContainers[*].securityContext.privileged must not be set
to true.
      pattern:
        spec:
          =(initContainers):
          - =(securityContext):
              =(privileged): "false"
          containers:
          - =(securityContext):
              =(privileged): "false"
```

In common with general Kubernetes object structures, the key fields are in the `spec:` section. First the `validationFailureAction` is used to dictate what happens when an object fails the policy. The two major options are `enforce`, which will block object creation, and `audit`, which will just log the failure and allow creation, an option that is useful for testing new rules.

The `match` section shows which resources will have the rule applied to them. For most PSP replacement policies, it will be pod resources that should be addressed, although it's worth noting that Kyverno policies can apply to any object type.

The `exclude` section is also used to show which resources to choose. In this case, the policy is configured to ignore the kube-system namespace, as there will likely be requirements for privileged containers there.

Lastly, the `pattern` section shows the test being applied, which is looking for the privileged section of the pod's `securityContext` and ensuring it's set to false.

The Kyverno documentation has a lot of detail on how to create policies to be enforced (`https://kyverno.io/docs/writing-policies/`).

Summary

Protecting workloads in Kubernetes is a vital mitigation, alongside strong RBAC controls, against the risks of privilege escalation and container breakout attacks. Implementing hardening mechanisms using security contexts is one of highest value activities developers can undertake from a security perspective.

The world of mandatory security policy enforcement is currently a developing one, and choosing the appropriate mechanism will require consideration of company priorities. For existing clusters where PSP is already deployed, it is reasonable to leave it in place, although plans should be started to look at migrating away from it before the feature is finally removed from Kubernetes.

The new built-in controller may be a good option for simple clusters that do not have complex policy requirements, as it implements only the pod security standards as options for workloads and thus lacks flexibility for complex requirements.

For more complex requirements, both OPA and Kyverno have great flexibility to apply policies to clusters. Kyverno's policy syntax is simpler than OPAs rego-based policies, so it would be a good option where only Kubernetes enforcement is required.

OPAs strength is that it is part of a larger policy enforcement ecosystem, so it can be used in other venues in addition to Kubernetes clusters. And while rego can be complex, it is also very flexible, so it's a good choice for more sophisticated requirements.

Index

A

M

N

O

P

R

V

W

X–Y–Z